Assessment of Student Achievement

Centre de ressources de la Faculté d'éducation
Université d'Ottawa - University of Ottawa
Faculty of Education Resource Centre

Canadian Edition

Norman E. Gronlund
Professor Emeritus
University of Illinois

Ian J. Cameron
Faculty of Education
University of Victoria

PEARSON

Toronto

To Mary Ann Gronlund and Dave, Derek, and Erik
Norman E. Gronlund

To Mary and Alexandra,
who have given me much more than I have given to them, and to my 5000
students, of many of whom the same can be said.
Ian J. Cameron

National Library of Canada Cataloguing in Publication

Gronlund, Norman Edward, 1920–

  Assessment of student achievement / Norman E. Gronlund, Ian J. Cameron.—Canadian ed.
Includes index.

ISBN 0-205-40310-7

  1. Achievement tests—Design and construction. 2. Examinations—Design and construction. I. Cameron, Ian J. II. Title.

LB3060.65.G76 2004   371.26'1   C2003-901990-X

ISBN 0-205-40310-7

Vice President, Editorial Director: Michael J. Young
Acquisitions Editor: Christine Cozens
Marketing Manager: Ryan St. Peters
Developmental Editor: Adrienne Shiffman
Production Editor: Martin Tooke
Copy Editor: Laurel Sparrow
Proofreader: Bonnie Di Malta
Production Coordinator: Heather Bean
Page Layout: Janet Zanette
Art Director: Julia Hall
Cover Design: Amy Harnden
Cover Image: Digital Vision

2 3 4 5 6 7 DPC 07 06 05 04
Printed and bound in Canada.

371.261
.G76
2004

Contents

Preface   vii

1   *Student Assessment in Canada   1*

Historical Differences in Assessment Between the United States and Canada   1

The Canadian Experience with Student Assessment   3

Demands for Accountability   4

Summary of Points   7

Learning Exercises   7

References and Additional Reading   8

Weblinks   8

2   *Achievement Assessment and Instruction   9*

Relation Between Instruction and Assessment   11

Assessment in the Instructional Process   12

Other Ways Assessments Can Aid Learning   16

Teachers' Standards for Student Assessment   18

Special Considerations   18

Summary of Points   18

Learning Exercises   19

References and Additional Reading   19

Weblinks   20

3   *Nature of Student Assessment   21*

Major Types of Assessment Methods   22

Guidelines for Effective Student Assessment   25

Validity and Reliability in Assessment Planning   29

Norm-Referenced and Criterion-Referenced Assessment   30

Standardized Tests   31

Summary of Points   34

Learning Exercises   35

References and Additional Reading   36

Weblinks   36

4   *Validity and Reliability*   37

Validity   38
Reliability   44
Summary of Points   52
Learning Exercises   53
References and Additional Reading   53
Weblinks   54

5   *Planning for Assessment*   55

Types of Intended Learning Outcomes   56
Role of Instructional Objectives   56
Assessment Methods and Their Applicability   60
Domains   61
Planning the Unit of Instruction   61
Special Considerations   62
Summary of Points   62
Learning Exercises   63
References and Additional Reading   63
Weblinks   63

6   *Paper and Pencil Tests: General Principles*   64

The Paper and Pencil Test   64
Preparing and Using Paper and Pencil Tests   65
Specifying the Instructional Objectives   66
Preparing the Test Specifications   68
Considerations In Constructing Relevant Test Items   70
General Guidelines for Item Writing   75
Arranging the Items in the Test   77
Preparing Directions   78
Reviewing and Evaluating the Assembled Test   79
Administering and Scoring the Test   80
Analyzing the Effectiveness of Test Items   80
Special Considerations   82
Summary of Points   83
Learning Exercises   83
References and Additional Reading   84
Weblinks   84

7   *Writing Selection Items: Multiple Choice*   85

Nature of Multiple-Choice Items   85
Uses of Multiple-Choice Items   87
Rules for Writing Multiple-Choice Items   90
Special Considerations   102
Summary of Points   103
Learning Exercises   104
References and Additional Reading   104
Weblinks   104

8   *Writing Selection Items: True–False, Matching,
and Interpretive Exercise*   105

True–False Items   105
Matching Items   111
The Interpretive Exercise   112
Special Considerations   116
Summary of Points   116
Learning Exercises   117
References and Additional Reading   118
Weblinks   118

9   *Writing Supply Items: Short Answer and Essay*   119

Short-Answer Items   120
Essay Questions   123
Special Considerations   130
Summary of Points   131
Learning Exercises   132
References and Additional Reading   132
Weblinks   132

10   *Assessing Achievement Through Product and Performance*   133

Components of Product and Performance Skills   134
Stating Objectives for Product and Performance Assessment   134
Restricted and Extended Product and Performance Tasks   135
Steps in Preparing Product and Performance Assessments   136
Specifying the Outcomes for Products   137
Defining the Extended Product   138
Marking Products   143
Improving Product Assessments   146

Minimizing Excess Help and Cheating   147

Elements of Performance   148

Specifying the Performance Outcomes   151

Selecting the Focus of the Assessment   152

Selecting an Appropriate Degree of Realism   153

Selecting the Performance Situation   155

Selecting the Method of Observing, Recording, and Scoring   158

Improving Performance Assessments   162

Special Considerations   162

Summary of Points   163

Learning Exercises   164

References and Additional Reading   165

Weblinks   165

11   *Portfolio Assessment*   166

Advantages of Using Classroom Portfolios   167

Planning for the Use of Portfolios   168

Evaluating the Portfolio   172

Special Considerations   175

Summary of Points   176

Learning Exercises   177

References and Additional Reading   177

Weblinks   177

12   *Grading and Reporting*   178

Selecting the Basis for Grading   179

Combining Data for Grading   183

Guidelines for Effective and Fair Grading   186

Reporting to Students and Parents   187

Using a Portfolio   188

Special Considerations   188

Summary of Points   189

Learning Exercises   190

References and Additional Reading   190

Weblinks   190

Appendix: Principles for Fair Student Assessment Practices for Education in Canada   191

Glossary   209

Index   212

Preface

You have in your hands a "Canadianized" version of an American textbook. Some people don't see the reason for such an adaptation. "Why go to all that trouble?" some ask. "The school systems aren't all that different." Others say, "Why not write a Canadian text and be done with it?"

The reason for adapting the American text is that the original book, written by Norman Gronlund, is an excellent text. Most of the chapters, especially on the technical side of student assessment, would be hard to improve upon. There are, however, enough significant differences between Canadian and American school practices in the field of measurement and assessment to warrant a Canadian edition. Chapter 1 details some of the differences in education in the United States and Canada, and the reasons for them, and then goes on to discuss Canadian history in assessment and evaluation in schools. It seems important to have a general discussion because of the pervasiveness of American media in Canada. Because Canadians see so much American television and read so many American publications, they get the idea that almost everything about the two countries is the same. And much of it is. But much is different, as well, and those differences are significant, especially in schools.

This Canadian edition has a number of important changes:

1. The chapter dealing with performance assessment (which treated product and performance assessment as one) has been expanded considerably, to recognize that there are important differences between products and performances.
2. The chapter on portfolio assessment has been altered to reflect the current experience with portfolio use in Canadian schools.
3. The chapter on standardized testing has been eliminated, and replaced by a very brief discussion, reflecting the limited use of such tests in most Canadian schools.
4. Considerable new material was added to chapters listing steps for preparing, using, and scoring performance and product assessments.
5. Considerable material on scoring keys for products and performances has been added.
6. A discussion of plagiarism (especially plagiarism from the Internet) has been added.
7. Learning exercises have been added to each chapter.

8. Material on special needs students has been added to appropriate chapters.
9. URLs for educational Internet sites have been included.
10. The entire document, *Principles for Fair Student Assessment Practices for Education in Canada*, has been included as an appendix.
11. And, of course, examples are all Canadian rather than American.

The book now presents a well-balanced Canadian treatment of testing and other types of assessment and the important role that assessment plays in instruction. The material is presented in a simple, direct, and understandable manner without slighting basic concepts or sacrificing technical accuracy. Numerous practical examples are provided, and checklists, boxed material, and summaries of main points are used to aid in learning the content. No prior knowledge of measurement or statistics is required to understand the material in the book. In short, it is a practical guide for beginners.

I would like to thank Robert Crocker (MUN) and Alexa Okrainec (Brandon University) for their valuable contributions as reviewers during development.

Ian Cameron

1

Student Assessment in Canada

This chapter will enable you to:

1. Explain the historical and current differences between schooling in the United States and that in Canada.

2. Explain how these differences have influenced student assessment practices in the two countries.

3. Discuss the current interest in comparative testing in Canada, and its possible impacts.

Historical Differences in Assessment Between the United States and Canada

One of the most important differences between Canadian and American assessment practices is that in the United States "testing" has received a bad reputation. It is seen as "non-authentic," a "device for sorting children," and various other unpleasant things. In fact, there are reasons for these views, which we will discuss shortly, but we want to establish that the testing once common in American schools was far less common in Canadian schools. In fact, the student assessment practices now being promoted in the United States are the kind that have long been used in Canada, and when an American writer says, "Testing has to go," he or she is not talking about the kind of testing with which Canadian teachers are familiar. When American educators say, "We've got to replace what we've been doing with this new model," and the new model is the model Canadian teachers have used for years, Canadian teachers are puzzled. The task of this section is to explain the differences in testing between the United States and Canada.

1

When the United States attained independence from Britain in 1776, education in that country was strictly a private affair: there were no public schools. In fact, the U.S. Constitution hardly mentioned education. For that reason, public schooling came into being in the United States in a fragmented fashion, with each town establishing its own school system—some elaborate, some simple. Each town elected a school board, which in turn hired teachers and chose textbooks, which became, ipso facto, the curriculum. Curricula were common among towns and across states only insofar as the texts were similar and as the teachers followed the texts.

As the nineteenth century progressed and the responsibility for education evolved to the state level, the degree of centralization and the curricula within and between states differed widely. Generally, such differences were not a great problem. If the local schools had the reputation of not preparing students for university (which was especially true in the southern states), the children of the rich and the ambitious middle class were sent off to private schools. Teachers in good public secondary schools and in private schools knew what universities wanted, and made sure their students were prepared (Calhoun 1969).

However, toward the beginning of the twentieth century, the task of schools started changing. More immigrants were arriving in the United States, many with little schooling or knowledge of English. The common belief was that the United States was a "melting pot" where all would have a common language, culture, and ideals, and schools were tasked with ensuring that this homogeneity was achieved. Further, fewer workers were required by agriculture, and more by industry. Technology was becoming more complex, and there was a greater need for workers who had achieved a certain level of literacy. Companies wanted men who possessed the basic education required in order to learn the job, and not all jobs required the same level of education. Workers on production lines didn't need much education, but they had to be reliable and to work hard at repetitive, boring tasks. Other jobs demanded more education and more adaptability. Still other jobs required a great deal of education and a high degree of intelligence. By 1920, there was a perceived need to sort young people into various categories, so industry could continue expanding.

All of these influences pushed the schools in the United States toward standardized testing: tests with common standards, designed to be used across the country. Which students have learned enough to be allowed into university? The ones who pass the test. How well are immigrants "becoming" Americans? Give them a test. How can we educate potential workers as quickly as possible? Test them to see if they are ready for the next grade. How can we provide industry with workers of different abilities and levels of skill? Sort them by means of a test. How can we prove that education really is a profession? Make testing a science. By the mid-1930s, standardized testing was well established as an industry, and by the end of the 1940s virtually every school system in the United States was using standardized tests developed by companies that did nothing else (Callahan 1962).

The trend to standardized testing had a profound effect on schools in the United States. It meant that schools wanting their students to attend university not only had to offer certain courses, but they had to ensure that their students attained a certain standard of performance. This meant that students had to meet certain standards at each grade level, which led, in turn, to more standardized testing designed to sort "good" students from "poor" students. These tests not only told teachers and schools whether their best students were up to the standards of their grade compared to students from across the country, but also (along with IQ tests) allowed schools to practise what amounted to educational triage: the highest scoring students were put into the "top" class, the next group into "average" classes, and the lowest scoring students into the "bottom" class. (This is not the place for a sociological discussion, but because the tests were culturally biased this practice led to de facto segregation, even in states where segregation was not the law. The history of educational testing is a fascinating topic, and one that students may find interesting. Two good starting places are Callahan (1962) and Tyack (1974).)

Furthermore, universities needed some sort of entrance exam, to ensure that students applying had attained a minimum standard of performance in certain specific subjects. This was the start of the Scholastic Aptitude Test (the SAT). In a short time the SAT defined the curriculum to some extent, and all students wishing to attend a good university in the United States had to study certain subjects in order to qualify for entrance, and had to pass a test based on those subjects.

So from 1830 (or so), when public education became widespread in the United States, testing became more and more centralized, more and more sophisticated, and more and more removed from the classroom. By the 1960s teachers taught and testers tested, and communication between the two groups was minimal at best. Standardized tests were relied upon to ascertain how well students were doing, and in many districts and states such tests were mandated. All students were to be tested at certain times in their school careers, in some jurisdictions as often as once a year. By the 1980s, however, it was becoming obvious that standardized testing had disadvantages, and there began to be a demand for testing based on what actually happened in classrooms, using not only paper and pencil tests but other forms of assessment as well. And now we are back to the start of this chapter: throughout the 1990s, books and articles in the United States spent a lot of time discussing the problems inherent in American assessment (relying on standardized tests) and explaining the advantages of classroom-based assessment.

Having said all that, there are still many external tests in American schools. Most states have mandatory tests, which are designed to set standards. "Accountability" is an important word in American education, and "accountability" usually means testing, even today.

The Canadian Experience with Student Assessment

Schooling in Canada followed a pattern very different from that in the United States. The first schools in what is now Canada were founded in Quebec by the Roman Catholic church. Because of the close ties between the church and state in Quebec (as opposed to the situation in the United States, where there was a constitutional separation), the Catholic schools in Quebec became, by default, public schools, or at least served the purpose. In effect, this meant that Quebec had a centralized school system, with a common curriculum, texts, and methodology. Teachers made up tests, but there was considerable circulation of tests among schools and towns. To a great extent, assessment was common across the province.

In Ontario, education in the early part of the nineteenth century was also centralized. Because it was a colony of Great Britain, the province was administered by an agent of the British government (the Lieutenant Governor) who set policies for the province.

This led to a more centralized form of government than was found in most American states, which had, in the not-distant past, fought a war over the principles of independence and autonomy. Included in the Ontario colonial government was the office of superintendent of education, a post held from 1844 to 1876 by Egerton Ryerson, a man who had much influence on Canadian education. Under his guidance, Ontario's curriculum was remarkably uniform: he chose the textbooks, set the curriculum, and influenced the teaching methods to a considerable degree. So in Ontario, as in Quebec, there was a commonality among schools across the province.

When Canada became a country in 1867, the Articles of Confederation specified that education would be a provincial concern, and it has remained so to this day.

When British Columbia joined Confederation in 1871 it became the most centralized province of all with regard to education. One of the first acts of British Columbia's new legislature was to appoint a provincial superintendent of education, John Jessop, who had been a pupil of Ryerson and had the same views regarding the importance of central control. New Brunswick, Nova Scotia, and Manitoba likewise had strong central governments during their formative years, and all had a central office of education.

So the history of education in Canada was one of central control by each province. As succeeding provinces joined the country, they maintained this tradition. Even the fact of dual education systems (most provinces had, and have, both non-sectarian and Catholic school systems) did not have much impact on the centralized nature of education in each province. The fact was that from the start of public schooling to the 1960s, students in each province had a very common educational experience. The experiences differed from province to province, but within each province schooling was quite centralized.

One result of this centralization was that standardized testing never became as widespread or as important in Canada as it was in the United States. By and large, assessment was and is designed and carried out at the classroom level, with some tests supplied by the central provincial authority. Various provinces, for instance, have had and still have "provincial exams,"—tests required for Grade 12 graduation. But because in all provinces there was, and is, a continual struggle to keep provincial costs down, no province supplied or supplies all the tests required through 12 years of school. Teachers continue to be responsible for the design and administration of the vast majority of the testing carried out in Canadian schools.

That said, both American and Canadian commercial standardized tests have always been available in Canada, but they have been neither as widely used nor ascribed the same importance as their counterparts in the United States.

So, in the twenty-first century, school systems in the United States continue to move from basing student assessment on standardized tests to a more classroom-centred approach, which Canadian schools have been following for decades.

Having examined some important differences between the United States and Canada, let us turn to a discussion of current issues in the two countries.

Demands for Accountability

In the United States, *A Nation at Risk: The Imperative for Educational Reform*—a document issued by the National Commission on Excellence in Education (1983)—started the current discussion of school quality in North America. That report pointed out shortcomings in student achievement, and recommended mechanisms of reform. "Report cards" showing student test performance were used to make educators more accountable for student achievement, and comparisons of schools and districts placed considerable pressure on superintendents, principals, and teachers to "get the scores up." Teachers reported in surveys that, as a result of the pressure, they focused their instruction on the skills tested, taught test-taking skills, and used the format of the externally mandated test when making their own classroom tests. An overwhelming majority of states and districts reported that students were doing better. Indeed, the results came to be known as the "Lake Wobegon effect," because almost all states and most districts were reporting that their students were scoring above the national norm. (The name comes from radio personality Garrison Keillor's description of his hometown of Lake Wobegon. "It is a place," he says at the end of his weekly monologue on The Prairie Home Companion radio program, "where all the women are strong, all the men are good looking, and all the children are above average.") That finding raised serious questions about the credibility of test results and about the possible negative side effects of high-stakes accountability.

Accountability in Canada

In Canada, the push for reform was not as strong as in the United States, and was generally satisfied by provincially prepared assessments. British Columbia led efforts in this regard with its Provincial Learning Assessment Program (PLAP), which was introduced in 1976 and tested students in Grades 4, 8, and 12 (later 4, 7, and 10) in different subjects each year.

Currently, the School Achievement Indicators Program (SAIP), operated by the Council of Ministers of Education Canada (CMEC), measures the achievements of a sample of 13- and 16-year-old students across Canada. The first assessment, in mathematics content and problem solving, was administered in 1993. This was followed by an assessment of reading and writing in 1994, and of science in 1996. A second cycle of assessments began in 1997 and was completed in 1999. SAIP results are reported according to the level achieved, with Level 1 being the lowest and Level 5 being the highest.

Reports show the performance of each jurisdiction compared with the results for Canada as a whole. For the reading and writing assessment, results for francophones by jurisdiction are compared with pan-Canadian francophone results, and results for anglophones by jurisdiction with pan-Canadian anglophone results.

Provincial Assessments

As well as nationwide testing, there is widespread use of testing at the provincial level. As of the year 2000, every province and territory (with the exceptions of Prince Edward Island and the Northwest Territories) was conducting annual provincewide testing, usually at the Grade 3, 6, and 9 levels, and usually measuring reading, writing, and mathematics, the traditional "3 Rs." Further, most provinces and territories have exit examinations, which typically account for 30 to 50 percent of a student's mark in the course. Naturally, these tests not only measure student achievement but help to set the curriculum. One result is that content (specific material to be learned) is becoming less important in subjects such as English and French, and skills (performance on generic tasks) are becoming more important.

International Assessments

The increased awareness of the need to compete in a global economy has stimulated interest not only in provincial and national assessments of student progress, but also in international comparisons. International assessments of achievement are fraught with many difficulties. Comparisons are complicated by differences in the selectivity of the educational systems of different countries, variations in the quality of the samples obtained, and differences in definitions of educational levels. In addition, it is difficult to agree on the content to be included in the assessment; even after an agreement on content is reached, there is the challenge of translation. It is well known that the difficulty of a test item can be altered substantially by subtle changes in wording when working in a single language. This problem is compounded when items must be translated from one language to another. All of these factors threaten the validity of international assessments of student achievement.

Despite the many limitations, international test results based on the Third International Mathematics and Science Study (TIMSS) attracted considerable attention. Although Canadian students compared reasonably well with their counterparts in other industrialized nations, their performance has been used by many to argue that students in this country are not doing well enough and to push for higher standards of student performance. In the latest (1999) TIMSS results, Canadian students had good results in both mathematics and science. Of the 38 participating countries, six had mathematics scores and five had science scores significantly higher than Canada's (Japan, Korea, Singapore, and Taiwan scored significantly higher than Canada in both mathematics and science in 1999). Scores for Canadian students in both mathematics and science improved markedly from 1995 to 1999, and Canada was one of only two countries that showed a statistically significant improvement in both subjects. The 1999 TIMSS results show that Quebec students did particularly well in mathematics, with an overall score within the group of the top six countries with scores significantly higher than the Canadian average. Alberta students did particularly well in science, placing among the top five countries with scores significantly higher than the Canadian average.

Results from the first PISA (the new OECD Programme for International Student Assessment) indicate that Canadian students were in the top three countries in reading, the top five or six in mathematics, and the top seven or eight in science. (Several countries had similar scores.) Full information on PISA is available at the Web site: www.pisa.oecd.org.

The impact of international tests on school systems cannot be overstated. When Canadian provinces decided to become involved in international assessments, they also agreed that each province would be treated as a separate jurisdiction: that is, the reports would treat each province as a country. British Columbia had the highest scores on these tests in the 1980s and early '90s, which led other provinces to examine their instructional practices and resulted in greater centralization of curriculum in several provinces. Possibly as a result, in 1999 Alberta posted scores higher than those of British Columbia on several international tests.

BOX 1.1 • *Content Standards*

CANADIAN CONTENT STANDARDS ON-LINE

Content standards developed by states and national professional associations may be found on the World Wide Web. The ministry of education in each province has a Web site with links to many other sites for provincial standards, standards of subject matter, professional associations, and discussions of standards. Enter the name of the province and the word "education" in any search engine.

Tests such as the SAIP and international assessments such as TIMSS serve a monitoring function, providing information on current status and progress. Several developments at the national level, however, reflect a desire to use testing and assessment not only to record progress but also as an instrument of educational reform.

Summary of Points

1.   Education practices in the United States and Canada look alike on the surface, but are actually quite different.
2.   Because schooling in the United States was a local matter, large-scale standardized testing was invented to provide standards for graduation and university entrance.
3.   Starting in the 1980s, large-scale testing fell into disrepute in the United States, leading many educators to recommend moving away from testing to "authentic" assessment, that is, assessment based on student products and performances as opposed to paper and pencil tests. This backlash carried over into Canada, although Canada had never relied on standardized testing to provide graduation or university entrance standards.
4.   Because schooling in Canada is the responsibility of each province, schooling has always been somewhat centralized, and there has not been the same need for standardized tests as in the United States
5.   The call for accountability in education in Canada and for each province to be "competitive" with one another and with the rest of the world has resulted in more emphasis on large-scale testing. However, these tests are based on curriculum and are more useful than traditional standardized tests.

Learning Exercises

1.   Discuss the potential effects of the pressure to compare schools, districts, and provinces in terms of student achievement test scores on instruction and student learning.
2.   Discuss the pros and cons of teaching to the specific content of externally mandated tests and assessments.

3.   Describe the purpose and function of the PISA assessment program. In what ways might this program influence school instruction?

References and Additional Reading

Calhoun, D. (1969). *The Education of Americans: A Documentary History.* Boston: Houghton Mifflin.

Callahan, R.E. (1962). *Education and the Cult of Efficiency.* Chicago: University of Chicago Press.

Centre for Research in Applied Measurement and Evaluation (2000). *Principles for Fair Student Assessment Practices for Education in Canada.* Edmonton: University of Alberta.

Cole, N.S., and Moss, P.A. (1989). "Bias in test use." In R. L. Linn (ed.), *Educational Measurement* (3rd ed.). Upper Saddle River, NJ: Merrill/ Prentice Hall.

National Commission on Excellence in Education (1983). *A Nation at Risk: The Imperative for Educational Reform.* Washington, DC: U.S. Government Printing Office.

Tyack, D.B. (1974). *The One Best System.* Cambridge, MA: Harvard University Press.

U.S. Congress, Office of Technology Assessment (1992). *Testing in American Schools: Asking the Right Questions* (OTA-SET-519). Washington, DC: U.S. Government Printing Office.

Widgor, A.K., and Garner, W.R. (eds.) (1982). *Ability Testing: Uses, Consequences, and Controversies, Part I.* Washington, DC: National Academy Press.

Willingham, W.W., and Cole, N.S. (1997). *Gender and Fair Assessment.* Mahwah, NJ: Lawrence Erlbaum Associates.

Weblinks

Alberta Government
Contains information about provincial testing.
http://www2.gov.ab.ca/home/school_and_students/

Council of Ministers of Education Canada
Information about Canada-wide testing.
http://www.cmec.ca/stats/pceip/1999/Indicatorsite/english/pages/page21e.html#2

Indian and Northern Affairs
Discussion of problems facing Native peoples in Canada.
http://www.oag-bvg.gc.ca/domino/reports.nsf/html/0004ce.html

2

Achievement Assessment and Instruction

This chapter will enable you to:

1. Explain why a variety of assessment methods are important in achievement assessment.
2. Write a definition of achievement assessment.
3. Describe the relation between instruction and assessment.
4. Distinguish among the various roles of assessment in the instructional process.
5. List the ways in which assessments can directly aid learning.

As Chapter 1 pointed out, Canadian schools have a tradition of using a variety of techniques for student assessment. Still, until the 1970s the paper and pencil test was the most common assessment technique. Then for about 20 years paper and pencil tests were out of fashion in many jurisdictions: many provinces did away with provincial examinations, and in fact efforts were made to avoid comparing schools, districts, or provinces. Now, at the beginning of the twenty-first century, the situation has changed yet again. Provincial exams and assessments are in fashion: comparisons among provinces, districts, and schools are common, and there is pressure on teachers to ensure that their students do well on tests.

This textbook takes the stance that while paper and pencil tests are important (and are in fact essential to a good assessment program), other methods of assessment are equally important, and teachers must use a variety of assessment methods. This is especially significant as large-scale testing becomes more prevalent, because teachers naturally want their students to do well on externally mandated tests, and tend to give students tests so the students can practise writing tests. As a result, student grades are once again being determined more by test results than by other assessment methods. Consider the following scenario.

In a province with no graduation exams, an English teacher bases his letter grades for the four reporting periods on tests (25 percent), products (40 percent), homework and class participation (20 percent), and performances (15 percent). Then the province introduces a graduation exam, worth 40 percent of the final grade. To ensure that his students can write the type of exam he knows they will be facing, the teacher continues to give tests worth 20 percent of the total grade. The percentage of the students' grade resulting from tests is now 60 percent rather than 25 percent, as it was originally, or 40 percent, as the provincial share would indicate. While provincial exams have important benefits, they lead to this result. Teachers must ensure that this does not happen, by reducing the percentage of their classroom marks that comes from testing.

Furthermore, some critics (especially in the United States, where paper and pencil testing was for many years by far the most common means of assessment) have called for more emphasis on **authentic assessment** of "real-life" **tasks** (e.g., solving problems that exist in the real world). Others have contended that paper and pencil testing should be replaced, at least in part, by types of **alternative assessment**. In Canada, the need is not to replace paper and pencil tests with authentic or alternative methods, but to avoid returning to the days when paper and pencil tests were the most important assessment technique. (See Box 2.1). If you want to determine whether students can write, have them write something. If you want to determine whether students can operate a machine, have them operate the machine. If you want to determine whether students can conduct an experiment, have them conduct an experiment. In short, if you want to determine whether they can perform a task, have them perform the task. There is little doubt that more emphasis on performance and product assessment in the schools improves the assessment of our intended learning outcomes. However, paper and pencil testing still has an important role to play, even as we focus more directly on performance and product-based tasks.

BOX 2.1 • *Commonly Used Assessment Terms*

Performance Assessments	Assessments requiring students to demonstrate their achievement of understandings and skills by actually performing a task or set of tasks (e.g., giving a speech, conducting an experiment, operating a machine).
Product Assessments	Assessments requiring students to demonstrate their achievement of understandings and skills by actually producing something (e.g., a story, a report, a map, a cake).
Alternative Assessments	A title for performance or product assessments that emphasizes that these assessment methods provide an alternative to traditional paper and pencil testing.
Authentic Assessments	A title for performance or product assessments that stresses the importance of focusing on the application of understandings and skills to real problems in "real-world" contextual settings.

Most types of performance or product have a knowledge component that is important to the performance or product. For example, good writing includes such factors as knowledge of vocabulary, grammar, and spelling. These are not well sampled by a writing task because we tend to use only the words we know, use sentence structures that we can punctuate easily, and substitute words we can spell for those we can't spell. Thus, in writing, we can structure the product to conceal our weaknesses. A separate test of vocabulary, grammar, and spelling can identify these weaknesses and be used to improve writing skill. Just don't interpret the test results as measures of "writing ability": the tests measure knowledge useful in writing, but writing ability is determined by assessing the actual writing (**product assessment**). Similarly, in operating machinery, the actual operation of the machine is the ultimate goal, but tests measuring knowledge of how to operate the machine and the safety precautions to follow may be needed before the hands-on **performance assessment**. Likewise, before conducting an experiment, tests can be used to determine how well students know the information needed for a well controlled experiment.

Throughout this book, the emphasis will be on achievement assessment that includes both paper and pencil testing and performance and product assessment. Tests can provide direct measures of many important learning outcomes, ranging from simple to complex, and they can provide needed information for assessing and improving actual real-life tasks. Thus, although we should strive for assessment that is as authentic as we can make it, within the constraints of the school setting, both tests and performance- and product-based tasks are needed for a complete assessment of student achievement. Further, so-called "authentic" assessment has its own problems, which will be discussed later.

As used in this book, **achievement assessment** is a broad category that includes all of the various methods for determining the extent to which students are achieving the intended learning outcomes of instruction. Because we are limiting our concern to achievement assessment, the single term *assessment* is used throughout the book as a matter of convenience.

Relation Between Instruction and Assessment

In preparing for any type of instructional program, our main concern is, "How can we most effectively bring about student learning?" As we ponder this question, our attention is naturally directed toward the methods and materials of instruction. However, at the same time we should also consider the role of assessment in the instructional process. When properly designed and appropriately used, assessment procedures can contribute to more effective instruction and greater student learning.

The close relation between instruction and assessment can be seen in Table 2.1. Both require that we clearly specify the learning outcomes to be achieved by students, and the provisions of well designed assessments closely parallel the characteristics of effective instruction. This relationship highlights the importance of broadening instructional planning to include assessment planning. The typical procedure of limiting instructional planning to the teaching–learning process is inadequate. Effective instruction requires that we expand our concern to a teaching–learning–assessment process, with assessment as a basic part of the instructional program. As with all instructional activities, the main function of assessment is to improve learning, which it can do in a number of ways.

TABLE 2.1 • *Relation Between Instruction and Assessment*

Instruction	Assessment
Instruction is most effective when:	*Assessment is most effective when:*
1. Directed toward a clearly defined set of intended learning outcomes.	1. Designed to assess a clearly defined set of intended learning outcomes.
2. The methods and materials of instruction are congruent with the outcomes to be achieved.	2. The nature and function of the assessments are congruent with the outcomes to be assessed.
3. The instruction is designed to fit the characteristics and needs of the students.	3. The assessments are designed to fit the relevant student characteristics and are fair to everyone.
4. Instructional decisions are based on information that is meaningful, dependable, and relevant.	4. Assessments provide information that is meaningful, dependable, and relevant.
5. Students are periodically informed concerning their learning progress.	5. Provision is made for giving the students early feedback of assessment results.
6. Remediation is provided for students not achieving the intended learning.	6. Specific learning weaknesses are revealed by the assessment results.
7. Instructional effectiveness is periodically reviewed and the intended learning outcomes and instruction modified as needed.	7. Assessment results provide information useful for evaluating the appropriateness of the objectives, the methods, and the materials of instruction.

Assessment in the Instructional Process

To be fully integrated with instruction, plans for assessment should be made during the planning for instruction. From the beginning of instruction to the end, teachers need to make numerous decisions. Carefully planned assessment procedures can improve the effectiveness of many of these decisions by providing more objective information on which to base judgments. Let us consider some of the decisions teachers need to make (1) at the beginning of instruction, (2) during instruction, and (3) at the end of instruction.

Beginning of Instruction (Placement Assessment)

Teachers need to answer two major questions before proceeding with the instruction:

1. To what extent do the students possess the skills and abilities that are needed to begin instruction?

2. To what extent have the students already achieved the intended learning outcomes of the planned instruction?

Information concerning the first question is frequently obtained from readiness pretests. These are tests given at the beginning of a course or unit of instruction that cover those prerequisite skills necessary for success in the planned instruction. For example, a test of computational skill might be given at the beginning of an algebra course, or a test of English grammar might be given at the beginning of a German course. Students lacking in prerequisite skills could be given remedial work, or they could be placed in a special section that had lower prerequisites.

The second question is frequently answered by a placement pretest covering the intended learning outcomes of the planned instruction. This might very well be the same test that is given at the end of the instruction; preferably it should be another form of the test. Here we are interested in determining whether students have already mastered some of the material we plan to include in our instruction. If they have, we might need to modify our teaching plans, encourage some students to skip particular units, and place other students at a more advanced level of instruction. The function of placement assessment is summarized in Figure 2.1.

In addition to the use of pretests, performance- and product-based tasks may also be useful for determining entry skills. In the area of writing, for example, obtaining writing samples at the beginning of instruction can establish a base for later assessments of progress. This type of preassessment would be especially valuable if portfolios of student work were to be maintained during the instruction.

The contribution that preassessment can make to instruction depends on the nature of the instruction, how well we know students, and how the results are to be used. A pretest in arithmetic may be quite useful at the beginning of an algebra course, whereas a pretest in a course that lacks a clearly defined set of prerequisite skills (e.g., social studies) may be of little value. Similarly, the results of a test of basic skills may be of great value to a new teacher unfamiliar with the students and of less value to an experienced teacher familiar with the students' backgrounds. In addition, preassessment will contribute little to the instructional program unless plans are made to remedy deficiencies, place students in the most beneficial position in the instructional sequence, or use the results as a base for assessing future progress. To be most effective, the use of preassessment should be considered during the instructional planning stage.

FIGURE 2.1 • Simplified model for the instructional role of placement assessment.

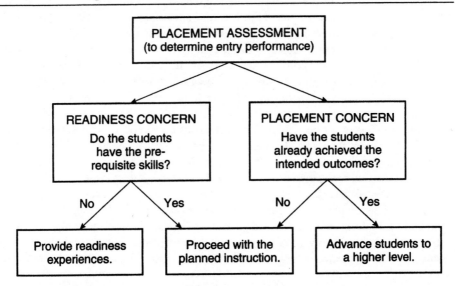

During Instruction (Formative and Diagnostic Assessment)

During the instructional program, our main concern is with the learning progress being made by students. Questions such as the following must be answered.

    1.   On which learning tasks are the students progressing satisfactorily? On which ones do they need help?

    2.   Which students are having such severe learning problems that they need remedial work?

    Tests used to monitor student progress during instruction are called formative tests. Formative tests are typically designed to measure the extent to which students have mastered the learning outcomes of a rather limited segment of instruction, such as a unit or a textbook chapter. These tests are similar to the quizzes and unit tests that teachers have traditionally used, but they place greater emphasis on (1) measuring all of the intended outcomes of the unit of instruction, and (2) using the results to improve learning (rather than to assign grades). The purpose is to identify the students' learning, successes, and failures so that adjustments in instruction and learning can be made. When the majority of students fail a test item, or set of items, the material is typically retaught in a group setting. When a minority of students experience learning failures, alternative methods of study are usually prescribed for each student (for example, reading assignments in a second book, computer instruction, and visual aids). These corrective prescriptions are frequently keyed to each item, or to each set of items designed to measure a separate learning task, so that students can begin immediately after testing to correct their individual learning errors.

    Formative assessment using performance-based tasks may involve periodic assessments of a product (e.g., writing sample, drawing) or of a process (e.g., giving a speech, operating a machine) with feedback to students concerning strengths and weaknesses. The aim here, as with formative testing, is to monitor learning progress and to provide corrective prescriptions to improve learning.

    When a student's learning problems are so persistent that they cannot be resolved by the corrective prescriptions of formative assessment, a more intensive study of the student's learning difficulties is called for. It is here that diagnostic assessment is useful. Diagnostic assessment attempts to answer such questions as the following: Are the students having difficulty in addition because they don't know certain number combinations, or because they don't know how to carry? Are the students' difficulties in reading German due to their inadequate knowledge of vocabulary, or to their poor grasp of certain elements of grammar? Are the students unable to apply scientific principles to new situations because they don't understand the principles, because their knowledge of particular concepts is weak, or because the new situations are too unfamiliar to them? Thus, diagnostic assessment focuses on the common sources of error encountered by students, so that the learning difficulties can be pinpointed and remedied.

    Diagnostic assessment can frequently be aided by the use of diagnostic tests. These tests typically include a relatively large number of test items in each specific area, with slight variations from one set of items to the next so that the cause of specific learning errors can be identified. In detecting errors in the addition of whole numbers, for example, we might construct a test that includes a set of items requiring no carrying, a set that requires simple carrying, and one that requires repeated carrying to determine if carrying is the source of the difficulty. Unfortunately, diagnostic tests are difficult to construct in most areas of instruction. Therefore, we must depend more heavily on observation and judgment.

Diagnosing learning problems is a matter of degree. Formative assessment determines whether a student has mastered the learning tasks being taught and, if not, prescribes how to remedy the learning failures. Diagnostic assessment is designed to probe deeper into the causes of learning deficiencies that are left unresolved by formative assessment. Of course, this is not to imply that all learning problems can be overcome by formative and diagnostic assessment. These are simply methods to aid in the identification and diagnosis of specific learning difficulties so that appropriate remedial steps can be taken. Diagnosing and remedying severe learning problems frequently require a wide array of assessment procedures and the services of specially trained personnel. All we are attempting to do here is to show how formative and diagnostic assessment can contribute to improved student learning during instruction. The model presented in Figure 2.2 summarizes the process.

End of Instruction (Summative Assessment)

At the end of a course or unit of instruction, we are concerned primarily with the extent to which the students have achieved the intended outcomes of the instruction. Questions such as the following must be answered:

1. Which students have mastered the learning tasks to such a degree that they should proceed to the next grade, course, or unit of instruction?

2. What letter grade should be assigned to each student?

FIGURE 2.2 • Simplified model for the instructional role of formative assessment.

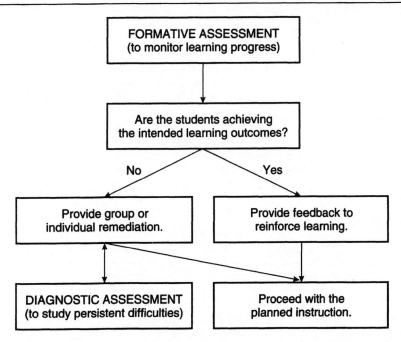

Achievement assessment at the end of instruction for the purpose of certifying mastery or assigning grades is called summative assessment. This assessment is typically comprehensive in coverage and includes both tests and performance assessments. Although the results are used primarily for grading, there should be some feedback to students and the results should be used for evaluating the effectiveness of the instruction. See Figure 2.3 for the summative assessment model.

It is important to note that summative assessment is a higher-stakes form of assessment than formative assessment. This means that the teacher must be more careful in the preparation and application of the assessment activity. When there are few or no marks involved, an error in describing an assignment may not matter much; when a student's mark for the term is at stake, it matters a lot.

Other Ways Assessments Can Aid Learning

As noted in the previous section, assessments can aid the teacher in making various instructional decisions having a direct influence on student learning. In addition, assessments can aid student learning in a number of other ways.

Student Motivation

A carefully planned assessment program can have a direct influence on student learning by (1) providing students with short-term goals, (2) clarifying the types of tasks to be learned, and (3) providing feedback concerning their learning progress. Short-term

FIGURE 2.3 • Simplified model for the instructional role of summative assessment.

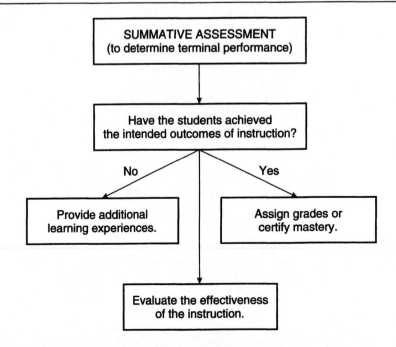

goals are more motivating than telling students, "Someday you will find this knowledge or skill useful." An expected assessment stimulates learning activity and directs it toward the learning tasks to be assessed. Its contribution to learning depends to a large extent on how faithfully our assessments reflect all of the important outcomes of the instruction and how we use the results. For example, if the application of principles is stressed in our assessment as well as in our teaching, we can expect students to direct greater efforts toward learning how to apply principles. Also, if the assessment results are reported to students as soon as possible, this feedback concerning their strengths and weaknesses in the application of principles will further clarify the nature of the task and indicate what changes are needed for effective performance. Thus, properly used assessments can motivate students to work toward the instructional objectives of a course by arousing greater learning activity, by directing it toward the intended learning outcomes, and by providing prompt knowledge of results.

Retention and Transfer of Learning

Because assessments tend to direct students' learning efforts toward the intended outcomes of instruction, they can be used as tools for increasing the retention and transfer of learning. In general, learning outcomes at the understanding, application, and interpretation levels are likely to be retained longer and to have greater transfer value than outcomes at the knowledge level. By including assessments of these more complex learning outcomes, we can direct attention to their importance and provide reinforcing practice in the skills, applications, and interpretations we are attempting to develop. Thus, assessments can be used to supplement and complement our teaching efforts in these areas and thereby increase the likelihood that the learning will be of greater permanent value to the students.

Student Self-Assessment

All instruction should be directed toward helping individuals better understand themselves so that they can make more intelligent decisions. Periodic assessment and feedback of the results can help students gain insight into what they can do well, the misconceptions that need correction, and the degree of skill they have in various areas. Such information provides the students with a more objective basis for assessing their own strengths and weaknesses. Properly used assessments tend to provide evidence of learning progress in such an objective and impartial way that the results can be accepted with little resistance or distortion. This assumes, of course, that the assessments are properly prepared and are being used to improve learning rather than to threaten or label students. In the latter instance, self-assessment is apt to be distorted by the psychological defense mechanisms an individual uses to maintain a positive self-image.

Evaluating Instructional Effectiveness

Assessment results can be used to evaluate the effectiveness of various aspects of the instructional process. For example, they can help determine the extent to which the instructional objectives were realistic, whether the methods and materials of instruction were appropriate, and how well the learning experiences were sequenced. When the majority of the students do poorly on an assessment, it may be the fault of the students but the difficulty is more likely to be found in the instruction. The teacher may be striving for learning outcomes that are unattainable by the students, using inappropriate materials, or using ineffective methods for bringing about the desired changes. An analysis of the students' responses and a class discussion of the results should provide clues to the source of the instructional difficulty so that corrective steps can be taken.

Teachers' Standards for Student Assessment

It is generally agreed that student assessment plays an important role in effective teaching and helps teachers make decisions about their teaching practices on the basis of the assessment results. *The Principles for Fair Student Assessment Practices for Education in Canada* is a document that was developed by a working group guided by a joint advisory committee. The advisory committee included two representatives appointed by each of the Canadian Education Association, Canadian School Boards Association, Canadian Association for School Administrators, Canadian Teachers' Federation, Canadian Guidance and Counselling Association, Canadian Association of School Psychologists, Canadian Council for Exceptional Children, Canadian Psychological Association, and Canadian Society for the Study of Education. In addition, the joint advisory committee included a representative of the provincial and territorial ministries and departments of education. (The entire document is reproduced in this text as Appendix 1.)

Special Considerations

The contents of this chapter apply equally, or perhaps especially, to special needs, Native, and ESL students. It is particularly important to include a variety of types of assessment for these students, and to monitor their progress carefully. In the case of special needs students who have an Individualized Education Plan (IEP), assessment is built into the plan. The learning outcomes will specify how well the student must achieve each outcome in order to be successful. The greatest assessment challenge with regard to special needs students not on IEPs, and Native and ESL students, is deciding whether standards that apply to other students also apply to them. This question will be considered in later chapters.

The purpose of assessment and evaluation for these students is the same as for other students—to inform the student and parents about the student's achievement in all areas of instruction. With the inclusion of special needs students in regular classrooms, most jurisdictions have adopted regulations concerning assessment, evaluation, and reporting for these students. In some cases, special needs students can achieve results that are comparable to other students', and can be assessed and reported on in similar ways. In other cases, assessment techniques have to be modified and, in some cases, changed entirely. Teachers should be guided by circumstances.

Summary of Points

1. In recent years there has been an increasing emphasis on large-scale paper and pencil testing. Teachers must ensure that they balance any such increase with less emphasis on testing in their own practices.

2. A well balanced assessment program should include both testing and perform-ance and product assessment, with each used where most appropriate.

3. Achievement assessment is a general category that includes a broad range of methods for determining the extent to which students are achieving the intend-ed learning outcomes of instruction.

4. Instruction is more effective when well designed assessments are an integral part of the instructional process.

5. Assessment procedures can be used for measuring entry performance (place-ment assessment), monitoring learning progress (formative and diagnostic assessment), or measuring end of instruction achievement (summative assess-ments).

6. Achievement assessments can contribute to student motivation, the retention and transfer of learning, student self-evaluation skills, and an evaluation of instructional effectiveness.

7. Teachers' standards for student assessment focus on their competence in select-ing assessment methods, developing assessment methods, administering and scoring them, interpreting and using assessment results, preparing valid grades, communicating assessment results, and recognizing inappropriate assessment methods and uses of assessment information.

Learning Exercises

1. List several instructional decisions and explain how each can be improved by the use of tests and other types of assessments.

2. Why is it necessary to specify what is to be evaluated before selecting or con-structing an assessment instrument?

3. What are some of the perceived advantages and disadvantages of paper and pencil tests relative to performance assessments?

References and Additional Reading

Airasian, P.W. (1997). *Classroom Assessment*, 3rd ed. New York: McGraw-Hill. Bloom, B.S., Madaus, G.T., and Hastings, J.T. (1981). *Evaluation to Improve Learning.* New York: McGraw-Hill.

Linn, R.L., and Gronlund, N.E. (2000). *Measurement and Assessment in Teaching*, 8th ed. Upper Saddle River, NJ: Merrill/Prentice-Hall.

McMillan, J.H. (2001). *Classroom Assessment: Principles and Practices for Effective Instruction*, 2nd ed. Boston: Allyn and Bacon.

Popham, W.J. (2002). *Classroom Assessment: What Teachers Need to Know*, 3rd ed. Boston: Allyn and Bacon.

Stiggins, R.J. (2001). *Student-Involved Classroom Assessment*, 3rd ed. Upper Saddle River, NJ: Merrill/Prentice-Hall.

Weblinks

British Columbia Ministry of Education
Information on provincial policy on assessment.
http://www.gov.bc.ca/bced/

Canadian Citizenship
Discussion of assessment in social studies.
http://www.arts.mcgill.ca/programs/misc/conference/myers.htm

Teachers Canada
A variety of resources for schoolteachers.
http://canadateachers.about.com/mbody.htm

3

Nature of Student Assessment

This chapter will enable you to:

1. Describe a situation where testing and performance or product assessment are needed and indicate why.
2. Describe the major types of assessment methods and give an example of each.
3. Distinguish between tests and performance and product assessments in terms of realism of tasks, complexity of tasks, assessment time needed, and judgment in scoring.
4. List the guidelines for effective student assessment.
5. Describe the meaning of validity and reliability and the role they play in preparing assessment procedures.
6. Distinguish between norm-referenced and criterion-referenced assessments.
7. Describe the uses and limitations of standardized tests.

As noted in Chapter 2, assessment is used as a broad category that includes all of the various methods used to determine the extent to which students are achieving the intended learning outcomes of instruction. This includes both testing and performance and product assessments. To assess a student's driving ability, for example, an **objective test** is used to measure knowledge of how to drive and follow the rules of the road, and driving over a prescribed course (performance assessment) is used to determine skill in driving the automobile. The test on rules of the road covers a much larger sample of driving rules than are likely to be encountered in the driving performance, but skill in driving can only be determined by sitting behind the wheel and driving. Both are important. The knowledge test tells how well the student knows what to do and the performance assessment tells how skillfully the student can do it.

Teachers have tended to favour selection-type tests (i.e., multiple choice, true–false, matching) because many questions can be asked in a relatively short time, they are easy to administer and score, and the results can be expressed in numbers that are easily recorded, compared, and reported to others. Unfortunately, teachers have also limited selection-type tests almost entirely to knowledge of facts and terms. Various studies have shown that between 80 and 90 percent of teacher-made tests focus on knowledge outcomes. There is little doubt that this overemphasis on selection-type tests and simple knowledge outcomes has led to the movement toward assessment techniques that measure more complex learning outcomes in realistic settings. The fact that paper and pencil tests can be designed to measure a wide array of complex learning outcomes has frequently been overlooked in the movement toward "authentic" assessment. It is our contention that education is best served by using both paper and pencil testing and the assessment of actual performance and products, with all of the assessment measures focusing on more complex learning tasks than typically has been the case in the past.

Major Types of Assessment Methods

Assessment methods vary widely but they can be summarized in four major categories; the typical characteristics of each major type of assessment are shown in Table 3.1. Selected-response tests require the student to choose the correct or best answer, as in multiple-choice, true–false, and matching tests. Supply-response tests require students to respond with a word, short phrase, or complete essay answer. Restricted-response performance and product assessments are concerned with the performance or products of a limited task that is highly structured, such as writing a brief paragraph on a given topic, selecting laboratory equipment, measuring humidity, or locating information with a computer. Extended-response performance assessments involve more comprehensive and less structured performance tasks, such as writing a short story, conducting a laboratory experiment, predicting weather, or using a computer to solve a problem. Besides requiring more extended performances, the assessment typically requires students to integrate and apply knowledge and skills to performance tasks in a realistic setting. If there is a product involved (e.g., a short story), students may also be expected to review and revise the product before submitting it, to add greater realism to the task.

TABLE 3.1 • *Summary Comparison of Assessment Methods*

Testing		Performance Assessment	
Selected Response	*Supply Response*	*Restricted Performance*	*Extended Performance*

	REALISM OF TASKS	
LOW ←——————————————————→ HIGH		

	COMPLEXITY OF TASKS	
LOW ←——————————————————→ HIGH		

	ASSESSMENT TIME NEEDED	
LOW ←——————————————————→ HIGH		

	JUDGMENT IN SCORING	
LOW ←——————————————————→ HIGH		

Realism of Tasks

By realism of assessment tasks, we mean the extent to which they simulate performance in the real world. Traditional selection-type tests are low in realism because they involve selecting a response from a given set of possible answers. The response is limited to the listed alternatives, and such highly structured problems seldom occur in the real world. The extended performance assessment is high in realism because it attempts to simulate performance in the real world. Assessing how well a student can drive an automobile, operate a machine, give a speech, or apply knowledge and understanding to a real-life problem (e.g., how to protect the environment) requires comprehensive sets of responses that approximate those occurring in the real world. In between these extremes are the supply-type tests (e.g., short answer and essay) and the restricted response performance assessments that provide a moderate amount of structure but greater freedom of response, and thus more realistic problems than the selection-type tests.

In addition to the movement to increase realism in assessment by increasing adoption of extended performance assessment, there has also been a trend toward making traditional paper and pencil tests more authentic (i.e., have greater realism). This has resulted in the designing of tests to measure more complex learning outcomes, and in the use of problems and procedures more like those in the real world. In a math problem, for example, students may be given more facts than are needed to solve the problem in order to see if they can select the facts needed to solve it. In solving a science problem, students might be given the freedom to select the procedure for solving the problem and be asked to justify the procedure used. In some cases this involves a shift from selection-type items to supply-type items, but in others it may be a combination of the two item types (e.g., explain why the selected answer was chosen).

Complexity of Tasks

Selected-response items tend to be low in the complexity of the problem presented and in the nature of the expected response. Although items can be designed to measure understanding and thinking skills, they typically present a single, limited problem and require choice of the correct or best answer. Extended performance problems, on the other hand, typically involve multiple learning outcomes, the integration of ideas and skills from a variety of sources, the availability of various possible solutions, and the need for multiple criteria for evaluating the results (e.g., preparing a plan for reducing drug traffic). Similarly, performance of a hands-on nature involves complex movement patterns that are guided by the integration of information and specific skills from various learning experiences (e.g., playing a musical instrument, operating a machine, repairing electronic equipment). As with the realism category, supply-type tests fall in between the two extremes. Essay tests, for example, can be designed to measure the ability to select, integrate, and express ideas, but the tasks are usually more limited and structured than in performance assessments.

Assessment Time Needed

A large number of selected-response items can be administered to a group of students in a relatively short time and the results can be quickly scored by hand or by machine.

This efficiency has no doubt been a major factor in their widespread use. Performance and product assessments tend to be extremely time consuming. Some tasks may require days or even weeks to complete (e.g., conduct an experimental study) and others may require assessing students one at a time (e.g., giving a speech, operating a machine). In most cases, evaluating the product or the performance is also difficult and time consuming. Supply-response tests, like the essay test, require more time to score than selected-response tests but less than that of performance and product assessments.

The greater amount of time needed for performance and product assessment may result in loss of content coverage because of the limited number of assessment problems that can be included in the instructional program. This raises a question concerning the extent to which the assessment results are generalizable to other comparable tasks. We can present "real-world" problems to students, but problems are frequently unique to a particular contextual setting and the real world changes. Thus, transfer of learning is a key consideration in performance and product assessment. We can justify the greater time needed only if the assessment is an integral part of instruction and transferable learning outcomes are emphasized (e.g., reasoning, critical thinking, psychomotor skills).

Judgment in Scoring

The amount of judgment involved in scoring varies widely. Each selected response item is marked right or wrong so the scoring is completely objective (i.e., different scorers will arrive at the same score). The essay test provides more freedom of response, and this introduces greater subjectivity into the scoring. Different scorers can and do arrive at different scores as they weight elements of the answer differently (e.g., completeness, organization, clarity of writing, and the like) and introduce other personal biases into their judgments. As the tasks become more comprehensive and complex, as in performance and product assessment, the demands on teacher judgment become even greater. Complex tasks that involve the integration of various types of information and skill and may have multiple solutions make it difficult, and in many cases undesirable, to have model answers as might be used with essay testing. With performance and product assessment, we are most likely to have to depend on identification of the **criteria** of a quality performance and then apply the criteria by means of a **rating scale**, a **scoring key**, or a set of **scoring rubrics**. Each of these steps is based on subjective judgment.

A review of these categories makes clear that each assessment method has its strengths and weaknesses. When we use selected-response tests, we can obtain comprehensive coverage of a content domain, and can administer, score, and interpret it easily, but we sacrifice realism and some types of complexity. When we use extended performance and product assessment, we can obtain a high degree of realism and increase the complexity of the tasks we can assess, but the time needed for assessment is frequently excessive and the evaluation of the student's achievement is highly judgmental. A useful rule would be to use the most efficient method as long as it is appropriate for assessing the intended learning outcomes, but don't neglect complex learning outcomes just because the assessment methods are time consuming and the results are difficult to score or judge.

Guidelines for Effective Student Assessment

The main purpose of a classroom assessment program is to improve student learning. This is most likely to result if assessment is closely integrated with instruction and is guided by a basic set of conditions. The following guidelines provide a general framework for using student assessment effectively.

 1. **Effective assessment requires a clear conception of all intended learning outcomes.** During both instructional and assessment planning, we need to ask ourselves— What are the intended learning outcomes of the instruction? What types of knowledge, understanding, application, and skills are we willing to accept as evidence that the instruction has been successful? Here, there is always the danger of focusing too narrowly on knowledge outcomes because they are easy to identify, state, and measure. Unless we include the more complex learning outcomes at this stage, they are likely to be neglected during assessment. We need to specify all intended learning outcomes in terms of student achievement and make plans to assess them all.

 2. **Effective assessment requires that a variety of assessment procedures be used.** The vast array of possible learning outcomes in any particular area of instruction means that various types of assessment procedures must be considered when planning for assessment. Selected-response tests may be used for some learning outcomes, and essay tests for others where ability to express ideas is important. In assessing performance skills, where we must depend largely on judgment, rating scales or checklists may be needed.

 In assessing the more complex learning outcomes, a combination of methods may be most suitable. Solving a complex problem, for example, may involve gathering information from diverse sources, analyzing it, integrating it, writing out a suggested solution, and making an oral presentation to a group. Similarly, locating and correcting a malfunction in a machine may involve reading a technical manual, identifying machine sounds, selecting proper tools, testing machine parts, and making the needed repairs. In addition to correcting the malfunction, speed of performance, following the proper sequence of steps, and similar factors may be an important part of the assessment. In evaluating performance skills, multiple assessment is likely to be the rule rather than the exception.

 3. **Effective assessment requires that the instructional relevance of the procedures be considered.** Instructionally relevant assessment means that the intended outcomes of instruction, the domain of learning tasks, and the assessment procedures will all be in close agreement. It also means that plans for using the assessment results in the instructional program must be considered. Will the classroom test be sufficiently diagnostic to provide for remedial action? Can the assessment of a complex skill be designed as an ongoing activity so that it can contribute directly to the instruction? These and similar questions are needed to obtain maximum integration of instruction and assessment. Remember, the main purpose of both instruction and assessment is to improve student learning. With a well designed assessment program, assessment activities may become barely distinguishable from instructional activities.

 4. **Effective assessment requires an adequate sample of student performance.** Assessment is always a matter of sampling. Our instruction typically covers numerous

knowledge and skill outcomes, but because of the limited time available for assessment and other constraints, we can only measure or judge a limited sample of student performance in any particular area. In preparing a classroom test, for example, there may be 100 terms that the students should know but we only have room for 20 terms in our test. Thus, we must select a representative sample from the 100 words because we want to be able to generalize from performance on the 20 terms as to how well students know the 100 terms. If our sample is adequate, we can estimate that 18 correct answers on the 20 terms indicates that a student knows about 90 percent of the 100 terms (with allowance for a margin of error, of course).

Sampling is also a problem in performance and product assessment. In fact, it is usually a greater problem. In assessing driving skill, for example, it would be impossible to include all possible driving problems in a brief driving test so we must settle for a representative sample of them. It is interesting to note that, for licensing purposes, some provinces are now including highway driving to obtain a more adequate sample of driving skill.

In the assessment of performance skills in the classroom, there are typically two problems of sampling. In a writing project, for example, we might ask (1) does the project include a representative sample of the writing skills we are stressing in our teaching, and (2) does performance on this project represent what writing performance would be like on other similar projects? Because extended performance assessment (e.g., giving a speech, conducting an experiment, applying math to a real-world problem) is so time consuming and context bound, the adequacy of sampling is always an important concern in planning the assessment.

5. **Effective assessment requires that the procedures be fair to everyone.** An assessment program that makes the intended learning outcomes clear to students, that uses assessment procedures that are instructionally relevant and adequately sample student performance, and uses assessment results to improve learning goes a long way toward creating an atmosphere of fairness. In addition, however, special efforts must be made to eliminate irrelevant sources of difficulty and bias of various types. Student performance may be inadequate because the directions were ambiguous, the reading level was inappropriate, or the performance called for knowledge or skills that were not intended as parts of the assessment task. Similarly, including racial or gender stereotypes in the assessment material may distort the results and create a feeling of unfairness. Fairness requires care in preparing and using assessment procedures, clearly communicating our intentions to students, and using the results to improve learning. As with sampling, performance and product assessments are likely to present greater problems (in this case, to be less fair) than paper and pencil testing. Paper and pencil tests are carried out under controlled conditions, with all students having the same chance to do well. Performances, and to a lesser extent products, are by nature less controlled, so students may have varying opportunities to do well. This does not mean that teachers should avoid performance and product assessments; it means that they should be careful to be as fair as they can be when planning and carrying out these types of assessment tasks.

6. **Effective assessment requires the specification of criteria for judging successful performance.** In the past, success was typically determined by comparing a stu-

dent's performance to that of others (norm-referenced interpretation). If performance surpassed that of others, it was considered excellent performance. If performance was lower than that of others, it was considered poor performance. Although this method of judging success has its merits and is useful in certain situations, it is not satisfactory as a measure of how well students are learning the intended outcomes of instruction. For this purpose we need criteria that describe what students can do when they perform successfully (e.g., type 40 words per minute with no more than two errors).

Establishing performance criteria is difficult in many areas but, if the intended learning outcomes are clearly stated in performance terms, the criteria for success can be more easily established. In assessing vocabulary, for example, we can describe success in terms of how well students can define each term and use it in a sentence, how well they can distinguish between similar terms, and how well they can use the terms in a writing project. Effective laboratory performance can be described in terms of the selection and manipulation of equipment, the accuracy of measurements, the procedures followed, and the written description and interpretation of results. By specifying success in performance terms, we can describe what students are achieving and how well. The degree of success can be expressed by scoring keys, scoring rubrics that describe degrees of effectiveness, rating scales, or whatever means is most useful for describing student performance.

Students should have a clear notion of what is expected of them and clearly specified criteria of successful performance can be used to clarify the learning tasks. In some cases, students may participate in defining the desired performance. In planning for oral reports, for example, discussing criteria and listing them on the board will cause students to focus on the criteria of a good oral report and help them improve their performance. This is one way that instruction and assessment can be blended together to the benefit of students.

7. **Effective assessment requires feedback to students that emphasizes strengths of performance and weaknesses to be corrected.** Feedback of assessment results to students is an essential factor in any assessment program. To be most effective, feedback should:

(a) be given as soon as possible following, or during, the assessment.

(b) be detailed and understandable to students.

(c) focus on successful elements of the performance and the errors to be corrected.

(d) provide remedial suggestions for correcting errors.

(e) be positive and provide a guide for improving both performance and self-assessment.

In performance and product assessment, our immediate goal is to improve achievement. But if we are to develop self-learners who will continue to improve on their own, then we need also to help them develop self-assessment skills. Thus, feedback must focus on both achievement and self-assessment skills. For example, we suggest not only how to modify performance but also how to check on the effect of the modifications on performance and how to determine future improvement. A final question concerning feedback might be, will this feedback to students make them more dependent on the teacher or will it contribute to more independent learning? The most desirable choice is obvious and is illustrated in Figure 3.1.

FIGURE 3.1 • Role of assessment feedback.

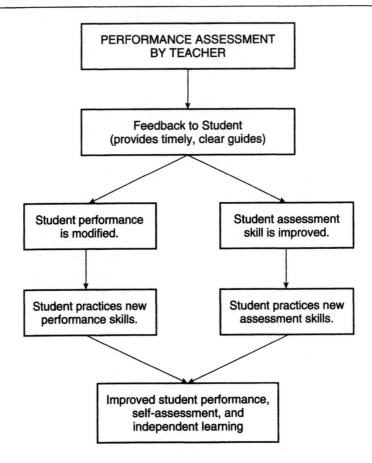

8. Effective assessment must be supported by a comprehensive grading and reporting system. All too frequently teachers have used various types of assessment procedures and then assigned grades on the basis of scores on an objective test. Instead, we need to have the grading and reporting system reflect the emphasis in our assessments. If half of our learning outcomes are assessed by tests and half by performance and product assessments, and a single grade is used, the two types of assessment should receive equal weight in the grade. With emphasis on performance and product assessment, more elaborate grading and reporting systems are needed to describe student achievement adequately. Reports based on the intended learning outcomes and portfolios of student work are becoming increasingly important for reporting learning progress to students, parents, and others. These more elaborate reports are in harmony with the comprehensive assessment procedures being used.

Because letter grades are still required for some purposes (e.g., college and university admission), it may be necessary to use both letter grades and a more elaborate report. In any event, the grading and reporting procedures should reflect and support the assessment procedures, be made clear to students at the beginning of instruction, and provide for periodic feedback to students concerning their learning progress.

Validity and Reliability in Assessment Planning

Two of the most important characteristics of a well designed assessment procedure are *validity* and *reliability*. These characteristics are of primary concern during assessment planning, and most of the suggestions in this book are directed toward preparing assessments that provide for valid and reliable interpretation of results. The technical issues of validity and reliability are discussed in considerable detail in Chapter 4, but a brief discussion of the importance of these concepts is in order here.

Validity refers to the appropriateness and meaningfulness of the inferences we make from assessment results for some intended use. For example, if we give a vocabulary test, we would like to be able to interpret the scores as a representative sample of the terms we have been teaching. If we do a good job of (1) clearly defining the domain of vocabulary items to be measured, (2) carefully preparing the test specifications, and (3) constructing a representative sample of relevant test items, our interpretations from the results are likely to be valid. We are now able to infer that high scores represent good knowledge of the vocabulary that has been taught. Note that it is the inference that is important. If we infer that high scores indicate good writing ability or good verbal ability, we are generalizing beyond the limited assessment domain being tested and the validity of our inference is in doubt, without further evidence. Thus, it is not the test scores that are valid or invalid but the inferences we make from them.

Performance and product assessments are typically viewed as providing more valid inferences concerning learning than traditional paper and pencil tests because they focus more directly on the types of tasks we are teaching. If we want to determine whether students can read, we have them read something. If we want to determine whether students can give a speech, we have them give a speech. If we want to determine whether students can operate a computer, we have them operate a computer. In each case, the task has the appearance of being valid (i.e., we have good face validity). However, it is not as simple as it seems. In performance and product assessment, the problem of defining the assessment domain, of specifying how the performance or product will be judged, and of obtaining a representative sample of tasks poses special problems. For example, there are many different types of reading, many different types of speeches, and many different types of problems to be solved on the computer. Each requires its own specifications and scoring rubrics, and because of the time consuming nature of performance and product assessment, the sampling tends to be limited. This restricts the extent to which we can infer that performance on one assessment task is generalizable to performance on other assessment tasks in the same area.

Reliability refers to the consistency of assessment results. For example, if a student earns a score of 60 on a test, we would like to be able to say that 60 accurately represents the student's test performance. Thus, if we tested the student at a different time or with a different sample of equivalent items, we would expect to obtain a similar score. Similarly, if a student receives a high rating on a writing project, we would like to say that it represents the student's writing skill and that if others rated the project the results would be similar. This consistency of results would indicate that they are relatively free from errors and thus we can rely on them (i.e., they have "rely-ability").

We cannot, of course, expect assessment results to be perfectly consistent over different occasions or over different samples of the same achievement domain. Such factors as ambiguities, variations in samples, fluctuations in motivation and attention, and luck can introduce errors that cause assessment results to vary. Likewise, in judging performance and product tasks, the personal biases of the rater can introduce error into the results. An important goal in assessment is to keep these various types of errors to a minimum so that our results are as reliable as possible.

In addition to being important in its own right, reliability is necessary to obtain valid inferences from assessment results. After all, if an individual's test score fluctuated widely on a given sample of items, we could not expect to draw valid inferences concerning the student's achievement. Similarly, if ratings varied widely on a student's writing project, valid inferences could not be made concerning writing skill. Thus, reliability provides the consistency of results that makes valid inferences possible. Of course, the consistency of results is just one important requirement for valid inferences. If a teacher asked her students to do as many push-ups as possible each Friday, she would probably obtain high reliability: the same students would perform the most push-ups each week, and the same students would perform the fewest. If, however, she then used the numbers of push-ups to determine the students' math grades, that would hardly be valid. We could be consistently assessing the wrong thing, using inappropriate procedures, or generalizing beyond the achievement domain being assessed. Thus, reliability is a necessary—but not a sufficient—condition for making valid inferences.

Both the validity and reliability of assessment results can be provided for during the preparation of assessment procedures. When we clearly specify the intended learning outcomes, define the achievement domain to be assessed, and select a relevant and representative set of assessment tasks, we are providing for valid inferences concerning learning. When we include an adequate number of tasks in our assessment and we use procedures that are free from ambiguity, irrelevant sources of difficulty, unintended clues, and other factors that might distort the results, we are providing for both reliability and validity.

Norm-Referenced and Criterion-Referenced Assessment

An achievement assessment can be used to provide (1) a relative ranking of students or (2) a description of the learning tasks a student can and cannot perform. Results of the first type are interpreted in terms of each student's relative standing among other students (for example, "He is third highest in a class of 35 students"). This method of interpreting student performance is called **norm-referenced interpretation**. Results of the second type are expressed in terms of the specific knowledge and skills each student can demonstrate (e.g., "She can identify the parts of a microscope and demonstrate its use"). This method of interpreting assessment results is called **criterion-referenced interpretation**. Both methods of describing assessment results are useful. The first tells how an individual's performance compares with that of others. The second tells in specific performance terms what an individual can do without reference to the performance of others.

Strictly speaking, the terms *norm-referenced* and *criterion-referenced* refer only to the method of interpreting the results. Thus, both types of interpretation could be applied to the same assessment. For example, we might say, "Joan surpassed 90 percent of the students (norm-referenced interpretation) by correctly completing 20 of the 25 chemical equations" (criterion-referenced interpretation). The two types of interpretation are likely to be most meaningful, however, when the assessment is designed specifically for the type of interpretation to be made. In general, norm-referenced interpretation is facilitated by a wide spread of scores so that reliable discriminations can be made among students at various levels of achievement. Criterion-referenced interpretation is facilitated by assessment tasks that provide a detailed description of student performance. In testing, this means a larger number of test items per task. In performance assessment, this means performance tasks that make clear what parts of the task a person can and cannot do.

Although norm-referenced and criterion-referenced interpretations apply to all types of achievement assessments, the differences can be most clearly indicated when applied to testing. A summary of some common characteristics of tests specifically designed for each type of interpretation is presented in Table 3.2 (page 32). It must be kept in mind, however, that these are primarily matters of emphasis. For example, norm-referenced tests are typically, but not exclusively, used for surveying achievement over a broad range of learning outcomes. By the same token, criterion-referenced tests are typically, but not exclusively, used for **mastery testing**. A review of the characteristics of each testing approach in Table 3.2 will reveal the differences that exist when each test is constructed to serve its principal use. It is not uncommon, however, to view the two test types as the ends of a continuum rather than as discrete categories, and to combine the best features of each in constructing achievement tests.

For most instructional purposes, criterion-referenced assessments are to be favoured. We can best help students improve learning by determining what tasks they can and cannot perform. Thus, the classroom assessment program should be based on instruments and procedures that provide for this type of interpretation. Norm-referenced interpretation is most useful when we are concerned about the relative ranking of students, as in the selection and classification of students (e.g., advance placement, grouping, giving awards, and relative grading).

Most of the discussions of procedures for constructing tests and making performance assessment will apply to all types of tests and assessments. Where there are significant differences due to the type of interpretation to be made, these will be noted.

Standardized Tests

As mentioned in Chapter 1, standardized achievement tests are not currently used in Canada to the extent they were in the past, nor to the extent they were and are used in the United States. More and more, provinces are adopting their own large-scale tests to see how well schools and districts are doing. Standardized tests are still used, however, so a brief discussion would seem to be in order.

TABLE 3.2 • *Summary Comparison of Two Basic Approaches to Achievement Testing*

	Norm-Referenced Testing	Criterion-Referenced Testing
Principal Use	Survey testing.	Mastery testing.
Major Emphasis	Measures individual differences in achievement.	Describes tasks students can perform.
Interpretation of Results	Compares performance to that of other individuals.	Compares performance to a clearly specified achievement domain.
Content Coverage	Typically covers a broad area of achievement.	Typically focuses on a limited set of learning tasks.
Nature of Test Plan	Table of specifications is commonly used.	Detailed domain specifications are favoured.
Item Selection Procedures	Items are selected that provide maximum discrimination among individuals (to obtain a reliable ranking). Easy items are typically eliminated from the test.	Includes all items needed to adequately describe performance. No attempt is made to alter item difficulty or to eliminate easy items to increase the spread of scores.
Performance Standards	Level of performance is determined by relative position in some known group (e.g., ranks fifth in a group of 20).	Level of performance is commonly determined by absolute standards (e.g., demonstrates mastery by defining 90 percent of the technical terms).

The most important features of standardized tests are that: (1) they are designed to provide a curve, closely approximating the **normal curve** of distribution, so they may not test basic skills (if everyone gets the correct answer to a question, there is no discrimination); and (2) because the tests are not curriculum specific (that is, they are not based on a particular curriculum), they test generic skills and knowledge widely considered to be important.

Thus, a **standardized achievement test** measures a standard set of broadly based educational outcomes, uses standard directions and standard scoring procedures, and provides for a comparison of a student's score to that of similar students who have taken the same test under the same conditions.

The score a student receives when a test has been scored according to the directions is called the **raw score**. On a classroom test, this is typically the number of items a student answers correctly. Although raw scores are used in classroom testing, the interpretations and comparisons made with standardized tests require that the raw scores be converted to some type of **derived score**. Raw scores won't work because tests may differ in the number of items in the test and the difficulty of the items. By converting raw scores to the same derived score scale, we provide a common basis for comparing relative performance.

The raw scores on a standardized test are converted to derived scores during the norming of the test. Attempts are made to obtain norm groups that contain a sample of students like those for whom the test is intended. National **norms**, for example, typically include students from the various geographic regions of Canada, urban and rural schools, and schools of different size. A balance of boys and girls, socioeconomic levels, and ethnic groups is also sought. Thus, national norms should approximate as closely as possible the student population throughout the country.

It is important to note that the scores in the norm group should not be viewed as goals or standards. They are simply the scores that a representative group of students have earned on the test. They aid in interpreting and comparing test performance but they do not represent levels of performance to strive for. They are average or typical scores obtained in average or typical schools.

The most common way of interpreting raw scores is by converting them into percentile rank or grade equivalents. A **percentile rank** indicates a student's relative position in a group in terms of the percentage of group members scoring at or below the student's raw score. For example, if a raw score of 33 equals a percentile rank of 80, it means 80 percent of the group members had raw scores equal to or lower than 33.

When interpreting percentile ranks, a number of cautions must be kept in mind. (1) Percentile ranks describe test performance in terms of the *percentage of persons* earning a lower score and *not* the percentage of items answered correctly. The **percentage correct score** is a criterion-referenced interpretation; *percentile rank* indicates relative standing and, therefore, is a norm-referenced score. (2) Percentile ranks are not equally spaced on the scale. A difference of 5 percentile ranks near the middle of the distribution of scores represents a smaller difference in test performance than a 5-percentile-rank difference at the ends of the distribution. This is because percentile ranks are based on the percentage of persons being surpassed and there is a larger percentage of persons in the middle of a score distribution to surpass than at the ends of the distribution. For example, at the high end of the distribution, a raw score difference of several points will make little difference in percentile rank because there are so few high scores. Although this limits some uses of percentile ranks (e.g., they can't be directly averaged), they remain one of the most useful and easiest to interpret types of derived scores.

Grade equivalent scores provide another widely used method of describing test performance. They are used primarily at the elementary school level. With these scores, a student's raw score on the test is converted to the grade level at which the score matches the average raw score of students in the norm group. As with other derived scores, tables in the test manual present parallel columns of raw scores and grade equivalents. Thus, all we need to do is consult the table and obtain the grade equivalent for any given raw score.

There are some important caveats to be noted when using grade equivalent scores. First, note that the grade equivalent score is expressed in terms of the grade level and the month in that school year. Scores are equated to the average score earned by students (in the norm group) in the middle of the grade at which the test is aimed. If a student in the middle of Grade 4 achieved a score of 4.4 on the reading portion, we would interpret his reading performance as average. In language, the same student might score 6.3, and be judged as two years advanced, and in math, a score of 7.6 would indicate he is more than three years advanced. Does that mean that he can do the work at these levels? No, it most likely means that he does Grade 4 work in these areas faster and more efficiently than do other Grade 4 students. The tests probably did not include Grade 6 and 7 material. The same misinterpretations can occur with low grade equivalents. If the student had a math score of 2.0, for example, it wouldn't mean he could only do Grade 2 math problems. It would more likely mean that he did Grade 4 problems more slowly and with more errors than other Grade 4 students. High and low grade equivalent scores are typically obtained by extrapolation and do not represent average scores earned by those groups. This is often necessary because students at lower grade levels may not have the knowledge and skill needed to take the test, and students at higher grade levels may have moved beyond the types of skills measured by the test.

Grade equivalent scores provide a simple method of interpreting test performance, but when using them and interpreting them to parents, the following common misinterpretations should be avoided.

1.   They are *not* standards to be achieved but simply the average scores of students in the norm group.

2.   They do *not* indicate the grade level at which a student can do the work.

3.   Extremely high and low grade equivalent scores are *not* as dependable indicators of test performance as those near the student's grade level.

In addition to these cautions to be observed when interpreting an individual's grade equivalent scores, a comparison of scores on tests in a **test battery** requires an additional caution. Growth in basic skills, for example, is uneven. In reading, growth is more rapid than in math, which depends more directly on the skills taught in school. Thus, a difference of a year in grade equivalent scores represents a larger difference in achievement on a reading test than on a math test. In addition, growth in achievement tends to slow down at different times for different skills, and when growth slows down, the differences in achievement between grade equivalent scores become smaller. Both the variations in growth of skills from one area to another and the variations in patterns of growth over time contribute to the unevenness of the units on our grade equivalent score scale. In comparing a student's grade equivalent scores on different tests from a test battery, it may be wise to look at the norm table to see how the raw scores spread out on each test. A high or low grade equivalent score might be discounted if the difference from other grade equivalent scores is based on relatively few raw score points.

Summary of Points

1. Student assessment must include the assessment of complex learning outcomes.
2. Assessment methods vary widely, but they can be classified as selected-response tests, supply-response tests, restricted-response performance and product assessments, or extended-response performance and product assessments.
3. Selected-response tests (e.g., multiple-choice tests) are lowest in realism and complexity of the tasks assessed, but require little time to administer and can be scored quickly and objectively.
4. Supply-response tests (e.g., essay tests) are higher in realism and the complexity of tasks they can measure (e.g., ability to originate, integrate, and express ideas) than selected-response tests, but they are more time consuming to use and more difficult to score.

5. Performance and product assessments, both restricted-response and extended-response, can be designed with high degrees of realism (i.e., like real-world problems) that focus on highly complex learning tasks, but they require large amounts of time to use and the scoring is judgmental and highly subjective.

6. A sound assessment policy would be to use the most efficient method available for assessing each intended learning outcome as long as it is appropriate, but don't neglect complex learning outcomes just because the assessment methods are more time consuming to use and more difficult to score or judge.

7. Effective assessment requires a clear conception of all intended learning outcomes, a variety of assessment procedures that are relevant to the instruction, an adequate sample of tasks, procedures that are fair to everyone, criteria for judging success, timely and detailed feedback to students, and a grading and reporting system that is in harmony with the assessment program.

8. Validity and reliability are the two most important characteristics of any assessment method and must be considered during the planning and preparation of assessment procedures.

9. Valid and reliable interpretations of assessment results require clearly defined intended learning outcomes, a representative sample of instructionally relevant tasks, a sound scoring system, and freedom from irrelevant factors that introduce error.

10. Assessment results can be interpreted by comparing a student's performance to that of others (norm-referenced) or by describing the student's performance on a clearly defined set of tasks (criterion-referenced).

11. Criterion-referenced interpretation is especially important for instructional uses of assessment results, but norm-referenced interpretation may be needed for selection and classification decisions.

12. In some cases, both criterion-referenced and norm-referenced interpretation may be used with the same assessment.

13. Standardized tests can be useful, but must be interpreted with care, especially when being discussed with parents.

Learning Exercises

1. Name three differences between restricted-response and extended-response performance tasks. When is each most suitable?

2. What are two sampling difficulties with product or performance assessment? How might you overcome these problems?

3. Which of the following represents a criterion-referenced interpretation and which a norm-referenced interpretation?
   (a) Mary's reading score placed her near the bottom of the class.
   (b) Chan defined 90 percent of the science terms correctly.
   (c) Mike can identify all of the parts of a sentence.
   (d) Teresa surpassed 85 percent of the Grade 6 students on the arithmetic test.

References and Additional Reading

Linn, R.L., and Gronlund, N.E. (2000). *Measurement and Assessment in Teaching*, 8th ed. Upper Saddle River, NJ: Merrill/Prentice-Hall.

McMillan, J.H. (2001). *Classroom Assessment: Principles and Practices for Effective Instruction*, 2nd ed. Boston: Allyn and Bacon.

Oosterhoff, A.C. (1999). *Developing and Using Classroom Assessments*, 2nd ed. Upper Saddle River, NJ: Prentice-Hall.

Smith, J.K., Smith, L.F., and DeLisi, R. (2001). *Natural Classroom Assessment*. Thousand Oaks, CA: Corwin Press.

Stiggins, R.J. (2001). *Student-Involved Classroom Assessment*, 3rd ed. Upper Saddle River, NJ: Merrill/Prentice-Hall.

Wiggins, G.P. (1998). *Educative Assessment: Designing Assessments to Inform and Improve Student Performance*. San Francisco, CA: Jossey-Bass.

Weblinks

Assessment, Evaluation, and Reporting
Simcoe (Ontario) school board site.
http://mariposa.scdsb.on.ca/SServices/assess/principles.htm

Standards and Assessments as Part of Effective Education
CMEC site on assessment; an important Canadian viewpoint.
http://www.interlog.com/~klima/ed/standards.html

Student Performance Indicator Definitions
Vermont state site for statewide testing program.
http://crs.uvm.edu/schlrpt/perform.htm

4

Validity and Reliability

This chapter will enable you to:

1. Distinguish between validity and reliability.
2. Describe the essential features of the concept of validity.
3. Describe how content-related evidence of validity is obtained.
4. List factors that can lower the validity of achievement assessments.
5. Describe procedures for obtaining criterion-related evidence of validity.
6. Describe procedures for obtaining construct-related evidence of validity.
7. Describe the role of consequences of using an assessment procedure on its validity.
8. Describe the methods for estimating test reliability and the type of information provided by each.
9. Describe how the standard error of measurement is computed and interpreted.
10. Explain how to determine the reliability of a performance-based assessment.

The two most important questions to ask about a test or other assessment procedure are: (1) to what extent will the interpretation of the results be appropriate, meaningful, and useful, and (2) to what extent will the results be free from errors? The first question is concerned with *validity*, the second with *reliability*. An understanding of both concepts is essential to the effective construction, selection, interpretation, and use of tests and other assessment instruments. Validity is the most important quality to consider in the preparation and use of assessment procedures. First and foremost, we want the results to provide a representative and relevant measure of the achievement domain under consideration. Our second consideration is reliability, which refers to the consistency of our assessment results. For example, if we tested individuals at a different time, or with a different sample of equivalent items, we would like to obtain approximately the same results. This consistency of results is important for two reasons. (1) Unless the results are fairly stable, we cannot expect them to be valid. For example, if an individual scored high on a test one time and low another time, it would be impossible to validly describe the achievement. (2) Consistency of results indicates smaller errors of measurement and, thereby, more dependable results. Thus, reliability provides the consistency needed to obtain validity and enables us to interpret assessment results with greater confidence.

Although it is frequently unnecessary to make elaborate validation and reliability studies of informal assessment procedures, an understanding of these concepts provides a conceptual framework that can serve as a guide for more effective construction of assessment instruments, more effective selection of standardized tests, and more appropriate interpretation and use of assessment results.

Validity

Validity is concerned with the interpretation and use of assessment results. For example, if we infer from an assessment that students have achieved the intended learning outcomes, we would like some assurance that our tasks provided a relevant and representative measure of the outcomes. If we infer that the assessment is useful for predicting or estimating some other performance, we would like some credible evidence to support that interpretation. If we infer that our assessment indicates that students have good "reasoning ability," we would like some evidence to support the fact that the results actually reflect that construct. If we infer that our use of an assessment had positive effects (e.g., increased motivation) and no adverse effects (e.g., poor study habits) on students, we would like some evidence concerning the consequences of its use. These are the kinds of considerations we are concerned with when considering the validity of assessment results.

Content-Related Evidence

Content-related evidence of validity is critical when we want to use performance on a set of tasks as evidence of performance on a larger domain of tasks. Let's assume, for example, that we have a list of 500 words that we expect our students to be able to spell correctly at the end of the school year. To test their spelling ability, we might give them a 50-word spelling test. Their performance on these words is important only insofar as it provides evidence of their ability to spell the 500 words. Thus, our spelling test would provide a valid measure to the degree to which it provided an adequate sample of the 500 words it represented. If we selected only easy words, only difficult words, or only words that represented certain types of common spelling errors, our test would tend to be unrepresentative and thus the scores would have low validity. If we selected a balanced sample of words that took these and similar factors into account, our test scores would provide a representative measure of the 500 spelling words and thereby provide for high validity.

It should be clear from this discussion that the key element in content-related evidence of validity is the adequacy of the **sampling**. An assessment is always a sample of the many tasks that could be included. Content validation is a matter of determining whether the sample of tasks is representative of the larger domain of tasks it is supposed to represent.

Content-related evidence of validity is especially important in achievement assessment. Here we are interested in how well the assessment measures the intended learning outcomes of the instruction. We can have greater assurance that an assessment provides valid results by (1) identifying the learning outcomes to be assessed, (2) preparing a plan that specifies the sample of tasks to be used, and (3) preparing an assessment procedure that closely fits the set of specifications. These are the best procedures we have for ensuring the assessment of a representative sample of the domain of tasks encompassed by the intended learning outcomes.

Although the focus of content-related evidence of validity is on the adequacy of the sampling, a valid interpretation of the assessment results assumes that the assessment was properly prepared, administered, and scored. Validity can be lowered by inadequate procedures in any of these areas (see Box 4.1). Thus, validity is "built in" during the planning and preparation stages and maintained by proper administration and scoring. Throughout this book we describe how to prepare assessments that provide valid results, even though we have not used the word *validity* as each procedure is discussed.

In summary, content-related evidence of validity is of major concern in achievement assessment, whether you are developing or selecting the assessment procedure. When constructing a test, for example, content relevance and representativeness are built in by following a systematic procedure for specifying and selecting the sample of test items, constructing high quality items, and arranging the test for efficient administration and scoring. In test selection, it is a matter of comparing the test sample to the domain of tasks to be measured and determining the degree of correspondence between them. Similar care is needed when preparing and using product and performance assessments. Thus, content-related evidence of validity is obtained primarily by careful, logical analysis.

Criterion-Related Evidence

Two types of studies are used in obtaining criterion-related evidence of validity. These can be explained most clearly using test scores, although they could be used with any type of assessment result. The first type of study is concerned with the use of test performance to predict future performance on some other valued measure called a *criterion*. For example, we might use scholastic aptitude test scores to predict course grades (the criterion). For obvious reasons, this is called a *predictive* study. The second type of

---

BOX 4.1 • *Factors That Lower the Validity of Assessment Results*

1. Tasks that provide an inadequate sample of the achievement to be assessed.
2. Tasks that do not function as intended, due to use of improper types of tasks, lack of relevance, ambiguity, clues, bias, inappropriate difficulty, or similar factors.
3. Improper arrangement of tasks and unclear directions.
4. Too few tasks for the types of interpretation to be made (e.g., interpretation by objective based on a few test items).
5. Improper administration—such as inadequate time allowed and poorly controlled conditions.
6. Judgmental scoring that uses inadequate scoring guides, or objective scoring that contains computational errors.

study is concerned with the use of test performance to estimate current performance on some criterion. For instance, we might want to use a test of study skills to estimate what the outcome would be of a careful observation of students in an actual study situation (the criterion). Since with this procedure both measures (test and criterion) are obtained at approximately the same time, this type of study is called a *concurrent* study.

Although the value of using a predictive study is rather obvious, a question might be raised concerning the purpose of a concurrent study. Why would anyone want to use test scores to estimate performance on some other measure that is to be obtained at the same time? There are at least three good reasons for doing this. First, we may want to check the results of a newly constructed test against some existing test that has a considerable amount of validity evidence supporting it. Second, we may want to substitute a brief, simple testing procedure for a more complex and time consuming measure. For example, our test of study skills might be substituted for an elaborate rating system if it provided a satisfactory estimate of study performance. Third, we may want to determine whether a testing procedure has *potential* as a predictive instrument. If a test provides an unsatisfactory estimate of current performance, it certainly cannot be expected to predict future performance on the same measure. On the other hand, a satisfactory estimate of present performance would indicate that the test may be useful in predicting future performance as well. This would inform us that a predictive study would be worth doing.

The key element in both types of criterion-related study is the *degree of relationship* between the two sets of measures: (1) the test scores and (2) the criterion to be predicted or estimated. This relationship is typically expressed by means of a correlation coefficient or an expectancy table.

Correlation Coefficients. Although the computation of correlation coefficients is beyond the scope of this book, the concept of correlation can easily be grasped. A **correlation coefficient** (*r*) simply indicates the degree of relationship between two sets of measures. A *positive* relationship is indicated when high scores on one measure are accompanied by high scores on the other; low scores on the two measures are similarly associated. A *negative* relationship is indicated when high scores on one measure are accompanied by low scores on the other. The extreme degrees of relationship it is possible to obtain between two sets of scores are indicated by the following values:

1.00	=	perfect positive relationship
0.00	=	no relationship
−1.00	=	perfect negative relationship

When a correlation coefficient is used to express the degree of relationship between a set of test scores and some criterion measure, it is called a **validity coefficient.** For example, a validity coefficient of 1.00 applied to the relationship between a set of aptitude test scores (the predictor) and a set of achievement test scores (the criterion) would indicate that each individual in the group had exactly the same relative standing on both measures, and would thereby provide a perfect prediction from the aptitude scores to the achievement scores. Most validity coefficients are smaller than this, but the extreme positive relationship provides a useful benchmark for evaluating validity coefficients. The closer the validity coefficient approaches 1.00, the higher the degree of relationship and, thus, the more accurate our predictions of each individual's success on the criterion will be.

A more realistic procedure for evaluating a validity coefficient is to compare it to the validity coefficients that are *typically* obtained when the two measures are correlated. For example, a validity coefficient of 0.40 between a set of aptitude test scores and achievement test scores would be considered small because we typically obtain coefficients in the 0.50 to 0.70 range for these two measures. Therefore, validity coefficients must be judged on a relative basis, the larger coefficients being favoured. To use validity coefficients effectively, one must become familiar with the size of the validity coefficients that are typically obtained between various pairs of measures under different conditions (e.g., the longer the time span between measures, the smaller the validity coefficient).

Expectancy Table. The expectancy table is a simple and practical means of expressing criterion-related evidence of validity and is especially useful for making predictions from test scores. The **expectancy table** is simply a twofold chart with the test scores (the predictor) arranged in categories down the left side of the table and the measure to be predicted (the criterion) arranged in categories across the top of the table. For each category of scores on the *predictor*, the table indicates the percentage of individuals who fall within each category of the *criterion*. An example of an expectancy table is presented in Table 4.1.

Note in Table 4.1 that of those students who were in the above-average group (**stanines** 7, 8, and 9) on the test scores, 43 percent received a grade of A, 43 percent a B, and 14 percent a C. Although these percentages are based on this particular group, it is possible to use them to predict the future performance of other students in this science course. Hence, if a student falls in the above-average group on this scholastic aptitude test, we might predict that he or she has 43 chances out of 100 of earning an A, 43 chances out of 100 of earning a B, and 14 chances out of 100 of earning a C in this particular science course. Such predictions are highly tentative, of course, due to the small number of students on which this expectancy table was built. Teachers can construct more dependable tables by accumulating data from several classes over a period of time.

Expectancy tables can be used to show the relationship between any two measures. Constructing the table is simply a matter of (1) grouping the scores on each measure into a series of categories (any number of them), (2) placing the two sets of categories on a twofold chart, (3) tabulating the number of students who fall into each position in

TABLE 4.1 • *Expectancy Table Showing the Relation between Scholastic Aptitude Scores and Course Grades for 30 Students in a Science Course*

Grouped Scholastic Aptitude Scores (Stanines)	Percentage in Each Score Category Receiving Each Grade				
	E	D	C	B	A
Above Average (7, 8, 9)			14	43	43
Average (4, 5, 6)		19	37	25	19
Below Average (1, 2, 3)	57	29	14		

the table (based on the students' standing on both measures), and (4) converting these numbers to percentages (of the total number in that row). Thus, the expectancy table is a clear means of showing the relationship between sets of scores. Although the expectancy table is more cumbersome to deal with than a correlation coefficient, it has the special advantage of being easily understood by persons without knowledge of statistics. Thus, it can be used in practical situations to clarify the predictive efficiency of a test.

Construct-Related Evidence

The construct-related category of evidence focuses on assessment results as a basis for inferring the possession of certain psychological characteristics. For example, we might want to describe a person's reading comprehension, reasoning ability, or mechanical aptitude. These are all hypothetical qualities, or *constructs,* that we assume exist in order to explain behaviour. Such theoretical constructs are useful in describing individuals and in predicting how they will act in many different specific situations. To describe a person as being highly intelligent, for example, is useful because that term carries with it a series of associated meanings that indicate what the individual's behaviour is likely to be under various conditions. Before we can interpret assessment results in terms of these broad behaviour descriptions, however, we must first establish that the constructs that are presumed to be reflected in the scores actually do account for differences in performance.

Construct-related evidence of validity for a test includes (1) a description of the theoretical framework that specifies the nature of the construct to be measured, (2) a description of the development of the test and any aspects of measurement that may affect the meaning of the test scores (e.g., test format), (3) the pattern of relationship between the test scores and other significant variables (e.g., high correlations with similar tests and low correlations with tests measuring different constructs), and (4) any other type of evidence that contributes to the meaning of the test scores (e.g., analyzing the mental process used in responding, determining the predictive effectiveness of the test). The specific types of evidence that are most critical for a particular test depend on the nature of the construct, the clarity of the theoretical framework, and the uses to be made of the test scores. Although the gathering of construct-related evidence of validity can be endless, in practical situations it is typically necessary to limit the evidence to that which is most relevant to the interpretations to be made.

The construct-related category of evidence is the broadest of the three categories. Evidence obtained in both the content-related category (e.g., representativeness of the sample of tasks) and the criterion-related category (e.g., how well the scores predict performance on specific criteria) are also relevant to the construct-related category because they help to clarify the meaning of the assessment results. Thus, the construct-related category encompasses a variety of types of evidence, including that from content-related and criterion-related validation studies.

The broad array of evidence that might be considered can be illustrated by a test designed to measure mathematical reasoning ability. Some of the evidence we might consider is:

1.   Compare the sample of test tasks to the domain of tasks specified by the conceptual framework of the construct. Is the sample relevant and representative (content-related evidence)?

2.   Examine the test features and their possible influence on the meaning of the scores (e.g., test format, directions, scoring, reading level of items). Is it possible that some features might distort the scores?

3.   Analyze the mental process used in answering the questions by having students "think aloud" as they respond to each item. Do the items require the intended reasoning process?

4.   Determine the internal consistency of the test by intercorrelating the test items. Do the items seem to be measuring a single characteristic (in this case, mathematical reasoning)?

5.   Correlate the test scores with the scores of other mathematical reasoning tests. Do they show a high degree of relationship?

6.   Compare the scores of known groups (e.g., mathematics majors and nonmajors). Do the scores differentiate between the groups as predicted?

7.   Compare the scores of students before and after specific training in mathematical reasoning. Do the scores change as predicted from the theory underlying the construct?

8.   Correlate the scores with grades in mathematics. Do they correlate to a satisfactory degree (criterion-related evidence)?

Other types of evidence could be added to this list, but it is sufficiently comprehensive to make clear that no single type of evidence is adequate. Interpreting test scores as a measure of a particular construct involves a comprehensive study of the development of the test, how it functions in a variety of situations, and how the scores relate to other significant measures.

Assessment results are, of course, influenced by many factors other than the construct they are designed to measure. Thus, construct validation is an attempt to account for all possible influences on the scores. We might, for example, ask to what extent the scores on our mathematical reasoning test are influenced by reading comprehension, computation skill, and speed. Each of these factors would require further study. Were attempts made to eliminate such factors during test development by using simple vocabulary, simple computations, and liberal time limits? To what extent do the test scores correlate with measures of reading comprehension and computational skill? How do students' scores differ under different time limits? Answers to these and similar questions will help us to determine how well the test scores reflect the construct we are attempting to measure and the extent to which other factors might be influencing the scores.

Construct validation, then, is an attempt to clarify and verify the inferences to be made from assessment results. This involves a wide variety of procedures and many different types of evidence (including both content-related and criterion-related). As evidence accumulates from many different sources, our interpretations of the results are enriched and we are able to make them with great confidence.

Consequence of Using Assessment Results

Validity focuses on the inferences drawn from assessment results with regard to specific uses. Therefore, it is legitimate to ask, What are the consequences of using the assessment? Did the assessment improve learning, as intended, or did it contribute to adverse effects (e.g., lack of motivation, memorization, poor study habits)? For example, assessment procedures that focus on simple learning outcomes only (e.g., knowledge of facts) cannot provide valid evidence of reasoning and application skills, are likely to narrow the focus of student learning, and tend to reinforce poor learning strategies (e.g., rote learning). Thus, in evaluating the validity of the assessment used, one needs to look at what types of influence the assessments have on students. The following questions provide a general framework for considering some of the possible consequences of assessments on students.

1. Did use of the assessment improve motivation?

2. Did use of the assessment improve performance?

3. Did the use of the assessment improve self-assessment skills?

4. Did the use of the assessment contribute to transfer of learning to related areas?

5. Did the use of the assessment encourage independent learning?

6. Did the use of the assessment encourage good study habits?

7. Did the use of the assessment contribute to a positive attitude toward schoolwork?

8. Did use of the assessment have an adverse effect in any of the above areas?

Judging the consequences of using the various assessment procedures is an important role of the teacher, if the results are to serve their intended purpose of improving learning. Both testing and performance assessments are most likely to have positive consequences when they are designed to assess a broad range of learning outcomes, they give special emphasis to complex learning outcomes, they are administered and scored (or judged) properly, they are used to identify students' strengths and weaknesses in learning, and the students view the assessments as fair, relevant, and useful for improving learning.

Reliability

Reliability refers to the consistency of assessment results. Would we obtain about the same results if we used a different sample of the same type task? Would we obtain about the same results if we used the assessment at a different time? If a performance assessment is being rated, would different raters rate the performance the same way? These are the kinds of questions we are concerned about when we are considering the reliability of assessment results. Unless the results are generalizable over similar samples of tasks, time periods, and raters, we are not likely to have great confidence in them.

Because the methods for estimating reliability differ for tests and product and performance assessments, these will be treated separately.

Estimating the Reliability of Test Scores

The score an individual receives on a test is called the *obtained score, raw score,* or *observed score*. This score typically contains a certain amount of error. Some of this error may be *systematic error,* in that it consistently inflates or lowers the obtained score. For example, readily apparent clues in several test items might cause all students' scores to be higher than their achievement would warrant, or short time limits during testing might cause all students' scores to be lower than their "real achievement." The factors causing systematic errors are mainly due to inadequate testing practices. Thus, most of these errors can be eliminated by using care in constructing and administering tests. Removing systematic errors from test scores is especially important because they have a direct effect on the validity of the inferences made from the scores.

Some of the error in obtained scores is *random error,* in that it raises and lowers scores in an unpredictable manner. Random errors are caused by such things as temporary fluctuations in memory, variations in motivation and concentration from time to time, carelessness in marking answers, and luck in guessing. Such factors cause test scores to be inconsistent from one measurement to another. Sometimes an individual's obtained score will be higher than it should be and sometimes it will be lower. Although these errors are difficult to control and cannot be predicted with accuracy, an estimate of their influence can be obtained by various statistical procedures. Thus, when we talk about estimating the *reliability* of test scores or the amount of *measurement error* in test scores, we are referring to the influence of random errors.

Reliability refers to the *consistency* of test scores from one measurement to another. Because of the ever present measurement error, we can expect a certain amount of variation in test performance from one time to another, from one sample of items to another, and from one part of the test to another. Reliability measures provide an estimate of how much variation we might expect under different conditions. The reliability of test scores is typically reported by means of a **reliability coefficient** or the standard error of measurement that is derived from it. Since both methods of estimating reliability require score variability, the procedures to be discussed are useful primarily with tests designed for norm-referenced interpretation.

As we noted earlier, a correlation coefficient expressing the relationship between a set of test scores and a criterion measure is called a *validity coefficient.* A **reliability coefficient** is also a correlation coefficient, but it indicates the correlation between two sets of measurements taken from the same procedure. We may, for example, administer the same test twice to a group, with a time interval in between (*test–retest* method); administer two equivalent forms of the test in close succession (*equivalent-forms* method); administer two equivalent forms of the test with a time interval in between (*test–retest with equivalent forms* method); or administer the test once and compute the consistency of the response within the test (*internal-consistency* method). Each of these methods of obtaining reliability provides a different type of information. Thus, reliability coefficients obtained with the different procedures are not interchangeable. Before deciding on the procedure to be used, we must determine what type of reliability evidence we are seeking. The four basic methods of estimating reliability and the type of information each provides are shown in Table 4.2 (page 46).

Test–Retest Method. The test–retest method requires administering the same form of the test to the same group after some time interval. The time between the two administrations may be just a few days or several years. The length of the time interval should fit the type of interpretation to be made from the results. Thus, if we are interested in

TABLE 4.2 • *Methods of Estimating Reliability of Test Scores*

Method	Type of Information Provided
Test–retest method	The stability of test scores over a given period of time.
Equivalent-forms method	The consistency of the test scores over different forms of the test (that is, different samples of items).
Test–retest with equivalent forms	The consistency of test scores over *both* a time interval and different forms of the test.
Internal-consistency methods	The consistency of test scores over different parts of the test.

Note: Scorer reliability should also be considered when evaluating the responses to *supply-type* items (for example, essay tests). This is typically done by having the test papers scored independently by two scorers and then correlating the two sets of scores. Agreement among scorers is not, however, a substitute for the methods of estimating reliability shown in the table.

using test scores only to group students for more effective learning, short-term stability may be sufficient. On the other hand, if we are attempting to predict vocational success or make some other long-range predictions, we would desire evidence of stability over a period of years.

Test–retest reliability coefficients are influenced both by errors within the measurement procedure and by the day-to-day stability of the students' responses. Thus, longer time periods between tests will result in lower reliability coefficients, due to the greater changes in the students. In reporting test–retest reliability coefficients, then, it is important to include the time interval. For example, a report might state: "The stability of test scores obtained on the same form over a three-month period was 0.90." This makes it possible to determine the extent to which the reliability data are significant for a particular interpretation.

Equivalent-Forms Method. With this method, two equivalent forms of a test (also called **alternate forms** or **parallel forms**) are administered to the same group during the same testing session. The test forms are equivalent in the sense that they are built to measure the same abilities (that is, they are built to the same set of specifications), but for determining reliability it is also important that they be constructed independently. When this is the case, the reliability coefficient indicates the adequacy of the test sample. That is, a high reliability coefficient would indicate that the two independent samples are apparently measuring the same thing. A low reliability coefficient would, of course, indicate that the two forms are measuring different behaviour and that therefore both samples of items are questionable.

Reliability coefficients determined by this method take into account errors within the measurement procedures and consistency over different samples of items, but they do not include the day-to-day stability of the students' responses.

Test–Retest Method with Equivalent Forms. This is a combination of both methods. Here, two different forms of the same test are administered with time intervening. This is the most demanding estimate of reliability, since it takes into account all possible sources of variation. The reliability coefficient reflects errors within the testing procedure, consistency over different samples of items, and the day-to-day stability of the students' responses. For most purposes, this is probably the most useful type of reliability, since it enables us to estimate how generalizable the test results are over the various conditions. A high reliability coefficient obtained by this method would indicate that a test score represents not only present test performance but also what test performance is likely to be at another time or on a different sample of equivalent items.

Internal-Consistency Methods. These methods require only a single administration of a test. One procedure, the *split-half* method, involves scoring the odd items and the even items separately and correlating the two sets of scores. This correlation coefficient indicates the degree to which the two arbitrarily selected halves of the test provide the same results. Thus, it reports on the internal consistency of the test. Like the equivalent-forms method, this procedure takes into account errors within the testing procedure and consistency over different samples of items, but it omits the day-to-day stability of the students' responses.

Since the correlation coefficient based on the odd and even items indicates the relationship between two halves of the test, the reliability coefficient for the total test is determined by applying the *Spearman–Brown prophecy formula*. A simplified version of this formula is as follows:

$$\text{Reliability of total test} = \frac{2 \times \text{reliability for } \frac{1}{2} \text{ test}}{1 + \text{reliability for } \frac{1}{2} \text{ test}}$$

Thus, if we obtained a correlation coefficient of .60 for two halves of a test, the reliability for the total test would be computed as follows:

$$\text{Reliability of total test} = \frac{2 \times .60}{1 + .60} = \frac{1.20}{1.60} = .75$$

This application of the Spearman–Brown formula makes clear a useful principle of test reliability: the reliability of a test can be increased by lengthening it. This formula shows how much reliability will increase when the length of the test is doubled. Application of the formula, however, assumes that the test is lengthened by adding items like those already in the test.

Another internal-consistency method of estimating reliability is by use of the **Kuder–Richardson Formula 20 (KR-20)**. Kuder and Richardson developed other formulas but this one is probably the most widely used with standardized tests. It requires a single test administration, a determination of the proportion of individuals passing each item, and the standard deviation of the total set of scores. The formula is not especially helpful in understanding how to interpret the scores, but knowing what the coefficient means is important. Basically, the KR-20 is equivalent to an average of all split-half coefficients when the test is split in all possible ways. Where all items in a test are measuring the same thing (e.g., math reasoning), the result should approximate the split-half reliability estimate. Where the test items are measuring a variety of skills or content areas (i.e., are less homogeneous), the KR-20 estimate will be lower than the split-half reliability estimate. Thus, the KR-20 method is useful with homogeneous tests but can be misleading if used with a test designed to measure heterogeneous content.

Internal-consistency methods are used because they require that the test be administered only once. They should not be used with speeded tests, however, because a spuriously high reliability estimate will result. If speed is an important factor in the testing (that is, if the students do not have time to attempt all the items), other methods should be used to estimate reliability.

Standard Error of Measurement. The **standard error of measurement** is an especially useful way of expressing test reliability because it indicates the amount of error to allow for when interpreting individual test scores. The standard error is derived from a reliability coefficient by means of the following formula:

$$\text{Standard error of measurement} = s\sqrt{1 - r_n}$$

where s = the standard deviation and r_n = the reliability coefficient. In applying this formula to a reliability estimate of .60 obtained for a test where $s = 4.5$, the following results would be obtained.

$$
\begin{aligned}
\text{Standard error of measurement} \ &= 4.5\sqrt{1 - .60} \\
&= 4.5\sqrt{.40} \\
&= 4.5 \times .63 \\
&= 2.8
\end{aligned}
$$

The standard error of measurement shows how many points we must add to—and subtract from—an individual's test score in order to obtain "reasonable limits" for estimating that individual's true score (that is, a score free of error). In our example, the standard error would be rounded to 3 score points. Thus, if a given student scored 35 on this test, that student's *score band,* for establishing reasonable limits, would range from 32 (35 − 3) to 38 (35 + 3). In other words, we could be reasonably sure that the score band of 32 to 38 included the student's true score (statistically, there are two chances out of three that it does). The standard errors of test scores provide a means of allowing for error during test interpretation. If we view test performance in terms of score bands (also called *confidence bands*), we are not likely to overinterpret small differences between test scores.

For the test user, the standard error of measurement is probably more useful than the reliability coefficient. Although reliability coefficients can be used in evaluating the quality of a test and in comparing the relative merits of different tests, the standard error of measurement is directly applicable to the interpretation of individual test scores.

Reliability of Criterion-Referenced Mastery Tests. As noted earlier, the traditional methods for computing reliability require score variability (that is, a spread of scores) and are therefore useful mainly with norm-referenced tests. When used with criterion-referenced tests, they are likely to provide misleading results. Since criterion-referenced tests are not designed to emphasize differences among individuals, they typically have limited score variability. This restricted spread of scores will result in low correlation estimates of reliability, even if the consistency of our test results is adequate for the use to be made of them.

When a criterion-referenced test is used to determine mastery, our primary concern is with how consistently our test classifies masters and nonmasters. If we administered two equivalent forms of a test to the same group of students, for example, we would like the results of both forms to identify the same students as having mastered the material. Such perfect agreement is unrealistic, of course, since some students near the cutoff score are likely to shift from one category to the other on the basis of errors of measurement (due to such factors as lucky guesses or lapses of memory). However, if too many students demonstrated mastery on one form but nonmastery on the other, our decisions concerning who mastered the material would be hopelessly confused. Thus, the reliability of mastery tests can be determined by computing the percentage of consistent mastery–nonmastery decisions over the two forms of the test.

The procedure for comparing test performance on two equivalent forms of a test is relatively simple. After both forms have been administered to a group of students, the resulting data can be placed in a two-by-two table like that shown in Figure 4.1. These data are based on two forms of a 25-item test administered to 40 students. Mastery was set at 80 percent correct (20 items), so all students who scored 20 or higher on both forms of the test were placed in the upper right-hand cell (30 students), and all those who scored below 20 on both forms were placed in the lower left-hand cell (6 students). The remaining students demonstrated mastery on one form and nonmastery on the other (4 students). Since 36 of the 40 students were consistently classified by the two forms of the test, we apparently have reasonably good consistency.

We can compute the percentage of consistency for this procedure with the following formula:

$$\% \text{ Consistency} = \frac{\text{Masters (both forms)} + \text{Nonmasters (both forms)}}{\text{Total number in group}} \times 100$$

$$\% \text{ Consistency} = \frac{30 + 6}{40} \times 100 = 90\%$$

This procedure is simple to use but it has a few limitations. First, two forms of the test are required. This may not be as serious as it seems, however, since in most mastery programs more than one form of the test is needed for retesting those students who fail to demonstrate mastery on the first try. Second, it is difficult to determine what percentage of decision consistency is necessary for a given situation. As with other measures of reliability, the greater the consistency, the more satisfied we will be, but what constitutes a minimum acceptable level? There is no simple answer to such a question because

FIGURE 4.1 • Classification of 40 students as masters or nonmasters on two forms of a criterion-referenced test.

		FORM B	
		NONMASTERS	MASTERS
FORM A	MASTERS	2	30
	NONMASTERS	6	2

it depends on the number of items in the test and the consequences of the decision. If a nonmastery decision for a student simply means further study and later retesting, low consistency might be acceptable. However, if the mastery–nonmastery decision concerns whether to give a student a high school certificate, as in some competency testing programs, then a high level of consistency will be demanded. Since there are no clear guidelines for setting minimum levels, we will need to depend on experience in various situations to determine what are reasonable expectations.

More sophisticated techniques have been developed for estimating the reliability of criterion-referenced tests, but the numerous issues and problems involved in their use go beyond the scope of this book. See Box 4.2 for factors that lower reliability of test scores.

Estimating the Reliability of Product and Performance Assessments

Product and performance assessments are commonly evaluated by using scoring keys or descriptive rubrics that describe a number of levels of performance, ranging from high to low (e.g., outstanding to inadequate). The performance for each student is then judged and placed in the category that best fits the quality of the performance. The reliability of these performance judgments can be determined by obtaining and comparing the scores of two judges who scored the performances independently. The scores of the two judges can be correlated to determine the consistency of the scoring, or the proportion of agreement in scoring can be computed.

Let's assume that a product, such as a writing sample, was obtained from 32 students, and two teachers independently rated the students' performance on a four-point scale where 4 is high and 1 is low. The results of the ratings by the two judges are shown in Table 4.3 (page 51). The ratings for Judge 1 are presented in the columns and those for Judge 2 are presented in the rows. Thus, Judge 1 assigned a score of 4 to seven students and Judge 2 assigned a score of 4 to eight students. Their ratings agreed on six of the students and disagreed by one score on three of the students. The number of rating agreements can be seen in the boxes on the diagonal from the upper right-hand corner to the lower left-hand corner. The percentage of agreement can be computed by adding

BOX 4.2 • *Factors That Lower the Reliability of Test Scores*

1. Test scores are based on too few items. (*Remedy:* Use longer tests or accumulate scores from several short tests.)
2. Range of scores is too limited. (*Remedy:* Adjust item difficulty to obtain larger spread of scores.)
3. Testing conditions are inadequate. (*Remedy:* Arrange opportune time for administration and eliminate interruptions, noise, and other disrupting factors.)
4. Scoring is subjective. (*Remedy:* Prepare scoring keys and follow carefully when scoring essay answers.)

the numbers in these diagonal boxes (6 + 7 + 6 + 5 = 24), dividing by the total number of students in the group (32), and multiplying by 100.

$$\text{Rater agreement} = \frac{24}{32} \times 100 = 75\%$$

By inspection, we can see that all ratings were within one score of each other. The results also indicate that Judge 2 was a more lenient rater than Judge 1 (i.e., gave more high ratings and fewer low ratings). Thus, a table of this nature can be used to determine the consistency of ratings and the extent to which leniency can account for the disagreements.

Although the need for two raters will limit the use of this method, it seems reasonable to expect two teachers in the same area to make periodic checks on the scoring of performance assessments. This will not only provide information on the consistency of the scoring, but will provide the teachers with insight into some of their rating idiosyncrasies. See Box 4.3 for factors that lower the reliability of performance assessment.

The percentage of agreement between the scores assigned by independent judges is a common method of estimating the reliability of performance assessments. It should be noted, however, that this reports on only one type of consistency—*the consistency of the scoring*. It does not indicate the consistency of performance over similar tasks or over different time periods. We can obtain a crude measure of this by examining the performance of students over tasks and time, but a more adequate analysis requires an understanding of **generalizability** (the extent to which an assessment procedure provides comparable results over different samples of similar tasks, different settings, and different administrations), which is too technical for treatment here.

TABLE 4.3 • *Classification of Students Based on Performance Ratings by Two Independent Judges*

		Ratings by Judge 1				
	Scores	*1*	*2*	*3*	*4*	*Row Totals*
	4			2	6	8
Ratings by Judge 2	**3**		3	7	1	11
	2	2	6			8
	1	5				5
	Column Totals	7	9	9	7	32

BOX 4.3 • *Factors That Lower the Reliability of Performance Assessments*

1. Insufficient number of tasks. (*Remedy:* Accumulate results from several assessments. For example, several writing samples.)

2. Poorly structured assessment procedures. (*Remedy:* Define carefully the nature of the tasks, the conditions for obtaining the assessment, and the criteria for scoring or judging the results.)

3. Dimensions of performance are specific to the tasks. (*Remedy:* Increase generalizability of performance by selecting tasks that have dimensions like those in similar tasks.)

4. Inadequate scoring guides for judgmental scoring. (*Remedy:* Use scoring rubrics or rating scales that specifically describe the criteria and levels of quality.)

5. Scoring judgments that are influenced by personal bias. (*Remedy:* Check scores or ratings with those of an independent judge. Receive training in judging and rating, if possible.)

Summary of Points

1. Validity is the most important quality to consider in assessment and is concerned with the appropriateness, meaningfulness, and usefulness of the specific inferences made from assessment results.

2. Validity is a *unitary concept* based on various forms of evidence (content-related, criterion-related, construct-related, and consequences).

3. Content-related evidence of validity refers to how well the sample of tasks represents the domain of tasks to be assessed.

4. Content-related evidence of validity is of major concern in achievement assessment and is built in by following systematic procedures. Validity is lowered by inadequate assessment practices.

5. Criterion-related evidence of validity refers to the degree to which assessment results are related to some other valued measure called a *criterion*.

6. Criterion-related evidence may be based on a predictive study or a concurrent study and is typically expressed by a correlation coefficient or expectancy table.

7. Construct-related evidence of validity refers to how well performance on assessment tasks can be explained in terms of psychological characteristics, or constructs (e.g., mathematical reasoning).

8. The construct-related category of evidence is the most comprehensive. It includes evidence from both content-related and criterion-related studies plus other types of evidence that help clarify the meaning of the assessment results.

9. Consequences of using the assessment is also an important consideration in validity—both positive and negative consequences.

10. Reliability refers to the consistency of scores (i.e., to the degree to which the scores are free from measurement error).

11. Reliability of test scores is typically reported by means of a reliability coefficient or a standard error of measurement.

12. Reliability coefficients can be obtained by a number of different methods (e.g., test–retest, equivalent-forms, internal-consistency) and each one measures a different type of consistency (e.g., over time, over different samples of items, over different parts of the test).

13. Reliability of test scores tends to be lower when the test is short, range of scores is limited, testing conditions are inadequate, and scoring is subjective.

14. The standard error of measurement indicates the amount of error to allow for when interpreting individual test scores.

15. Score bands (or *confidence bands*) take into account the error of measurement and help prevent the overinterpretation of small differences between test scores.

16. The reliability of criterion-referenced mastery tests can be obtained by computing the percentage of agreement between two forms of the test in classifying individuals as masters and nonmasters.

17. The reliability of performance-based assessments is commonly determined by the degree of agreement between two or more judges who rate the performance independently.

Learning Exercises

1. If a fellow teacher told you that a particular reading test had high validity, what types of questions would you ask?

2. A high school science teacher prepared a set of assessment tasks to be used in all sections of biology, without consulting the teachers of the other sections. What effect might this have on the assessment's validity? Why?

3. Which method of estimating reliability provides the most useful information for each of the following? Why?
   (a) Selecting a scholastic aptitude test for predicting future achievement.
   (b) Reassessing students to determine standing relative to a fixed performance standard.
   (c) Determining whether a test measures a homogeneous characteristic.
   (d) Determining the degree to which essay scores obtained from different raters are affected by differences in the stringency of raters.

References and Additional Reading

American Educational Research Association (1999). *Standards for Educational and Psychological Testing.* Washington, DC: AERA.

Linn, R.L., and Gronlund, N.E. (2000). *Measurement and Assessment in Teaching,* 8th ed. Upper Saddle River, NJ: Merrill/Prentice-Hall.

Oosterhoff, A.C. (2001). *Classroom Applications of Educational Measurement,* 3rd ed. Upper Saddle River, NJ: Merrill/Prentice-Hall.

Thorndike, R. (1997). *Measurement and Evaluation in Psychology and Education,* 6th ed. Upper Saddle River, NJ: Prentice-Hall.

Weblinks

A Framework for Assessment and Evaluation
Considerations of school assessment.
http://www.edu.gov.mb.ca/metks4/docs/policy/reporting/framwork.html

Assessment, Evaluation, and Reporting
Simcoe (Ontario) school board site.
http://mariposa.scdsb.on.ca/SServices/assess/principles.htm

Standards and Assessments as Part of Effective Education
CMEC site on assessment; an important Canadian viewpoint.
http://www.interlog.com/~klima/ed/standards.html

5

Planning for Assessment

This chapter will enable you to:

1. List the types of learning outcomes to consider in planning for the assessment of student achievement.
2. State instructional objectives as intended learning outcomes and define them in performance terms.
3. Describe the various types of assessments, and discuss where each is most appropriate.
4. Prepare a preliminary plan for the number and type of assessment activities for a unit of instruction.

Planning for the assessment of student achievement involves a consideration of the following questions:

1. What do we expect students to learn?
2. What *types* of student performance are we willing to accept as evidence of learning?
3. What assessment instruments will best evaluate the students' performance?

The first question focuses on the goals of the curriculum as set by the school and influenced by the district and province. In recent years, provinces have developed **content standards** that provide guidelines for determining what students should know and be able to do. This has caused districts and schools to modify curricula and put greater emphasis on the more complex learning outcomes.

The second question focuses on the importance of specifying instructional objectives in performance terms and including all types of desired learning outcomes. These objectives must, of course, be in harmony with the goals of the curriculum and will reflect the provincial content standards to the same degree as does the school curriculum. In final analysis, the assessment of student achievement is determined by what the students are expected to learn, and this is determined by the goals of the school curriculum. The instructional objectives are simply a means of stating the curriculum goals in more specific terms so that they are useful in both instruction and assessment.

The third question focuses on the match between the instructional objectives and the procedures of assessment. The objectives specify the intended learning outcomes in performance terms, and the assessment method is used to determine the extent to which students' performance is satisfactory. For some outcomes, a test will provide adequate evidence. In other cases, some type of observational technique will be needed to evaluate the ongoing nature of the performance (e.g., giving a speech) or to evaluate a resulting product (e.g., a written report). The key to effective assessment is to use the most direct and relevant method available.

Types of Intended Learning Outcomes

In planning for the assessment of student achievement, a number of types of learning outcomes might be considered. Although the goals of the school and the nature of the instructional content will determine what specific types of learning outcomes are to be assessed, a review of the various types of outcomes shown in Table 5.1 will prevent any serious omissions. The list is not exhaustive, but it makes clear the range of outcomes to consider—beyond that of knowledge—when preparing objectives for instruction and assessment.

Well designed classroom tests can be used to measure many of the outcomes in the cognitive areas, but skills and products require the use of scoring keys, checklists, rating scales, or holistic scoring rubrics.

Role of Instructional Objectives

Well stated instructional objectives provide a description of the intended learning outcomes in performance terms—that is, in terms of the types of performance students can demonstrate to show that they have achieved the knowledge, understanding, or skill described by the objective. By describing the performance that we are willing to accept as evidence of learning, we provide a focus for instruction, student learning, and assessment. Objectives help keep all three in close harmony. For example, for an objective emphasizing problem-solving strategies, we teach students how to apply problem-solving strategies, they practise applying the strategies, and we assess their skill in applying problem-solving strategies with new problems. Thus, the instructional targets, the learning targets, and the assessment targets are all the same. If the students are made aware of the objectives at the beginning of instruction, both teacher and students are working toward common goals, and instruction and assessment are both part of the same process.

Stating Instructional Objectives

In stating instructional objectives, it is helpful to keep in mind that we are not describing the teaching procedures or the learning process. We are simply describing the student

TABLE 5.1 • *Some Types of Intended Learning Outcomes*

Types	Sample Categories
Knowledge, Comprehension, and Application	Facts Concepts Principles Methods Process
Reasoning Ability	Analyzing Comparing Inferring Generalizing Evaluating
Observable Skills	Speaking Oral reading Laboratory skills Psychomotor skills Work-study skills
Products	Writing Drawing Designing Constructing Problem solving

performance to be demonstrated at the end of the learning experience as evidence of learning. This permits us to use a variety of procedures, materials, and learning activities to achieve the desired outcomes.

A useful procedure is first to state the general objectives that focus on the broader learning outcomes, and then define each general objective in more specific terms, as follows.

1. Understands Scientific Concepts

    1.1 Describes the concept in his or her own words.

    1.2 Describes the role of the concept in science.

    1.3 Distinguishes the concept from similar scientific concepts.

    1.4 Uses the concept in writing about science.

    1.5 Applies the concept in solving problems.

The specific learning outcomes listed under the general objective are not meant to be exhaustive, but they should provide a representative sample of the types of performance that we are willing to accept as evidence that the objective has been achieved. The general procedure for stating instructional objectives is presented in Box 5.1 (page 58). The specific application of these steps is described and illustrated later for a unit on test planning.

BOX 5.1 • *Stating Instructional Objectives*

The following steps provide guidelines for stating instructional objectives that are useful in instruction and assessment.

1. State the general objectives as follows:
   1.1 Write each as an intended learning outcome.
   1.2 State each in performance terms.
   1.3 Start each with a verb (e.g., "knows," "comprehends").
   1.4 Write each so it is general enough to identify a domain of specific learning outcomes.

2. List and state the specific learning outcomes as follows:
   2.1 Clarify each general objective with a representative sample of specific learning outcomes.
   2.2 Begin each with an action verb indicating observable student performance (e.g., "selects," "describes").
   2.3 Include a sufficient number to indicate attainment of the general objective.
   2.4 Check to be sure the specific learning outcomes are relevant to the general objectives and that the general objectives are in harmony with the school goals.

Sources of Help in Locating Sample Objectives

In getting started with the identification and selection of instructional objectives, it helps to review various sources for ideas. Illustrative categories of intended learning outcomes and sample objectives can be found in the following sources.

   1. **Taxonomy of Educational Objectives.** (Commonly referred to as *Bloom's Taxonomy.*) This is an older guide but it provides a classification of objectives in the cognitive, psychomotor, and affective domains. Each domain includes categories and subcategories that are designed to identify and classify all possible educational outcomes. For example, the cognitive domain includes the following major categories (Bloom 1956):

   (a) Knowledge (remembering previous learning material).

   (b) Comprehension (grasping the meaning of material).

   (c) Application (using information in concrete situation).

   (d) Analysis (breaking down material into its parts).

   (e) Synthesis (putting parts together into a whole).

   (f) Evaluation (judging the value of a thing using criteria).

These categories are listed in the order of increasing complexity and are clarified in the taxonomy by subdivisions that further describe the types of educational outcomes included. For detailed descriptions of all three domains of the taxonomy with illustrative objectives for each category, see Gronlund (2000) at the end of this chapter.

2. **Instructors' guides accompanying student textbooks.** These guides typically contain objectives but they tend to focus on lower level outcomes, may be poorly stated, and are likely to lack close harmony with the goals of the curriculum. However, they are worth a review for ideas on possible learning outcomes to consider. It may be possible to modify some to put them in more usable form.

3. **Publications of educational organizations.** Although usually stated at a more general level than needed, the content standards of professional associations provide an excellent starting point for considering instructional objectives.

4. **The Canadian Education Research Information System (CERIS).** CERIS provides links to various sources. Its Web address is http://ceris.schoolnet.ca/e/.

5. **Curriculum frameworks and guides.** Many local and provincial curriculum frameworks or guides contain lists of instructional objectives, and are available on-line.

6. **Provincial content standards.** The content standards adopted by provinces also provide a good starting point for identifying instructional objectives. Although the content standards for the province or district in which a teacher is working obviously are most relevant, useful ideas may also be derived from standards of other provinces. For access to provincial content standards, enter the name of the province in any search engine with the word "education" (e.g., "Manitoba Education").

Examples of content standards in different subjects from three provinces are illustrated in Box 5.2. The subject areas and grade ranges for provincial content standards vary from province to province. In some provinces, Alberta, for example, curriculum objectives are organized as core or optional outcomes, while other provinces, including British Columbia and Nova Scotia, do not identify outcomes as being of greater or lesser importance. Some provinces have grade-level specific standards; others have standards adopted for a range of grades. The standards also vary from province to province in terms of their specificity and emphases within a content area.

BOX 5.2 • *Examples of Provincial Standards Statements*

British Columbia, Grade 5 Reading
"It is expected that students will: read, listen and view for specific purposes; use strategies, including developing questions, rereading, reading and reviewing, to clarify meaning and build understanding." (British Columbia Ministry of Education Performance Standards 1998)

Alberta, Grade 1 Science
"Students will bring focus to investigative activities, based on their own questions and those of others." (Alberta Learning Curriculum Guide, K to Grade 12, Science 1996)

Ontario, Grade 9 Introduction to Business
"By the end of this course, students will: describe the concept of demand and the conditions that give rise to demand." (The Ontario Curriculum, Grade 9 to 12: Program Planning and Assessment 2000)

Assessment Methods and Their Applicability

There are various ways of describing methods of assessment and their applicability. Table 5.2 offers one way of looking at this issue. In the first column, the possible methods of assessment are listed. Across the top are listed the domains of learning. (There are many lists of domains: this seems to be comprehensive enough to provide a reasonable degree of discrimination, but not so lengthy as to preclude remembering the categories.) Within the cells is a one-word description of the usefulness of the assessment method when assessing the domain.

Methods

While all of these methods are described in greater or lesser detail in the following chapters, here is a brief description of each assessment type.

Paper and pencil tests need little description. They are the traditional tests with which everyone is familiar.

A *product* is anything the teacher can hold or stand on the floor to examine. Products include essays, worksheets, projects, maps, cakes, woodwork projects, samples of printing, paintings, poems, stories, and so on.

A *performance* consists of an activity performed by the student while the teacher watches and scores. The performance may be done in front of others, typically the class. Performances include public speaking, dribbling a basketball, playing an instrument, using a microscope, tumbling, debating, etc.

An *interview* consists of a teacher talking to a student one-on-one. It will always include a discussion, and may also involve a performance. Interviews are often used to test reading or understanding of complex or abstract material.

Observation consists of the teacher watching students during class activities, and noting the achievement and behaviour of specific students. Observation differs from performance in that the students do not know they are being assessed.

A *reflective essay or journal* is a place where students can write about what they have learned during a class, a day, or a unit. The task can be structured by the teacher, or it can be informal.

TABLE 5.2 • *Methods of Assessment*

Method	Domain			
	Content	**Process**	**Skill**	**Affective**
Test	Excellent	Possible	No	Possible
Product	Possible	Good	Good	No
Performance	Possible	Possible	Excellent	No
Interview	Good	Excellent	Possible	Good
Observation	No	Possible	Possible	Excellent
Essay or Journal	Good	Good	Possible	Good

Domains

Domains are areas of psychological or physiological activity. Psychologists use the concept to group together activities that seem to be controlled by certain parts of the body or mind. For example, when one is driving a car, the *affective* domain controls feelings about other drivers, the need to get to a destination at a certain time, and so on. The *sensorimotor* domain controls which way the wheel is turned, whether the clutch or the brake is touched, how the gears are shifted. The *cognitive* domain makes decisions as to whether one should be in the right or left lane, whether to turn a corner, and whether it is appropriate to stop at a crosswalk. To some extent, domains are artificial: different authorities specify different numbers and names of domains depending on what is being discussed.

Content consists of facts (dates, names, places, parts of speech, formulae, definitions), all the things one has to know to live in our world. Content can be thought of as the lower levels of the taxonomy, but this does not mean content is simple, unimportant, or trivial.

Process is defined as doing something with content (synthesizing, transferring, interpolating)—the higher levels of the taxonomy.

Skills are often psychomotor skills—actions involving the muscles of the body—but might include speaking, playing an instrument, singing, and so on.

The *affective* domain concerns attitudes, behaviour, and feelings. Learning outcomes that require students to work with others, to appreciate literature, to value the ecosystem, are aimed at the affective domain.

Each cell in Table 5.2 (page 60) contains a descriptor suggesting how effective the assessment method is for measuring student achievement in that particular domain. Content, for instance, can best be measured by tests, while interviews and journals are also good. Products and performances are not as useful for measuring content simply because, unless the directions are very explicit, the student may not include the content you want to assess, and then you do not know whether it has been mastered or not. Advantages and problems with each method will be addressed in the appropriate later chapter.

Planning the Unit of Instruction

The best time to decide how many assessment activities you will have for a unit and what form they will take is before you teach the unit. Do not wait until you are well into the unit to consider assessment—do it when you are in the planning stage. Indeed, many teachers plan their assessment first, and then plan the unit around the assessment.

There is no hard and fast rule regarding the number of assessments there should be in a unit of instruction. Generally speaking, the higher the grade level the fewer assessments, but the longer and more complex each will be. In Grade 1, teachers mark everything the students do, and the students will produce something in every subject block, so teachers will have between five and ten assessments per student per day, mostly of student writing, drawing, or observations of actions and behaviour. By Grade 5 or 6, students will be studying seven or eight subjects, and teachers might be collecting two or three assessment marks each day. By Grade 12, teachers in each subject area will collect perhaps one assessment mark per week (or two if the school is on a semester system), including homework, tests, assignments, performances, and observations. The types of assessment will vary from subject to subject, but generally the more content there is (social studies and science, for instance) the more tests there will be. Subjects that have a large verbal component (second languages and drama, for instance) will have fewer tests and more performance.

It is also important to space the assessment tasks out, to ensure that you are not asking students to hand in a major assignment at the same time as the unit test. Further, try to schedule interesting activities at times when student interest is apt to be waning. Students are more willing to work hard on a project in October than in mid-December. December is a good time to have performances.

Finally, you will plan a mix of outcomes aimed at all levels of the taxonomy. Generally, the lower the grade level the more knowledge and understanding objectives there will be, and the higher the grade level the higher the objectives. Assessment must measure student success at all levels taught.

Special Considerations

Obviously, goals and objectives may have to be modified for special needs students. In the case of students who have an Individualized Education Plan, or IEP, the plan itself will contain the goals and objectives appropriate for the student. In the case of students who do not have such a plan, but who cannot achieve the goals and objectives of the regular students, teachers should meet with the parents and decide to what extent the regular goals and objectives are applicable, and the degree of modification needed. It is important that the goals and objectives be as close as possible to those of the other students, but that the special needs student be able to achieve success.

With regard to planning, it is at this stage that special needs students should be considered. It is best to decide the extent to which they will be measured along with the regular students before instruction takes place rather than during instruction or afterwards.

If the nature of the student's handicap or difference is such that he or she will not be able to achieve success in regular classroom activities, alternative assessments should be planned at the beginning of the course of study. If an essay is planned and the special needs student cannot write an essay, the teacher must decide what the student will do in its place. If an exam is planned and the special needs student cannot write, but should be able to answer the questions orally, the teacher should advise the student at the beginning of the course that alternative arrangements will be made, so the student will not worry about writing the exam.

Communication with the parents is of the utmost importance, so the teacher, the student, and the parents know the expectations and agree that they are appropriate.

Summary of Points

1. Assessment planning should be guided by what the students are expected to learn as specified by the school goals and the more detailed instructional objectives.
2. Assessment planning requires a consideration of all possible types of learning outcomes in a given content area, not just those that can be measured by a test.

3. Assessment of performance skills and products typically requires some type of observation procedure, such as a scoring key, checklist, rating scale, or holistic scoring rubric (see Chapters 10 and 11).
4. Different domains of learning require different assessment procedures.
5. The time to plan assessment activities is at the beginning of a unit of instruction. Vary the activities according to the grade, the subject area, and the time of year.

Learning Exercises

1. List several instructional objectives that are best measured with objective test items. List several that require the use of product assessments.

2. Which assessment method would you use to measure achievement for each of the following objectives?
    (a) Students will understand the events of Confederation.
    (b) Students will be able to measure and record daily temperatures.
    (c) Students will appreciate literature.
    (d) Students will be able to do 20 push-ups.

3. Assume that you are going to prepare a brief unit test for a course in your major teaching area. How would you proceed? How would your procedure differ if it were to be an end-of-course summative test or assessment?

References and Additional Reading

Bloom, B.S., et al. (ed.) (1956). *Taxonomy of Educational Objectives: Cognitive Domain.* New York: David McKay Co.

Carey, L.M. (2001). *Measuring and Evaluating School Learning*, 3rd ed. Boston: Allyn and Bacon.

Gronlund, N.E. (2000). *How to Write and Use Instructional Objectives*, 6th ed. Upper Saddle River, NJ: Merrill/Prentice Hall.

Linn, R.L., and Gronlund, N.E. (2000). *Measurement and Assessment in Teaching*, 8th ed. Upper Saddle River, NJ: Merrill/Prentice-Hall.

Oosterhoff, A.C. (2001). *Classroom Application of Educational Measurement*, 3rd ed. Upper Saddle River, NJ: Merrill/Prentice-Hall.

Stiggins, R.J. (2001). *Student-Involved Classroom Assessment*, 3rd ed. Upper Saddle River, NJ: Merrill/Prentice-Hall, 2001.

Weblinks

Education World
A key site for teachers that contains many suggestions.
http://db.education-world.com/perl/browse?cat_id=1855

Resources in Language Testing Page
A British site containing links to resources on testing language competency.
http://www.surrey.ac.uk/ELI/ltr.html

Teachers Canada
A variety of resources and links concerning assessment.
http://canadateachers.about.com/cs/evaluation/

6

Paper and Pencil Tests: General Principles

This chapter will enable you to:

1. List the advantages of and problems with paper and pencil tests.
2. Prepare a set of specifications for a test.
3. Describe the relative merits of selection- and supply-type test items.
4. Match test items to the specific learning outcomes they measure.
5. Describe the factors to consider when preparing items for a test.
6. Describe how to arrange items in a test.
7. Write clear directions for a test.
8. Review and evaluate an assembled test.
9. Administer a test properly.
10. Make a simple item analysis.

The Paper and Pencil Test

As noted in Chapter 1, paper and pencil tests have had a somewhat checkered past. At one time they were one of many assessment devices used in schools, then they became by far the most popular method of assessment, then overuse of standardized tests in the United States led to a backlash against all testing, and recently Canada has embraced large-scale testing at the provincial, national, and international levels. But as pointed out in Chapter 5, paper and pencil tests have an important place in student assessment. To fail to make use of the most efficient assessment method because the method was misused in the past would be as unsound as the misuse itself.

Advantages of Paper and Pencil Tests

Paper and pencil tests (referred to hereafter simply as "tests") have many advantages as assessment devices.

Tests are efficient. An experienced teacher can make up a test for a unit of study in two or three hours, can have 30 students write it in an hour, and can mark it in one to four hours, depending on the types of questions asked. At the end of that time, the teacher will have a reasonably accurate picture of the students' understanding of the unit. Compared to an essay (which takes less teacher time to formulate, but much longer to mark, and assesses a much narrower range of knowledge) tests are very efficient.

Tests are fair. Because all students write the same test under the same conditions, the results are controlled by the students. Students who review lessons systematically and carefully will generally achieve better results than students who do not study, or who do all their review the night before the test. Students must do their own work—unlike assessments done outside of the classroom. Tests are generally more objective than other types of assessment.

Tests are reliable and valid. Because they are written under controlled conditions, and because the teacher controls the questions, the results are also controlled. The teacher can make the test easy or difficult. He or she can test a great deal of material to a limited degree, or a small amount of material in considerable depth.

Test results can be easily analyzed. Because all students must answer the same questions, the teacher knows which students understand all the material, which understand part of it (and where the weaknesses lie), and which students have poor understanding.

Problems With Paper and Pencil Tests

Although tests can be structured to ask high-level questions and to assess students' reasoning skills, it is much easier to ask low-level questions, so that is generally the level of achievement assessed by tests.

Many students are nervous about tests. Although research shows that test results correlate highly with other assessments, many students feel they cannot demonstrate their achievement properly on a test.

Students who have limited reading and writing skills may be unable to demonstrate their knowledge on a test. This is obvious in the primary grades, and with ESL students, but may be less obvious if a student has a learning disability.

Preparing and Using Paper and Pencil Tests

The preparation and use of a test that measures the intended learning outcomes in a balanced manner involves the following steps:

1. Specifying the instructional objectives.
2. Preparing the test specifications.
3. Constructing relevant test items.
4. Arranging the items in the test.
5. Preparing clear directions.
6. Reviewing and evaluating the assembled test.
7. Administering the test and making an item analysis.

Each of these steps will be described in the following chapters. Performance and product assessment will be described in Chapter 10.

Specifying the Instructional Objectives

As noted earlier, the first step in preparing instructional objectives is to list the general objectives as intended learning outcomes. The following list illustrates the procedure for a unit on planning an achievement test.

At the end of this unit in achievement test planning, the student will demonstrate that he or she:

1. knows the meaning of common terms.
2. knows specific facts about test planning.
3. knows the basic procedures for planning an achievement test.
4. comprehends the relevant principles of testing.
5. applies the principles in test planning.

These statements of general learning outcomes have deliberately been kept free of specific course content so that with only slight modification they can be used with various units of study. As we shall see later, the test specifications provide a means of relating intended outcomes to specific subject matter topics.

This list of general outcomes could, of course, be expanded by making the statements more specific, and in some cases it may be desirable to do so. The number of general learning outcomes to use is somewhat arbitrary, but somewhere between 5 and 15 items provide a list that is both useful and manageable. Typically, a shorter list is satisfactory for a unit of study, while a more comprehensive list is needed for summative testing at the end of a course.

Defining the General Outcomes in Specific Terms

When a satisfactory list of general learning outcomes has been identified and clearly stated, the next step is to list the specific types of student performance that are to be accepted as evidence that the outcomes have been achieved. For example, what specific types of performance will show that a student "knows the meaning of common terms" or "comprehends the relevant principles of testing"? For these two areas, the specific learning outcomes may be listed as follows:

1. Knows the meaning of common terms.

   1.1 Identifies the correct definitions of terms.

   1.2 Identifies the meaning of terms when used in context.

   1.3 Distinguishes between terms on basis of meaning.

   1.4 Selects the most appropriate terms when describing testing procedures.

4. Comprehends the relevant principles of testing.

   4.1 Describes each principle in his or her own words.

   4.2 Matches a specific example to each principle.

4.3 Explains the relevance of each principle to the major steps in test planning.

4.4 Predicts the most probable effect of violating each of the principles.

4.5 Formulates a test plan that is in harmony with the principles.

Note that the terms used to describe the specific learning outcomes indicate student performance that can be demonstrated to an outside observer. That is, they are *observable* responses that can be called forth by test items. The key terms are listed below to emphasize what is meant by defining learning outcomes in *specific performance terms*.

Identifies	Matches
Distinguishes between	Explains
Selects	Predicts
Describes	Formulates

Action verbs such as these indicate precisely what the student is able to do to demonstrate achievement. Such vague and indefinite terms as "learns," "sees," "realizes," and "is familiar with" should be avoided, since they do not clearly indicate the terminal performance to be measured.

Sample action verbs for stating specific learning outcomes at each level of the cognitive domain of the taxonomy are presented in Table 6.1. Although certain action verbs may be used at several different levels (e.g., "identifies"), the table provides a useful guide for defining intended outcomes in performance terms. For more comprehensive lists of action verbs, see Gronlund (2000) listed at the end of this chapter.

In defining the general learning outcomes in specific performance terms, it is typically impossible to list all of the relevant types of performance. The proportion that need be listed depends to a large extent on the nature of the test. In planning a test that is to be used to describe which learning tasks a student has mastered (criterion-referenced test), we should like as comprehensive a list as possible. For a test that is used to rank students in order of achievement (norm-referenced test), however, it is usually satisfactory

TABLE 6.1 • *Illustrative Action Verbs for Defining Objectives in the Cognitive Domain of the Taxonomy*

Taxonomy Categories	Sample Verbs for Stating Specific Learning Outcomes
Knowledge	Identifies, names, defines, describes, lists, matches, selects, outlines
Comprehension	Classifies, explains, summarizes, converts, predicts, distinguishes between
Application	Demonstrates, computes, solves, modifies, arranges, operates, relates
Analysis	Differentiates, diagrams, estimates, separates, infers, orders, subdivides
Synthesis	Combines, creates, formulates, designs, composes, constructs, rearranges, revises
Evaluation	Judges, criticizes, compares, justifies, concludes, discriminates, supports

to include sufficient specific types of performance to clarify what the typical student is like who has achieved the intended outcomes.

Preparing the Test Specifications

The writing of test items should be guided by a carefully prepared set of test specifications. The function of the specifications is to describe the achievement domain being measured and to provide guidelines for obtaining a representative sample of test tasks. Although the nature and detail of test specifications can be expected to vary considerably, here we shall describe one of the more commonly recommended procedures. In the construction of an **achievement test**, one of the most widely used devices has been a two-way chart called a *table of specifications*.

Building a Table of Specifications

Preparing a **table of specifications** involves (1) selecting the learning outcomes to be tested, (2) outlining the subject matter, and (3) making a two-way chart. The two-way chart describes the sample of items to be included in the test.

Selecting the Learning Outcomes to Be Tested. The learning outcomes for a particular course will depend on the specific nature of the course, the objectives attained in previous courses, the philosophy of the school, the special needs of the students, and a host of other local factors that have a bearing on the instructional program. Despite the variation from course to course, most lists of instructional objectives will include learning outcomes in the following areas: (1) knowledge, (2) intellectual abilities and skills, (3) general skills (laboratory, performance, communication, work–study), and (4) attitudes, interests, and appreciations. It is in the first two areas covered by the cognitive domain of the taxonomy that achievement testing is most useful. Learning outcomes in the other areas are typically evaluated by rating scales, checklists, anecdotal records, inventories, and similar nontest evaluation procedures. Thus, the first step is to separate from the list of learning outcomes those that are testable by paper and pencil tests. The selected list of learning outcomes should, of course, be defined in specific terms, as described in the previous section. Clarifying the specific types of performance to be called forth by the test will aid in constructing test terms that are most relevant to the intended learning outcomes.

Outlining the Subject Matter. The stated learning outcomes specify how students are expected to react to the subject matter of a course. Although it is possible to include both the student performance and the specific subject matter toward which the student is to react in the same statement, it is usually desirable to list them separately. The reason for this is that the student can react in the same way to many different areas of subject matter, and he can react in many different ways to the same area of subject matter. For example, when we state that a student can "define a term in her own words," "recall a specific fact," or "identify an example of a principle," these types of performance can be applied to almost any area of subject matter. Since particular types of student performance can overlap a variety of subject matter areas, and vice versa, it is more convenient to list each aspect of performance and subject matter separately and then to relate them in the table of specifications.

The content of a course may be outlined in detail for teaching purposes, but for test planning only the major categories need be listed. The following outline of subject matter topics based on a unit on achievement testing illustrates sufficient detail for the test plan.

A. Role of testing in the instructional process
  1. Instructional decisions and test types.
  2. Influence of tests on learning and instruction.

B. Principles of achievement testing
  1. Relation to instructional objectives.
  2. Representative sampling.
  3. Relevance of items to outcomes.
  4. Relevance of test to use of results.
  5. Reliability of results.
  6. Improvement of learning.

C. Norm-referenced versus criterion-referenced testing

D. Planning the test
  1. Determining the purpose of the test.
  2. Identifying the intended learning outcomes.
  3. Preparing the test specifications.
  4. Constructing relevant test items.

Making the Two-Way Chart. When the learning outcomes have been selected and clearly defined and the course content outlined, the two-way chart should be prepared. This is the table of specifications. It relates outcomes to content and indicates the relative weight to be given to each of the various areas. As noted earlier, the purpose of the table is to provide assurance that the test will measure a representative sample of the learning outcomes and the subject matter topics to be measured.

Table 6.2 (page 70) gives an example of a table of specifications for a summative test on a unit on achievement testing. Note that only the general learning outcomes and the major subject matter categories have been included. A more detailed table may be desirable for test purposes, but this is sufficient for illustration.

The number in each cell of the table indicates the number of test items to be devoted to that area. For example, 15 items in the test will measure knowledge of terms; four of them pertain to the "role of tests" in instruction," four to "principles of testing," four to "norm-referenced versus criterion-referenced," and three to "planning the test." The number of items assigned to each cell is determined by the weight given to each learning outcome and each subject matter area.

A number of factors will enter into assigning relative weights to each learning outcome and each content area. How important is each area in the total learning experience? How much time was devoted to each area during instruction? Which outcomes have the greater retention and transfer value? What relative importance do curriculum specialists assign to each area? These and similar criteria must be considered. In the final analysis, however, the weights assigned in the table should faithfully reflect the emphasis given during instruction. In Table 6.2, for example, it is assumed that twice as much emphasis was given to "planning the test" (20 items) as was given to "norm-referenced

TABLE 6.2 • *Table of Specifications for a Summative Test on a Unit for Achievement Testing*

Outcomes Content	Knows			Comprehends Principles	Applies Principles	Total Number of Items
	Terms	Facts	Procedures			
Role of Tests in Instruction	4	4		2		10
Principles of Testing	4	3	2	6	5	20
Norm-Referenced versus Criterion-Referenced	4	3	3			10
Planning the Test	3	5	5	2	5	20
Total Number of Items	15	15	10	10	10	60

versus criterion-referenced" (10 items). Similarly, it is assumed that knowledge outcomes were given approximately two-thirds of the emphasis during instruction (40 items), and that comprehension and application outcomes were each given approximately one-sixth of the total emphasis (10 items each).

In summary, preparing a table of specifications includes the following steps:

1. Identify the learning outcomes and content areas to be measured by the test.
2. Weight the learning outcomes and content areas in terms of their relative importance.
3. Build the table in accordance with these relative weights by distributing the test items proportionately among the relevant cells of the table.

The resulting two-way table indicates the type of test needed to measure the learning outcomes and course content in a balanced manner. Thus, the table of specifications serves the test maker like a blueprint. It specifies the number and the nature of the items in the test, and it thereby provides a guide for item writing.

Considerations In Constructing Relevant Test Items

The construction of a set of relevant test items is greatly simplified if the intended learning outcomes have been clearly defined and the test specifications carefully prepared. The quality of the test will then depend on how closely the test maker can match the specifications. Here we shall confine our discussion to some of the general specifications in preparing test items. More detailed procedures and rules for item writing will be described in the chapters that follow.

Selecting the Types of Test Items To Use

The items used in achievement tests can be classified as either *selection-type* items or *supply-type* items. The selection-type item presents students with a set of possible responses from which they are to select the most appropriate answer. The supply-type item requires students to create and supply their own answers. These two major categories can be used to classify the most widely used item types as follows.

Selection-Type Items

1. Multiple choice
2. True–false
3. Matching
4. Interpretive exercise

Supply-Type Items

1. Short answer
2. Essay (restricted response)
3. Essay (extended response)

These categories are sometimes referred to as *recognition* and *recall* items. This is a case of mislabelling that confuses the method of responding with the mental reaction needed to make the response. When measuring knowledge of facts, test responses might be limited to either the recognition or recall of the answer. However, when measuring complex learning outcomes with selection-type items, the answer is not achieved through mere recognition of a previously learned answer. It typically involves some use of higher mental processes to arrive at a solution (e.g., verbal or mathematical reasoning) before the correct answer can be selected. Similarly, a short-answer item may require reasoning or problem solving rather than simply recalling and supplying factual information. Essay answers, of course, typically require analysis, synthesis, and evaluation skills in addition to recall. Using the *selection* and *supply* labels makes clear how the responses are made but it does not imply limits on the types of learning outcomes that can be measured with each.

In deciding which item types to use in a test, a guiding principle should be: *Use the item types that provide the most direct measures of student performance specified by the intended learning outcome.* Thus, if you want to determine whether students can spell, have them spell from dictation. If you want to determine whether students can solve mathematics problems, have them solve problems and supply the answers. If you want to determine whether students can write, have them write something. Use selection-type items for supply-type outcomes only if there is a compelling reason for doing so (e.g., electronic scoring) and then take into account, during interpretation of the results, that a less direct measure has been used. In some cases, of course, both types of items are useful in the same area. For example, a writing project may provide the best evidence of writing skill but a selection-type test would provide the most systematic coverage of the elements of grammar needed for effective writing.

There are achievement areas where either selection-type items or supply-type items would measure equally well. In these cases, our choice between them must be based on other item characteristics. The preparation of good selection-type items is difficult and students can get a proportion of answers correct by guessing. However, these disadvantages are offset by the fact that (1) they provide an extensive sample of student performance (because of the large number of items used), (2) they can be scored quickly and objectively (i.e., scorers agree on the answers), (3) they eliminate bluffing, (4) they eliminate the influence of writing skill, and (5) they provide for the identification of specific learning errors. In comparison, supply-type items are easier to construct (although harder than commonly believed) but more difficult to score. The scoring of short-answer items is contaminated by answers of varying degrees of correctness and by adjustments needed for misspellings. The scoring of essay tests is tedious, time consuming, and influenced by bluffing, writing skill, and the shifting of standards during scoring. Another major shortcoming of supply-type items is the limited sample of learning tasks that can be measured. The short-answer item is restricted primarily to measuring knowledge outcomes. Although the essay test is especially suited to measuring complex learning outcomes, its sampling is limited by the relatively few questions that can be included in a test.

Table 6.3 presents a summary comparison of the relative merits of selection-type and supply-type items. Although this should serve as a guide in selecting the types of items to use in a given test, as noted earlier, the most important question to ask is: *Does this item type provide the most direct measure of the intended learning outcome?* If the various item types are equal in this regard, the selection-type items would be favoured

TABLE 6.3 • *Summary of the Relative Merits of Selection-Type Items and Supply-Type Items*

Characteristic	Selection-Type Items	Supply-Type Items	
		Short Answer	Essay
Measures factual information	Yes	Yes	Yes*
Measures understanding	Yes	No**	Yes
Measures synthesis	No**	No**	Yes
Easy to construct	No	Yes	Yes
Samples broadly	Yes	Yes	No
Eliminates bluffing	Yes	No	No
Eliminates writing skill	Yes	No	No
Eliminates blind guessing	No	Yes	Yes
Easy to score	Yes	No	No
Scoring is objective	Yes	No	No
Pinpoints learning errors	Yes	Yes	No
Encourages originality	No	No	Yes

*The essay test can measure knowledge of facts, but because of scoring and sampling problems it probably should not be used for this purpose.
**These items can be designed to measure limited aspects of these characteristics.

because of the broad sampling, the objective scoring, and the pinpointing of specific learning errors.

Matching Items to Specific Learning Outcomes

Effective achievement testing requires that a set of test items be constructed that calls forth the performance described in the intended learning outcomes. While we can never be certain of a perfect correspondence between outcome and item, the following examples illustrate how items should be written to measure the specific type of performance stated in the specific learning outcome.

EXAMPLES

Specific Learning Outcome: Defines terms in student's own words.
Directions: Define each of the following terms in a sentence or two.

1. Taxonomy
2. Cognitive
3. Measurement
4. Evaluation

Specific Learning Outcome: Identifies procedural steps in planning for a test.
1. Which one of the following steps should be completed first in planning for an achievement test?[1]
    A. Select the types of test items to use.
    B. Decide on the length of the test.
    *C. Define the intended learning outcomes.
    D. Prepare the test specifications.

Specific Learning Outcome: Identifies the hierarchical order of the categories in the cognitive domain of the taxonomy.
1. Which one of the following categories in the taxonomy indicates the highest level of learning?
    A. Analysis
    B. Application
    C. Comprehension
    *D. Synthesis

Specific Learning Outcome: Distinguishes between sound and unsound principles of achievement testing.
Directions: Read each of the following statements. If the statement indicates a sound principle of achievement testing, circle the S; if it indicates an unsound principle, circle the U.

*S	U	1.	*The specific learning outcomes to be tested should be stated in terms of student performance.*
S	*U	2.	*Achievement testing should be limited to outcomes that can be measured objectively.*
*S	U	3.	*Each achievement test item should measure a clearly defined type of student performance.*

---

[1] The correct answer is indicated throughout this book by an asterisk.

Specific Learning Outcome: Identifies examples of properly stated learning outcomes.
1. Which one of the following learning outcomes is properly stated in performance terms?
    A. Student realizes the importance of tests in teaching.
    B. Student has acquired the basic principles of achievement testing.
    C. Student demonstrates a desire for more experience in test construction.
    *D. Student predicts the most probable effect of violating a test construction principle.

It should be noted in these examples that each specific learning outcome provides a precise definition of the student performance to be measured, and the test item simply provides a task that makes measurement of the specified performance possible.

Improving the Functioning Content of Items

If test items are to call forth the performance described in the intended learning outcomes, great care must be taken in phrasing the items. We need to eliminate all barriers that might prevent a knowledgeable person from responding and all clues that might lead the uninformed to the correct answer. Only those who have achieved the outcome being measured should get the item right. All others (no matter how intelligent) should miss it.

Some of the common *barriers* to be avoided during test preparation are:

- vocabulary that is unnecessarily difficult.
- sentence structure that is unnecessarily complex.
- statements containing ambiguity.
- unclear pictorial materials.
- directions that are vague.
- material reflecting race, ethnic, or gender bias.

Awareness of such barriers during the planning and preparation of the test is the first step in their elimination. Essentially, we can avoid these barriers by (1) writing each test item so that it presents a clearly formulated task, (2) stating the items in simple, clear language, (3) keeping the items free from biased and nonfunctional material, and (4) using a test format and directions that contribute to effective test taking. Much of the material presented later in this book is directed toward constructing tests that prevent extraneous factors from distorting the test results.

Some of the common *clues* to be avoided during test preparation are:

- verbal associations that give away the answer.
- grammatical inconsistencies that eliminate wrong answers.
- specific determiners that make certain answers probable (e.g., sometimes) and others improbable (e.g., always).
- stereotyped or textbook phrasing of correct answers.
- length or location of correct answers.
- material in an item that aids in answering another item.

Just as in controlling extraneous factors that provide barriers to the correct answer, clues such as these can be eliminated by being aware of them and by following sound principles of test construction. Many of the rules for item writing and test preparation in the chapters that follow provide guidelines for this purpose.

Determining the Number of Test Items To Use

The number of items to use should be indicated in the test specifications, as noted earlier, and is modified by a number of practical constraints, such as the following:

1. Age of the students tested.
2. Time available for testing.
3. Type of test items used.
4. Type of interpretation to be made.

As a general rule of thumb, tests should be limited to 10 minutes per grade level. At the Grade 3 level, the testing time typically should be no more than 30 minutes so that proper motivation is maintained. Grade 6 students can be expected to maintain concentration for about 60 minutes. At the high school and college or university levels, students can be given tests lasting several hours (for example, a final examination), but most tests are limited to a testing time of 50 to 60 minutes because of the length of the typical class period.

In matching the number of items to available testing time, we are faced with the problem of estimating how many items students can complete per minute. Unfortunately, there are no simple answers. The size of the final product depends on the type of test item, the complexity of the learning outcome measured, and the age of the students. As a guideline, high school and college students should be able to answer one multiple-choice item, three short-answer items, or three true–false items per minute when the items are measuring knowledge outcomes. For measuring more complex learning outcomes such as comprehension and application, and for testing younger age groups, more time per item is needed. In estimating the number of items to be used, keep in mind the slower students in the group, for it is desirable to give most students an opportunity to complete the test. Keep in mind, however, that the more items there are, the more reliable and valid is the test. Do not limit test length because of two or three students. Make arrangements for them to complete the test in a different room, or at a different time. Testing just before lunch or recess will accommodate students who require more time to complete the test. Experience in testing a given group of students is frequently the only dependable guide for determining proper test length.

In addition to our concern with total test length, consideration must be given to the number of test items needed for each type of interpretation to be made. This issue is especially crucial in criterion-referenced interpretation, where we want to describe student performance in terms of each intended learning outcome. For this purpose we should use at least 10 items per outcome. Where practical constraints make it necessary to use fewer than 10 items for an intended outcome, only tentative judgments should be made and these should be verified by other means. In some cases it is possible to combine items into larger item clusters for a more meaningful interpretation. See Box 6.1 (page 76) for a summary checklist for evaluating the test plan.

General Guidelines for Item Writing

Some general suggestions apply to the writing of all item types. These provide a general framework for writing items that function as intended and that contribute to more valid and reliable results.

BOX 6.1 • *Checklist for Evaluating the Test Plan*

1. Is the purpose of the test clear?
2. Have the intended learning outcomes been identified and defined?
3. Are the intended learning outcomes stated in performance (measurable) terms?
4. Have test specifications been prepared that indicate the nature and distribution of items to be included in the test?
5. Does the specified set of items provide a representative sample of the tasks contained in the achievement domain?
6. Are the types of items appropriate for the learning outcomes to be measured?
7. Is the difficulty of the items appropriate for the students to be tested and the nature of the measurement (e.g., mastery or survey)?
8. Is the number of items appropriate for the students to be tested, the time available for testing, and the interpretations to be made?
9. Does the test plan include built-in features that contribute to valid and reliable scores?
10. Have plans been made for arranging the items in the test, writing directions, scoring, and using the results?

1.   **Select the type of test item that measures the intended learning outcome most directly.** Use a supply-type item if supplying the answer is an important element of the task (e.g., writing). Use a selection-type item if appropriate (e.g., identification) or if both types are equally appropriate.

2.   **Write the test item so that the performance it elicits matches the performance in the learning task.** The intended learning outcome specifies the learning task in performance terms and the test task should call forth the same performance.

3.   **Write the test item so that the test task is clear and definite.** Keep the reading level low, use simple and direct language, and follow the rules for correct punctuation and grammar.

4.   **Write the test item so that it is free of nonfunctional material.** Material not directly relevant to the problem being presented increases the reading load and may detract from the intent of the item. Use extraneous material only where its detection is part of the task (e.g., in math problems).

5.   **Write the test item so that irrelevant factors do not prevent an informed student from responding correctly.** Avoid trick questions that might cause a knowledgeable student to focus on the wrong aspect of the task. Use clear, unambiguous statements that maximize the performance to be measured and minimize all other influences. For example, word problems measuring mathematical reasoning should keep reading level and computational demands simple if an uncontaminated measure of reasoning ability is desired.

6.   **Write the test item so that irrelevant clues do not enable the uninformed student to respond correctly.** Removing unwanted clues from test items requires alertness

during item writing and a review of the items after setting them aside for a while. The most common clues for each item type will be considered in the following chapters. It is also important to prevent the information given in one item from providing an answer to another item in the test.

7.   Write the test item so that the difficulty level matches the intent of the learning outcome, the age group to be tested, and the use to be made of the results. When difficulty is being evaluated, check to be certain that it is relevant to the intended learning outcome and that the item is free from sources of irrelevant difficulty (e.g., obscure materials, overly fine discriminations).

8.   Write the test item so that there is no disagreement concerning the answer. Typically the answer should be one that experts would agree is the correct or best answer. Most problems arise here when students are to provide the best answer (best procedure, best explanation). This involves a matter of judgment and to be defensible the answer must be clearly best and identified as such by experts in the area. Where experts disagree, it may be desirable to ask what a particular authority would consider to be the best method, the best reason, and the like. When attributed to a source, the answer can be judged as correct or incorrect. One way around this difficulty is to ask, "What did class discussion say was…?"

9.   Write the test items far enough in advance that they can be later reviewed and modified as needed. A good time to write test items is shortly after the material has been taught, while the questions and context are still clearly in mind. In any event, reviewing and editing items after they have been set aside for a while can detect flaws that were inadvertently introduced during the original item writing.

10. Write more test items than called for by the test plan. This will enable you to discard weak or inappropriate items during item review and make it easier to match the final set of items to the test specifications.

Arranging the Items in the Test

After the final selection of the items to be included in a test, a decision must be made concerning the best arrangement of items. This arrangement will vary with the type of test being prepared, but the following guidelines should be helpful.

1.   For instructional purposes, it is usually desirable to group together items that measure the same outcome. Each group of items can then be identified by an appropriate heading (e.g., knowledge, comprehension, application). The inclusion of the headings helps to identify the areas where students are having difficulty and to plan for remedial action.

2.   Where possible, all items of the same type should be grouped together. This arrangement makes it possible to provide only one set of directions for each item type. It also simplifies the scoring and the analysis of the results.

3.   The items should be arranged in terms of increasing difficulty. This arrangement has a motivational effect on students and will prevent them from getting "bogged down" by difficult items early in the test.

Because most classroom tests include only a few item types, it is usually possible to honour all three of these guidelines. When this is not feasible, the item arrangement should be used that best fits the nature of the test and use to be made of the results.

Preparing Directions

The directions for an achievement test should be simple and concise and yet contain information concerning each of the following: (1) purpose of the test, (2) time allowed to complete the test, (3) how to record the answers, and (4) whether to guess when in doubt about an answer. The following sample directions for a multiple-choice test cover these four points.

EXAMPLE

Directions: This is a test of what you have learned during the first five weeks of the course. The results of this test will be used to clarify any points of difficulty and thus help you complete the course successfully.

There are 60 multiple-choice items, and you have one hour to complete the test. For each item, select the answer that *best* completes the statement or answers the question, and circle the letter of that answer. Since your score will be the number of items answered correctly, *be sure to answer every item.*

When two or more item types are included in the same test, it is usually desirable to provide general directions for the test as a whole and specific directions for each part. When this is done, the general directions should contain the information about purpose, time allowed, and what to do about guessing, and the specific directions should describe how to record the answers for that particular part. Also, some items, such as key-type exercises, require special directions for each item.

The use of separate answer sheets requires some elaboration of the instructions for recording the answers. If students are not familiar with the use of separate answer sheets, it might also be desirable to present a sample item with the correct answer properly marked. There is a variety of separate answer sheets, and the specific instructions will have to be adapted to the particular type used. Unless machine scoring is to be used, however, a teacher-made answer sheet that simply lists the letters of the alternatives for each item is usually satisfactory.

The Problem of Guessing

In our set of sample directions, the students were told, "Since your score will be the number of items answered correctly, be sure to answer every item." This is an attempt to equalize the variation among students in their tendency to guess when in doubt about the answer. The directions make it unnecessary to correct for guessing. Although a correction for guessing may be appropriate for standardized tests, it is not needed for classroom tests where the students have an opportunity to respond to all items. It is only where students are unable to complete the test (e.g., speed test) that the correction for guessing might be appropriate for classroom tests. Here, the purpose is to prevent students from rapidly and randomly marking the remaining items just before time is up in an attempt to improve their score (see Box 6.2 for a correction formula).

BOX 6.2 ● *Correcting for Guessing*

Use the correction for guessing formula only when students have insufficient time to consider all of the items in the test (e.g., speed test). Then, warn the students that there will be a correction for guessing. Use the following formula to correct the scores.

Score = Right – Wrong/n – 1

In this formula, *n* equals the number of alternatives, and thus:

True-false items	$S = R - W$
Multiple-choice items	$S = R - W/2$ (3 alternatives)
	$S = R - W/3$ (4 alternatives)
	$S = R - W/4$ (5 alternatives)

Reviewing and Evaluating the Assembled Test

After assembling the items into a test, it is desirable to review the test as a whole to be sure it meets the criteria of a good test. The types of questions to consider are listed in Box 6.3.

BOX 6.3 ● *Checklist for Evaluating the Assembled Test*

1.	*Balance*	Do the items measure a representative sample of the learning tasks in the achievement domain?
2.	*Relevance*	Do the test items present relevant tasks?
3.	*Conciseness*	Are the test tasks stated in simple, clear language?
4.	*Soundness*	Are the items of proper difficulty, free of defects, and do they have answers that are defensible?
5.	*Independence*	Are the items free from overlapping, so that one item does not aid in answering another?
6.	*Arrangement*	Are items measuring the same outcome grouped together?
		Are items of the same type grouped together?
		Are items in order of increasing difficulty?
7.	*Numbering*	Are the items numbered in order throughout the test?
8.	*Directions*	Are there directions for the whole test and each part?
		Are the directions concise and at the proper reading level?
		Do the directions include time limits and how to record answers?
		Do the directions tell what to do about guessing?
9.	*Spacing*	Does the spacing on the page contribute to ease of reading and responding?
10.	*Typing*	Is the final copy free of typographical errors?

Administering and Scoring the Test

The administration of a carefully prepared informal achievement test is largely a matter of providing proper working conditions, keeping interruptions to a minimum, and arranging enough space between students to prevent cheating. The written directions should be clear enough to make the test self-administering, but in some situations it may be desirable to give the directions orally as well. With young students, a blackboard illustration may also be useful. Above all, make certain that all the students know exactly what to do, and then provide them with the most favourable conditions in which to do it.

Scoring is facilitated if all answers are recorded on the left side of each test page, as we suggested earlier. Under this arrangement, scoring is simply a matter of marking the correct answers on a copy of the test and placing it next to the column of answers on each student's paper. If a separate answer sheet is used, it is usually better to punch out the letters of the correct answers on a copy of the answer sheet and use this as a scoring stencil. The stencil is laid over each answer sheet and the correctly marked answers appear through the holes. Where no mark appears, a red line can be drawn across the hole. This indicates to the student the correct answer for each item missed. If machine scoring is to be used, simply scan the students' papers to make certain that only one answer was marked for each item.

Unless corrected for guessing, a student's score on an objective test is typically the number of answers marked correctly. Thus, each test item is counted as one point. Although teachers frequently desire to count some items more heavily than others because of their importance or difficulty, such weighting of scores complicates the scoring task and seldom results in an improved measure of achievement. A better way to increase the relative weight of an area is to construct more items in that area.

Analyzing the Effectiveness of Test Items

After a test has been administered, the items should be analyzed for their effectiveness. One method of evaluating the test is to review the test item-by-item when it is handed back to students for a discussion of the results. Significant comments made during the discussion can be recorded on a blank copy of the test. The flexibility of this procedure makes it possible to pursue comments about particular items, to ask students why they selected the response they did (both correct and incorrect selections), and to spend as much time on each item as seems warranted. This procedure may bring forth some unjustified criticisms of the test, but it will also help identify defective items in need of revision. The extra time used in discussing the test results will not be wasted because students will be obtaining a review of the course material covered by the test.

Simple Item Analysis Procedure

The discussion of test results and review of the items can be much more effective if a simple tally of student responses is made on the master copy of the test. Recording the results of the 10 highest scoring students (H) and 10 lowest scoring students (L), like that in Figure 6.1, makes the results easily interpretable. The answer is circled and the numbers to the left of each alternative indicate how many students in each group selected that alternative.

The result in Figure 6.1 provides all the information we need to estimate the following types of item analysis information.

1. The difficulty of the item (percentage of students answering the item correctly).
2. The discriminating power of the item (how well the item discriminates between high and low scorers).
3. The effectiveness of each alternative (all should be chosen and each one more frequently by the low scoring group).

By simply looking at the answer sheet in Figure 6.1, we can see that eight students in the high-scoring group and four students in the low-scoring group selected the correct answer. Also, more students in the low-scoring group selected each wrong alternative than in the high-scoring group, indicating that the distracters seem to be distracting those students who haven't learned the meaning of the term.

Because we are using 10 students in the high-scoring group and 10 students in the low-scoring group, we can mentally calculate the usual indexes of difficulty and discriminating power by using the following simple steps.

1. Determine the percentage of high scorers and low scorers passing the item by adding a zero.

   H = 8 out of 10 = 80
   L = 4 out of 10 = 40

FIGURE 6.1 • Test copy with item analysis data to left of items (H = 10 highest scorers, L = 10 lowest scorers).

UNIT TEST

Name _____ Date _____

Directions:

    This test measures the knowledge, understandings, and applications you have acquired during the first four weeks.

    There are 65 objective items, and you will have the full class period to complete the test.

    Select the best answer for each item and circle the letter of that answer.

    Your score will be the number of items answered correctly, so *be sure to answer every item.*

KNOWLEDGE OF TERMS

H	L	
		1. An assessment instrument is properly classified as *objective* when
1	3	A. the instrument uses objective-type questions.
1	2	B. the responses called forth by the instrument are free of opinion.
0	1	C. those preparing the instrument used standard procedures of construction.
8	4	Ⓓ there is agreement among scorers concerning the correctness of the answers.

2. Obtain *item difficulty* by adding the percentage correct in the high and low groups and dividing by 2. Add a percent sign to the answer.

    $$\frac{80 + 40}{2} = 60\%$$

3. Obtain *discriminating power* by subtracting the percentage correct in the low group from the percentage correct in the high group. Add a decimal point to the answer.

    $$80 - 40 = 0.40$$

The description of the procedure makes it sound more complicated than it is, but making a few mental calculations like this will reveal its simplicity. Item difficulty typically uses the percent sign and, of course, can range from 0% to 100%. Our **difficulty index** is based on the high- and low-scoring groups only, but this provides a satisfactory approximation of item difficulty. The **discrimination index** typically uses the decimal point and thus ranges from 0 to 1.00.

This simple method of analyzing the test results can be used as an aid in discussing the items when reviewing the test. Items that most students answer correctly can be skipped over or treated lightly, items missed by most students can be discussed in more detail, and defective items can be pointed out to students rather than defended as fair. Also, the frequency with which each incorrect answer is chosen may reveal common errors and misconceptions that can be corrected on the spot or serve as a basis for remedial work. Discussing the reasons students have selected the right or wrong answer for an item can sometimes be revealing. We assume that if they selected the correct answer they had learned the material, but that may not be the case. Having students discuss the reasons for their choices provides insights into student thinking that may contribute to both improved teaching and improved test construction skills.

Although the method of **item analysis** presented here is a crude one, it is probably satisfactory for most classroom tests. We are using it primarily as a basis for reviewing the items with students and for any insights the results might give us for improving test items in the future. A more detailed description of item analysis and cautions in interpreting item-analysis data can be found in Linn and Gronlund (2000).

Because of the small number of students involved in classroom testing, item-analysis information must be interpreted with great caution. If a test item is reused with a new group, the results may be quite different, due to changes in the instruction, the study habits of students, or some other factor. The tentative nature of the item-analysis data is not of great concern, however, when used to review tests with students for the purpose of improving learning.

Special Considerations

Special needs students can often achieve success with simple test items, provided they can read the item. If their reading level is too low, arrangements should be made to have the student take the test orally, preferably at the same time as the other students are writing the test. It is important that the assistant understand that he or she is not to help the student answer the question. If the assistant can offer an interpretation of the question, that should be made clear.

Summary of Points

1. Paper and pencil tests tend to be efficient, fair, objective, reliable, valid, and easily analyzed.
2. Tests tend to assess lower-level thinking, some students fear tests, and students with poor reading and writing skills will find tests difficult.
3. Preparing and using an achievement test includes specifying the instructional objectives in performance terms, preparing a table of specifications, constructing relevant test items, arranging the items in the test, preparing clear directions, reviewing and evaluating the assembled test, administering the test, and making an item analysis.
4. Test specifications typically consist of a twofold table of specifications that indicates the sample of performance tasks to be measured.
5. The types of test items used in a test should be determined by how directly they measure the intended learning outcomes and how effective they are as measuring instruments.
6. Each test item should provide a task that matches the student performance described in a specific learning outcome.
7. The functioning content of test items can be improved by eliminating irrelevant barriers and unintended clues during item writing.
8. The difficulty of a test item should match the difficulty of the learning task to be measured. Beware of irrelevant sources of difficulty (e.g., obscure material).
9. An achievement test should be short enough to permit all students to attempt all items during the testing time available.
10. A test should contain sufficient test items for each type of interpretation to be made. Interpretations based on fewer than 10 items should be considered highly tentative.
11. Following a general set of guidelines during item writing will result in higher-quality items that contribute to the validity and reliability of the test results.
12. Item arrangement within the test will vary with the type of test used. Where possible, items should be grouped by major learning outcome (e.g., knowledge, comprehension, application); similar items should be grouped together and should be arranged in order of increasing difficulty.
13. Test directions should clearly indicate the purpose of the test, the time allowed, how to record the answers, and to answer every item.
14. A correction for guessing should be used for speed tests only.
15. Review and evaluate the assembled test before using.
16. Administer the test under controlled conditions.
17. Item analysis provides a means of evaluating the items and is useful in reviewing the test with students.

Learning Exercises

1. What are the advantages of using a two-way chart when preparing specifications for tests and assessments? For what type of testing and assessment is it most useful? Why?

2. Why is it important for classroom tests and assessments to measure a representative sample of intended learning outcomes?

3. (a) List several learning outcomes that are best measured with objective test items.

   (b) List several that require the use of product or performance assessment tasks.

References and Additional Reading

Bloom, B.S., et al. (ed.) (1956). *Taxonomy of Educational Objectives: Cognitive Domain*. New York: David McKay Co.

Carey, L.M. (2001). *Measuring and Evaluating School Learning*, 3rd ed. Boston: Allyn and Bacon.

Gronlund, N.E. (2000). *How to Write and Use Instructional Objectives*, 6th ed. Upper Saddle River, NJ: Merrill/Prentice-Hall.

Linn, R.L., and Gronlund, N.E. (2000). *Measurement and Assessment in Teaching*, 8th ed. Upper Saddle River, NJ: Merrill/Prentice-Hall.

Oosterhoff, A.C. (2001). *Classroom Application of Educational Measurement*, 3rd ed. Upper Saddle River, NJ: Merrill/Prentice-Hall.

Stiggins, R.J. (2001). *Student-Involved Classroom Assessment*, 3rd ed. Upper Saddle River, NJ: Merrill/Prentice-Hall.

Weblinks

Creating Effective Classroom Tests
Useful tutorial for test-makers.
http://taesig.8m.com/createcon.html

Education World
Information on test construction.
http://db.education-world.com/perl/browse?cat_id=1855

Grammar Quizzes
A number of tests and quizzes for ESL students.
http://esl.about.com/library/quiz/blgrammarquiz.htm

7

Writing Selection Items: Multiple Choice

This chapter will enable you to:

1. Describe the characteristics of multiple-choice items.
2. Describe the strengths and limitations of multiple-choice items.
3. Distinguish between well stated and poorly stated multiple-choice items.
4. Identify and correct faults in poorly stated multiple-choice items.
5. Match multiple-choice items to intended learning outcomes.
6. Construct multiple-choice items that are well stated, relevant to important learning outcomes, and free of defects.

Multiple-choice items are the most widely used and highly regarded of the selection-type items. They can be designed to measure a variety of learning outcomes, from simple to complex, and can provide the highest quality items. Because they play such an important role in achievement testing, they will be treated in this chapter in considerable detail. Other selection-type items (true–false, matching, and interpretive exercise) will be described in the following chapter.

Nature of Multiple-Choice Items

The multiple-choice item consists of a stem, which presents a problem situation, and several alternatives (options or choices), which provide possible solutions to the problem. The stem may be a question or an incomplete statement. The alternatives include the correct answer and several plausible wrong answers called *distracters*, the function of which is to distract those students who are uncertain of the answer.

The following items illustrate the question form and the incomplete-statement form of a multiple-choice item.

EXAMPLE

Which one of the following item types is an example of a supply-type test item?

    A. Multiple-choice item
    B. True–false item
    C. Matching item
  *D. Short-answer item

An example of a supply-type test item is the:

    A. multiple-choice item.
    B. true–false item.
    C. matching item.
  *D. short-answer item.

Although stated differently, both stems pose the same problem. Note, however, that the incomplete statement is more concise. This is typically the case. The question form is easier to write and forces the test maker to pose a clear problem but tends to result in a longer stem. An effective procedure for the beginner is to start with a question and shift to the incomplete statement whenever greater conciseness can be obtained.

The alternatives in the preceding example contain only one correct answer, and the distracters are clearly incorrect. Another type of multiple-choice item is the best-answer form in which the alternatives are all partially correct but one is clearly better than the others. This type is used for more complex achievement, as when the student must select the best reason for an action, the best method for doing something, or the best application of a principle. Thus, whether the correct-answer or best-answer form is used depends on the learning outcomes to be measured.

EXAMPLE

Which item is best for measuring computational skill?

    A. Multiple-choice item
    B. True–false item
    C. Matching item
  *D. Short-answer item

The examples given illustrate the use of four alternatives. Multiple-choice items typically include three, four, or five choices. The larger number will, of course, reduce the student's chances of obtaining the correct answer by guessing. Theoretically, with five alternatives there is only one chance in five of guessing the answer, whereas with four alternatives there is one chance in four. It is frequently difficult to obtain five plausible choices, however, and items are not improved by adding obviously wrong answers merely to have five alternatives. There is no reason why the items in a given test should all have the same number of alternatives. Some might contain three, some four, and some five, depending on the availability of plausible distracters. This would pose a problem only if the test were to be corrected for guessing—a practice that is not recommended for classroom achievement tests.

Uses of Multiple-Choice Items

The multiple-choice item can be used to measure knowledge outcomes and various types of complex learning outcomes. The single-item format is probably most widely used for measuring knowledge, comprehension, and application outcomes. The interpretive exercise consisting of a series of multiple-choice items based on introductory material (e.g., paragraph, picture, or graph) is especially useful for measuring analysis, interpretation, and other complex learning outcomes. The interpretive exercise will be described in the following chapter. Here, we confine the discussion to the use of single, independent, multiple-choice items.

Knowledge Items

Knowledge items typically measure the degree to which previously learned material has been remembered. The items focus on the simple recall of information and can be concerned with the measurement of terms, facts, or other specific aspects of knowledge.

EXAMPLE

Outcome: Identifies the meaning of a term.
Reliability means the same as:

    *A. consistency.
    B. relevancy.
    C. representativeness.
    D. usefulness.

The wide variety of knowledge outcomes that can be measured with multiple-choice items is best shown by illustrating some of the types of questions that can be asked in various knowledge categories. Sample questions stated as incomplete multiple-choice stems are presented in Box 7.1 (page 88).

The series of questions shown in Box 7.1, of course, provides only a sample of the many possible questions that could be asked. Also, the questions are stated in rather general terms. The stems for multiple-choice items need to be more closely related to the specific learning outcome being measured.

Comprehension Items

Comprehension items typically measure at the lowest level of understanding. That does not mean that comprehension is not important, nor does it imply that comprehension is always simple. Understanding the theory of relativity could hardly be thought of as simple, nor could understanding the relationship between Lear and his children in *King Lear*. Comprehension items determine whether the students have grasped the meaning of the material without requiring them to apply it. Comprehension can be measured by requiring students to respond in various ways, but it is important that the items contain some novelty, otherwise you are simply measuring memory. The following test items illustrate the measurement of common types of learning outcomes at the comprehension level.

BOX 7.1 • *Illustrative Knowledge Questions**

1.11   Knowledge of Terminology

What word means the same as _____?
Which statement best defines the term _____?

1.12   Knowledge of Specific Facts

Where would you find _____?
Who first discovered _____?

1.13   Knowledge of Conventions

What is the correct form for _____?
Which of the following rules applies to _____?

1.14   Knowledge of Trends and Sequences

What is the most important cause of _____?
Which of the following indicates the proper order of _____?

1.15   Knowledge of Classifications and Categories

What are the major classifications of _____?
What are the characteristics of _____?

1.16   Knowledge of Criteria

What is the most important criterion for selecting _____?

1.17   Knowledge of Methodology

What is the best way to _____?
What would be the first step in making _____?

1.18   Knowledge of Principles and Generalizations

Which statement best summarizes the belief that _____?
Which of the following principles best explains _____?

1.19   Knowledge of Theories and Structures

Which statement is most consistent with the theory of _____?
Which of the following best describes the structure of _____?

*Based on Bloom (1956), *Taxonomy of Educational Objectives.*

EXAMPLES

Outcome: Identifies an example of a term.
Which one of the following statements contains a specific determiner?

        A. Canada is a continent.
        B. Canada was discovered in 1200.
     *C. Canada has some big industries.
        D. Canada's population is increasing.

Outcome: Interprets the meaning of an idea.

The statement that "test reliability is a necessary but not a sufficient condition of test validity" means that:

    A. a reliable test will have a certain degree of validity.
    *B. a valid test will have a certain degree of reliability.
    C. a reliable test may be completely invalid and a valid test completely unreliable.

Outcome: Identifies an example of a concept or principle.
Which of the following is an example of a criterion-referenced interpretation?

    A. Jorge earned the highest score in science.
    B. Erik completed his experiment faster than his classmates.
    C. Edna's test score was higher than 50 percent of the class.
    *D. Tricia set up her laboratory equipment in five minutes.

Outcome: Predicts the most probable effect of an action.
What is most likely to happen to the reliability of the scores for a multiple-choice test when the number of alternatives for each item is changed from three to four?

    A. It will decrease.
    *B. It will increase.
    C. It will stay the same.
    D. There is no basis for making a prediction.

In this last example, the student must recognize that increasing the number of alternatives in the items produces the same effect as lengthening the test.

These examples would, of course, represent measurement at the comprehension level only where the situations were new to the students. If the solutions to these particular problems were encountered during instruction, the items would need to be classified as knowledge outcomes.

Some of the many learning outcomes at the comprehension level that can be measured by multiple-choice items are illustrated by the incomplete questions in Box 7.2.

BOX 7.2 • *Illustrative Comprehension and Application Questions*

Comprehension Questions

Which of the following is an example of _____?

What is the main thought expressed by _____?

What are the main differences between _____?

What are the common characteristics of _____?

Application Questions

Which of the following methods is best for _____?

What steps should be followed in applying _____?

Which situation would require the use of _____?

Which principle would be best for solving _____?

Application Items

Application items also measure understanding, but typically at a higher level than that of comprehension. Here, the students must demonstrate that they not only grasp the meaning of information but can also apply it to concrete situations that are new to them. Thus, application items determine the extent to which students can transfer their learning and use it effectively in solving new problems. Such items may call for the application of various aspects of knowledge, such as facts, concepts, principles, rules, methods, and theories. Both comprehension and application items are adaptable to practically all areas of subject matter, and they provide the basic means of measuring understanding.

The following examples illustrate the use of multiple-choice items for measuring learning outcomes at the application level.

EXAMPLES

Outcome: Distinguishes between properly and improperly stated outcomes.
Which one of the following learning outcomes is properly stated in terms of student performance?

     A. Develops an appreciation of the importance of testing.
   *B. Explains the purpose of test specifications.
     C. Learns how to write good test items.
     D. Realizes the importance of validity.

Outcome: Improves defective test items.
Directions: Read the following test item and then indicate the best change to make to improve the item.
Which one of the following types of learning outcomes is most difficult to evaluate objectively?

1. A concept
2. An application
3. An appreciation
4. None of the above

The best change to make in the previous item would be to:

     A. change the stem to incomplete-statement form.
     B. use letters instead of numbers for each alternative.
     C. remove the indefinite articles "a" and "an" from the alternatives.
   *D. replace "none of the above" with "An interpretation."

When writing application items, care must be taken to select problems that the students have not encountered previously and therefore cannot solve on the basis of general knowledge alone. Each item should be so designed that it calls for application of the particular fact, concept, principle, or procedure indicated in the intended learning outcome. See Box 7.2 for some of the many questions that might be asked at the application level, and Box 7.3 for strengths and limitations of multiple-choice items.

Rules for Writing Multiple-Choice Items

An effective multiple-choice item presents students with a task that is both important and clearly understood, one that can be answered correctly by anyone who has achieved

BOX 7.3 • *Multiple-Choice Items*

Strengths
1. Learning outcomes from simple to complex can be measured.
2. Highly structured and clear tasks are provided.
3. A broad sample of achievement can be measured.
4. Incorrect alternatives provide diagnostic information.
5. Scores are less influenced by guessing than true–false items.
6. Scoring is easy, objective, and reliable.

Limitations
1. Constructing good items is time consuming.
2. It is frequently difficult to find plausible distracters.
3. This item is ineffective for measuring some types of problem solving and the ability to organize and express ideas.
4. Score can be influenced by reading ability.

the intended learning outcome. Nothing in the content or structure of the item should prevent an informed student from responding correctly. Similarly, nothing in the content or structure of the item should enable an uninformed student to select the correct answer. The following rules for item writing are intended as guides for the preparation of multiple-choice items that function as intended.

1. Design each item to measure an important learning outcome. The problem situation around which an item is to be built should be important and should be related to the intended learning outcome to be measured. The items in the previous section illustrate how to match items to intended outcomes. When writing the item, focus on the functioning content of the item and resist the temptation to include irrelevant material or more obscure and less significant content to increase item difficulty. Remember that the purpose of each item is to call forth the type of performance that will help determine the extent to which the intended learning outcomes have been achieved.

Items designed to measure complex achievement must contain some novelty. For example, where a knowledge item might require the identification of a textbook definition of a term, a comprehension item may require the identification of a modified form of it, and an application item may require the identification of an example of its proper use. Both the comprehension and application items would function as intended, however, only if the material was new to the students. Thus, items measuring complex achievement should require students to demonstrate that they have grasped the meaning of the material and can use it in situations that are new to them.

2. Present a single, clearly formulated problem in the stem of the item. The task set forth in the stem of the item should be so clear that a student can understand it without reading the alternatives. In fact, a good check on the clarity and completeness of a multiple-choice stem is to cover the alternatives and determine whether the stem could be answered without the choices. Try this on the two sample items that follow.

EXAMPLES

Poor: A table of specifications:

     A. indicates how a test will be used to improve learning.
    *B. provides a more balanced sampling of content.
     C. arranges the instructional objectives in order of their importance.
     D. specifies the method of scoring to be used on a test.

Better: What is the main advantage of using a table of specifications when preparing an achievement test?

     A. It reduces the amount of time required.
    *B. It improves the sampling of content.
     C. It makes the construction of test items easier.
     D. It increases the objectivity of the test.

The first of these examples is no more than a collection of true–false statements with a common stem. The problem presented in the stem of the improved version is clear enough to serve as a supply-type, short-answer item. The alternatives simply provide a series of possible answers from which to choose.

Note also in the second version that a single problem is presented in the stem. Including more than one problem usually adds to the complexity of the wording and reduces the diagnostic value of the item. When students fail such an item, there is no way to determine which of the problems prevented them from responding correctly.

    3.   State the stem of the item in simple, clear language. The problem in the stem of a multiple-choice item should be stated as precisely as possible and should be free of unnecessarily complex wording and sentence structure. Anyone who possesses the knowledge measured by a test item should be able to select the correct answer. Poorly stated item stems frequently introduce sufficient ambiguity to prevent a knowledgeable student from responding correctly. Also, complex sentence structure may make the item more a measure of reading comprehension than of the intended outcome. The first of the two examples that follow is an extreme instance of this problem.

EXAMPLE

Poor: The paucity of plausible, but incorrect, statements that can be related to a central idea poses a problem when constructing which one of the following types of test items?

     A. Short answer
     B. True–false
    *C. Multiple choice
     D. Essay

Better: The lack of plausible, but incorrect, alternatives will cause the greatest difficulty when constructing:

     A. short-answer items.
     B. true–false items.
    *C. multiple-choice items.
     D. essay items.

Another common fault in stating multiple-choice items is to load the stem with irrelevant and, thus, nonfunctioning material. This is probably caused by the instructor's desire to continue to teach the students—even while testing them. The following example illustrates the use of an item stem as "another chance to inform students."

EXAMPLE

Poor. Testing can contribute to the instructional program of the school in many important ways. However, the main function of testing in teaching is:

Better. The main function of testing in teaching is:

The first version increases reading time and makes no contribution to the measurement of the specific outcome. Time spent in reading such irrelevant material could be spent more profitably in thinking about the problem presented. But if the purpose of an item is to measure a student's ability to distinguish between relevant and irrelevant material, this rule must, of course, be disregarded.

4.   **Put as much of the wording as possible in the stem of the item.** Avoid repeating the same material in each of the alternatives. By moving all of the common content to the stem, it is usually possible to clarify the problem further and to reduce the time the student needs to read the alternatives. Note the improvement in the following item when this rule is followed.

EXAMPLE

Poor. In objective testing, the term *objective*:
  A. refers to the method of identifying the learning outcomes.
  B. refers to the method of selecting the test content.
  C. refers to the method of presenting the problem.
  *D. refers to the method of scoring the answers.

Better. In objective testing, the term *objective* refers to the method of:
  A. identifying the learning outcomes.
  B. selecting the test content.
  C. presenting the problem.
  *D. scoring the answers.

In many cases, the problem is not simply to move the common words to the stem but to reword the entire item. The following example illustrates how an item can be improved by revising the stem and shortening the alternatives.

EXAMPLE

Poor. Instructional objectives are most apt to be useful for test-construction purposes when they are stated in such a way that they show:
  A. the course content to be covered during the instructional period.
  *B. the kinds of performance students should demonstrate upon reaching the goal.
  C. the things the teacher will do to obtain maximum student learning.
  D. the types of learning activities to be participated in during the course.

Better. Instructional objectives are most useful for test-construction purposes when they are stated in terms of:
  A. course content.
  *B. student performance.
  C. teacher behaviour.
  D. learning activities.

It is, of course, impossible to streamline all items in this manner, but economy of wording and clarity of expression are important goals to strive for in test construction. Items function better when slim and trim.

5. State the stem of the item in positive form, wherever possible. A positively phrased test item tends to measure more important learning outcomes than a negatively stated item. This is because knowing such things as the best method or the most relevant argument typically has greater educational significance than knowing the poorest method or the least relevant argument. The use of negatively stated item stems results all too frequently from the ease with which such items can be constructed rather than from the importance of the learning outcomes measured. The test maker who becomes frustrated by the inability to think of a sufficient number of plausible distracters for an item, as in Item 1 of the following example, suddenly realizes how simple it would be to construct the second version, in Item 2.

EXAMPLE

Item 1: Which one of the following is a category in the taxonomy of the cognitive domain?
  *A. Comprehension
  B. (distracter needed)
  C. (distracter needed)
  D. (distracter needed)

Item 2: Which one of the following is not a category in the taxonomy of the cognitive domain?
  A. Comprehension
  B. Application
  C. Analysis
  *D. (answer needed)

Note in the second version that the categories of the taxonomy serve as distracters and that all that is needed to complete the item is a correct answer. This could be any term that appears plausible but is not one of the categories listed in the taxonomy. Although such items are easily constructed, they are apt to have a low level of difficulty and are likely to measure relatively unimportant learning outcomes. Being able to identify answers that do not apply provides no assurance that the student possesses the desired knowledge.

This solution to the lack of sufficient distracters is most likely to occur when the test maker is committed to the use of multiple-choice items only. A more desirable procedure for measuring the "ability to recognize the categories in the taxonomy of the cognitive domain" is to switch to a modified true–false form, as in the following example.

EXAMPLE

Directions: Indicate which of the following are categories in the taxonomy of the cognitive domain, by circling Y for yes and N for no.
  *Y   N   Comprehension
  Y   N*   Critical Thinking
  Y   N*   Reasoning
  *Y   N   Synthesis

In responding to this item, the student must make a separate judgment for each statement—the statement either is or is not one of the categories. Thus, the item calls for the type of performance stated in the learning outcome, yet it avoids the problems of an insufficient number of distracters and of negative phrasing.

6. Emphasize negative wording whenever it is used in the stem of an item. In some instances the use of negative wording is basic to the measurement of an important learning outcome. Knowing that you should not cross the street against a red light or should not mix certain chemicals, for example, is so important that these precepts might be directly taught and directly tested. Any potentially dangerous situation may require a negative emphasis. There are also, of course, less dire circumstances where negative phrasing is useful. Almost any set of rules or procedures places some emphasis on practices to be avoided.

When negative wording is used in the stem of an item, it should be emphasized by being underlined or capitalized and by being placed near the end of the statement.

EXAMPLE

Poor: Which one of the following is not a desirable practice when preparing multiple-choice items?

    A. Stating the stem in positive form.
    B. Using a stem that could function as a short-answer item.
    C. Underlining certain words in the stem for emphasis.
  *D. Shortening the stem by lengthening the alternatives.

Better: All of the following are desirable practices when preparing multiple-choice items EXCEPT:

    A. stating the stem in positive form.
    B. using a stem that could function as a short-answer item.
    C. underlining certain words in the stem for emphasis.
  *D. shortening the stem by lengthening the alternatives.

The improved version of this item assures that the item's negative aspect will not be overlooked, and it furnishes the student with the proper mind-set just before reading the alternatives.

7. Make certain that the intended answer is correct or clearly best. When the correct-answer form of a multiple-choice item is used, there should be only one correct answer and it should be unquestionably correct. With the best-answer form, the intended answer should be one that competent authorities would agree is clearly the best. In the latter case it may also be necessary to include "of the following" in the stem of the item to allow for equally satisfactory answers that have not been included in the item.

EXAMPLE

Poor: What is the best method of selecting course content for test items?

Better: Which one of the following is the best method of selecting course content for test items?

The proper phrasing of the stem of an item can also help avoid equivocal answers when the correct-answer form is used. In fact, an inadequately stated problem frequently makes the intended answer only partially correct or makes more than one alternative suitable.

EXAMPLE

Poor: What is the purpose of classroom testing?

Better:
One purpose of classroom testing is:
   (or)
The main purpose of classroom testing is:

It is, of course, also necessary to check each of the distracters in the item to make certain that none of them could be defended as the correct answer. This will not only improve the quality of the item but will also prevent a disruptive argument during the discussion of the test results.

   8.   Make all alternatives grammatically consistent with the stem of the item and parallel in form. The correct answer is usually carefully phrased so that it is grammatically consistent with the stem. Where the test maker is apt to slip is in stating the distracters. Unless care is taken to check them against the wording in the stem and in the correct answer, they may be inconsistent in tense, article, or grammatical form. This, of course, could provide a clue to the correct answer, or at least make some of the distracters ineffective.

   A general step that can be taken to prevent grammatical inconsistency is to avoid using the articles "a" or "an" at the end of the stem of the item.

EXAMPLE

Poor: The recall of factual information can be measured best with a:
   A. matching item.
   B. multiple-choice item.
 *C. short-answer item.
   D. essay question.

Better: The recall of factual information can be measured best with:
   A. matching items.
   B. multiple-choice items.
 *C. short-answer items.
   D. essay questions.

The indefinite article "a" in the first version makes the last distracter obviously wrong. By simply changing the alternatives from singular to plural, it is possible to omit the article. In other cases, it may be necessary to add an article ("a," "an," or as appropriate) to each alternative or to rephrase the entire item.

   Stating all of the alternatives in parallel form also tends to prevent unnecessary clues from being given to the students. When the grammatical structure of one alternative differs from that of the others, some students may more readily detect that alternative as a correct or an incorrect response.

EXAMPLE

Poor: Why should negative terms be avoided in the stem of a multiple-choice item?
 *A. They may be overlooked.
   B. The stem tends to be longer.
   C. The construction of alternatives is more difficult.
   D. The scoring is more difficult.

Better. Why should negative terms be avoided in the stem of a multiple-choice item?
    *A. They may be overlooked.
    B. They tend to increase the length of the stem.
    C. They make the construction of alternatives more difficult.
    D. They may increase the difficulty of the scoring.

In the first version, some students who lack the knowledge called for are apt to select the correct answer because of the way it is stated. The parallel grammatical structure in the second version removes this clue.

9. Avoid verbal clues that might enable students to select the correct answer or to eliminate an incorrect alternative. One of the most common sources of extraneous clues in multiple-choice items is the wording of the item. Some such clues are rather obvious and are easily avoided. Others require the constant attention of the test maker to prevent them from slipping in unnoticed. Let's review some of the verbal clues commonly found in multiple-choice items.

  (a) Similarity of wording in both the stem and the correct answer is one of the most obvious clues. Key words in the stem may unintentionally be repeated verbatim in the correct answer, a synonym may be used, or the words may simply sound or look alike.

EXAMPLE

Poor. Which one of the following would you consult first to locate research articles on achievement testing?
    A. Journal of Educational Psychology
    B. Journal of Educational Measurement
    C. Journal of Consulting Psychology
    *D. Review of Educational Research

The word "research" in both the stem and the correct answer is apt to provide a clue to the correct answer to the uninformed but testwise student. Such obvious clues might better be used in both the stem and an incorrect answer, in order to lead the uninformed away from the correct answer.

  (b) Stating the correct answer in textbook language or stereotyped phraseology may cause students to select it because it looks better than the other alternatives, or because they vaguely recall having seen it before.

EXAMPLE

Poor. Learning outcomes are most useful in preparing tests when they are:
    *A. clearly stated in performance terms.
    B. developed cooperatively by teachers and students.
    C. prepared after the instruction has ended.
    D. stated in general terms.

The pat phrasing of the correct answer is likely to give it away. Even the most poorly prepared student is apt to recognize the often repeated phrase "clearly stated in performance terms," without having the foggiest notion of what it means.

  (c) Stating the correct answer in greater detail may provide a clue. Also, when the answer is qualified by modifiers that are typically associated with true statements (for example, "sometimes," "may," "usually"), it is more likely to be chosen.

EXAMPLE

Poor. Lack of attention to learning outcomes during test preparation:
      A. will lower the technical quality of the items.
      B. will make the construction of test items more difficult.
      C. will result in the greater use of essay questions.
   *D. may result in a test that is less relevant to the instructional program.

    The term "may" is rather obvious in this example, but this type of error is common and appears frequently in a subtler form.

    (d) Including absolute terms in the distracters enables students to eliminate them as possible answers because such terms ("always," "never," "all," "none," "only,") are commonly associated with false statements. This makes the correct answer obvious, or at least increases the chances that the students who do not know the answer will guess it.

EXAMPLE

Poor. Achievement tests help students improve their learning by:
      A. encouraging them all to study hard.
   *B. informing them of their progress.
      C. giving them all a feeling of success.
      D. preventing any of them from neglecting assignments.

    Such absolutes tend to be used by the inexperienced test maker to assure that the incorrect alternatives are clearly wrong. Unfortunately, they are easily recognized by the student as unlikely answers, making them ineffective as distracters.

    (e) Including two responses that are all-inclusive makes it possible to eliminate the other alternatives, since one of the two must obviously be the correct answer.

EXAMPLE

Poor. Which one of the following types of test items measures learning outcomes at the recall level?
   *A. Supply-type items
      B. Selection-type items
      C. Matching items
      D. Multiple-choice items

    Since the first two alternatives include the only two major types of test items, even poorly prepared students are likely to limit their choices to these two. This, of course, gives them a 50–50 chance of guessing the correct answer.

    (f) Including two responses that have the same meaning makes it possible to eliminate them as potential answers. If two alternatives have the same meaning and only one answer is to be selected, it is fairly obvious that both alternatives must be incorrect.

EXAMPLE

Poor. Which one of the following is the most important characteristic of achievement-test results?

A. Consistency
B. Reliability
*C. Relevance
D. Objectivity

In this item, both "consistency" and "reliability" can be eliminated because they mean essentially the same thing.

Extraneous clues to the correct answer must be excluded from test items if the items are to function as intended. It is frequently good practice, however, to use such clues to lead the uninformed away from the correct answer. If not overdone, this can contribute to the plausibility of the incorrect alternatives.

10. Make the distracters plausible and attractive to the uninformed. The distracters in a multiple-choice item should be so appealing to the students who lack the knowledge called for by the item that they select one of the distracters in preference to the correct answer. This is the ideal, of course, but one toward which the test maker must work continually. The art of constructing good multiple-choice items depends heavily on the development of effective distracters.

You can do a number of things to increase the plausibility and attractiveness of distracters:

(a) Use the common misconceptions or errors of students as distracters.

(b) State the alternatives in the language of the student.

(c) Use "good-sounding" words ("accurate," "important,") in the distracters as well as in the correct answer.

(d) Make the distracters similar to the correct answer in both length and complexity of wording.

(e) Use extraneous clues in the distracters, such as stereotyped phrasing, scientific-sounding answers, and verbal associations with the stem of the item. But don't overuse these clues to the point where they become ineffective.

(f) Make the alternatives homogeneous, but in doing so beware of fine discriminations that are educationally insignificant.

The greater plausibility resulting from the use of more homogenous alternatives can be seen in the improved version of the following item.

EXAMPLE

Poor. Obtaining a dependable ranking of students is of major concern when using:
   *A. norm-referenced summative tests.
   B. behaviour descriptions.
   C. checklists.
   D. questionnaires.

Better. Obtaining a dependable ranking of students is of major concern when using:
   *A. norm-referenced summative tests.
   B. teacher-made diagnostic tests.
   C. mastery achievement tests.
   D. criterion-referenced formative tests.

The improved version not only increases the plausibility of the distracters but it also calls for a type of discrimination that is more educationally significant.

11. Vary the relative length of the correct answer to eliminate length as a clue. There is a tendency for the correct answer to be longer than the alternatives because of the need to qualify statements to make them unequivocally correct. This, of course, provides a clue to the testwise student. Learning this fact, the inexperienced test maker frequently makes a special effort to avoid ever having the correct answer longer than the other alternatives. This, of course, also provides a clue, and the alert student soon learns to dismiss the longest alternative as a possible answer.

The relative length of the correct answer can be removed as a clue by varying it in such a manner that no apparent pattern is provided. That is, it should sometimes be longer than the distracters, sometimes shorter, and sometimes of equal length—but never consistently or predominantly of one relative length. In some cases it is more desirable to make the alternatives approximately equal length by adjusting the distracters rather than the correct answer.

EXAMPLE

Poor: One advantage of multiple-choice items over essay questions is that they:
    A. measure more complex outcomes.
    B. depend more on recall.
    C. require less time to score.
  *D. provide for a more extensive sampling of course content.

Better: One advantage of multiple-choice items over essay questions is that they:
    A. provide for the measurement of more complex learning outcomes.
    B. place greater emphasis on the recall of factual information.
    C. require less time for test preparation and scoring.
  *D. provide for a more extensive sampling of course content.

Lengthening the distracters, as was done in the improved version, removes length as a clue and increases the plausibility of the distracters, which are now more similar to the correct answer in complexity of wording.

12. Avoid using the alternative "all of the above," and use "none of the above" with extreme caution. When test makers are having difficulty in locating a sufficient number of distracters, they frequently resort to the use of "all of the above" or "none of the above" as the final option. These special alternatives are seldom used appropriately and almost always render the item less effective than it would be without them.

The inclusion of "all of the above" as an option makes it possible to answer the item on the basis of partial information. Since students are to select only one answer, they can detect "all of the above" as the correct choice simply by noting that two of the alternatives are correct. They can also detect it as a wrong answer by recognizing that at least one of the alternatives is incorrect; of course, their chance of guessing the correct answer from the remaining choices then increases proportionally. Another difficulty with this option is that some students, recognizing that the first choice is correct, will select it without reading the remaining alternatives.

Obviously, the use of "none of the above" is not possible with the best-answer type of multiple-choice item, since the alternatives vary in appropriateness and the criterion of absolute correctness is not applicable. When used as the right answer in a correct-answer type of item, this option may be measuring nothing more than the ability to detect incorrect answers. Recognizing that certain answers are wrong is no guarantee that the student knows what is correct. For example, a student may be able to answer the following item correctly without being able to name the categories in the taxonomy.

EXAMPLE

Poor. Which of the following is a category in the taxonomy of the cognitive domain?
    A. Critical Thinking
    B. Scientific Thinking
    C. Reasoning Ability
*D. None of the above

All students need to know to answer this item correctly is that the taxonomy categories are new and different from those that they have commonly associated with intellectual skills. Items such as this provide rather poor evidence for judging a student's achievement.

The alternative "none of the above" is probably used more widely with computational problems that are presented in multiple-choice form. The publishers of standardized achievement tests have resorted to multiple-choice items for such problems in order to make machine scoring possible, and they have resorted to the alternative "none of the above" in order to reduce the likelihood of the student estimating the answer without performing the entire computation. Although this use of "none of the above" may be defensible, there is seldom a need to use multiple-choice items for computational problems in classroom tests. The supply-type item that requires the student to solve the problems and record the answers provides the most direct and useful measure of computational skill. This is another case in which it is desirable to switch from multiple-choice items to another item type in order to obtain more effective measurement.

13. Vary the position of the correct answer in a random manner. The correct answer should appear in each alternative position about the same number of times, but its placement should not follow a pattern that may be apparent to the person taking the test. Students who detect that the correct answer never appears in the same position more than twice in a row, or that A is the correct answer on every fourth item, are likely to obtain a higher score than their knowledge would warrant. Such clues can be avoided by random placement of the correct answer.

The easiest way to randomly assign the position of the correct answer in a multiple-choice item is to develop a code with the aid of a book: simply open any book at a random place, look at the right-hand page, and let the last digit of the page number determine the placement of the correct answer. Since the right-hand page always ends in an odd number, the code might be as follows: the digit 1 indicates that the correct answer will be placed in position A, 3 = B, 5 = C, 7 = D, and 9 = E.

Sufficient variation without a discernible pattern might also be obtained by simply placing the responses in alphabetical order, based on the first letter in each, and letting the correct answer fall where it will.

When the alternative responses are numbers, they should always be listed in order of size, preferably in ascending order. This will eliminate the possibility of a clue, such as the correct answer being the only one that is not in numerical order.

14. Control the difficulty of the item either by varying the problem in the stem or by changing the alternatives. It is usually preferable to increase item difficulty by increasing the level of knowledge called for by making the problem more complex. However, it is also possible to increase difficulty by making the alternatives more homogeneous. When this is done, care must be taken that the finer discriminations called for are educationally significant and are in harmony with the learning outcomes to be measured.

15. Make certain each item is independent of the other items in the test. Occasionally information given in the stem of one item will help the students answer another item. This can be remedied easily by a careful review of the items before they are assembled into a test.

A different type of problem occurs when the correct answer to an item depends on knowing the correct answer to the item preceding it. The student who is unable to answer the first item, of course, has no basis for responding to the second. Such chains of interlocking items should be avoided. Each item should be an independently scorable unit.

16. Use an efficient item format. The alternatives should be listed on separate lines, under one another, like the examples in this chapter. This makes the alternatives easy to read and compare. It also contributes to ease of scoring since the letters of the alternatives all appear on the left side of the paper. A copy of the test can be used as a scoring stencil: Simply circle the letters of the correct answers on the copy, then place the copy next to the student's paper so that the columns of letters correspond.

The use of letters in front of the alternatives is preferable to the use of numbers, since numerical answers in numbered items may be confusing to the students.

17. Follow the normal rules of grammar. If the stem is in question form, begin each alternative with a capital letter and end with a period or other appropriate punctuation mark. Omit the period with numerical answers, however, to avoid confusion with decimal points. When the stem is an incomplete statement, start each alternative with a lower-case letter and end with whatever terminal punctuation mark is appropriate.

18. Break (or bend) any of these rules if it will improve the effectiveness of the item. These rules for constructing multiple-choice items are stated rather dogmatically as an aid to the beginner. As experience in item writing is obtained, situations are likely to occur where ignoring or modifying a rule may be desirable. In a problem-solving item, for example, it may be useful to include extraneous information in the stem to see if students can select what is needed to solve the problem. Until sufficient experience in item writing is gained, however, following the rules in this chapter will yield test items of fairly good quality.

Special Considerations

Special needs students often have problems with multiple-choice questions; this is especially true of students who are mentally handicapped. Many of these students find it difficult to remember the alternatives, especially if the alternatives are long and complex. If that is the case, and it is not practical to provide an alternative section, the student may have to omit the multiple-choice section. If an assistant is available, or if the teacher is conducting the test orally at a later time, the question can often be asked in a different way, perhaps as a true–false or short-answer question. If the test is being administered orally, it is tempting to ask the multiple-choice questions orally along with other questions, but it may be difficult for some students to keep the question and the possible answers in their heads, again especially if the alternatives are long and complex. Second language students should have no particular difficulty in this regard, but may need some time to understand the concept of multiple choice generally, as multiple choice is far more common in North America than in other cultures. The same comment applies to Native students who have not been exposed to multiple-choice tests. Many teachers in Indian Band schools avoid multiple-choice tests because they feel such tests do not fit Native culture. That may be correct, but does Native students no favour when they attend public schools and have to cope with such tests.

Summary of Points

1. The multiple-choice item is the most highly regarded and useful selection-type item.
2. The multiple-choice item consists of a stem and a set of alternative answers (options or choices).
3. The multiple-choice item can be designed to measure various intended learning outcomes, ranging from simple to complex.
4. Knowledge items typically measure the simple remembering of material.
5. Comprehension items measure the extent to which students have grasped the meaning of material.
6. Application items measure whether students can use information in concrete situations.
7. Items designed to measure achievement beyond the knowledge level must contain some novelty.
8. The stem of a multiple-choice item should present a single, clearly formulated problem that is related to an important learning outcome.
9. The intended answer should be correct or clearly best, as agreed upon by authorities.
10. The distracters (incorrect alternatives) should be plausible enough to lead the uninformed away from the correct answer.
11. The items should be written in simple, clear language that is free of nonfunctioning content.
12. The items should be free of irrelevant sources of difficulty (e.g., ambiguity) that might prevent an informed examinee from answering correctly.
13. The items should be free of irrelevant clues (e.g., verbal associations) that might enable an uninformed examinee to answer correctly.
14. The item format should provide for efficient responding and follow the normal rules of grammar.
15. The rules of item writing provide a framework for preparing effective multiple-choice items, but experience in item writing may result in modifications to fit particular situations.

Learning Exercises

1. List two advantages of the multiple-choice items, and two disadvantages.

2. In an area in which you are teaching or plan to teach, construct one multiple-choice item in each of the following areas: knowledge, understanding, and application.

3. Describe the relative merits of using correct-answer and best-answer multiple-choice items. What types of learning outcomes are best measured by each type of multiple-choice item?

References and Additional Reading

Carey, L.M. (2001). *Measuring and Evaluating School Learning*, 3rd ed. Boston: Allyn and Bacon.

Haladyna, T.M. (1997). *Writing Test Items to Evaluate Higher Order Thinking*. Boston: Allyn and Bacon.

Linn, R.L., and Gronlund, N.E. (2000). *Measurement and Assessment in Teaching*, 8th ed. Upper Saddle River, NJ: Merrill/Prentice-Hall.

Oosterhoff, A.C. (2001). *Classroom Applications of Educational Measurement*, 3rd ed. Upper Saddle River, NJ: Merrill/Prentice-Hall.

Weblinks

How to Write Multiple-Choice Questions
United States Department of Education
http://www.quizplease.com/qphelp/qphowto0.htm

Multiple-Choice Questions
University of Cape Town
http://www.uct.ac.za/projects/cbe/mcqman/mcqman01.html

Writing Multiple-Choice Questions that Demand Critical Thinking
University of Oregon
http://www.uoregon.edu/~tep/assessment/mc4critthink.html

8

Writing Selection Items: True–False, Matching, and Interpretive Exercise

This chapter will enable you to:

1. Describe the characteristics of each item type.
2. Describe the strengths and limitations of each item type.
3. Distinguish between well stated and poorly stated items of each type.
4. Identify and correct faults in poorly stated items of each type.
5. Match each item type to intended learning outcomes.
6. Construct items of each type that are well stated, relevant to important learning outcomes, and free of defects.

While the multiple-choice item provides the most generally useful format for measuring achievement at various levels of learning, multiple-choice items take longer to make up, and take more space than other select formats. Under certain conditions, other select formats are more efficient, and almost as effective. For example: (1) when there are only two possible alternatives, a true–false item can be used; (2) when there are a number of similar factors to be related, a matching item can be used; and (3) when the items are to measure analysis, interpretation, and other complex outcomes, an interpretive exercise can be used.

True–False Items

True–false items are typically used to measure the ability to identify whether statements of fact are correct. The basic format is simply a declarative statement that the student must judge as true or false. There are modifications of this basic form in which the student must respond "yes" or "no," "agree" or "disagree," "right" or "wrong," "fact" or "opinion," and the like. Such variations are usually given the more general name of *alternative-response* items. In any event, this item type is characterized by the fact that only two responses are possible.

EXAMPLE

T   *F   True–false items are classified as a supply-type item.

In some cases the student is asked to judge each statement as true or false, and then to change the false statements so that they are true. When this is done, a portion of each statement is underlined to indicate the part that can be changed. In the example given, for instance, the words "supply-type" would be underlined. The key parts of true statements, of course, must also be underlined. The problem with having students change false statements to true is that you lose the major advantage of select questions: that they can be answered quickly and therefore allow a greater number of questions to be asked.

Another variation is the cluster-type true–false format. In this case, a series of items is based on a common stem.

EXAMPLE

Which of the following terms indicate observable student performance? Circle Y for yes and N for no.

*Y	N	1.	Explains
*Y	N	2.	Identifies
Y	*N	3.	Learns
*Y	N	4.	Predicts
Y	*N	5.	Realizes

This item format is especially useful for replacing multiple-choice items that have more than one correct answer. Such items are impossible to score satisfactorily. This is avoided with the cluster-type item because it makes each alternative a separate scoring unit of one point. In our example, the student must record whether each term does or does not indicate observable student performance. Thus, this set of items provides an even better measure of the "ability to distinguish between performance and nonperformance terms" than would the single-answer multiple-choice item.

Despite the limitations of the true–false item, there are situations where it should be used. Whenever there are only two possible responses, the true–false item, or some adaptation of it, is likely to provide the most effective measure. Situations of this type include a simple "yes" or "no" response in classifying objects, determining whether a rule does or does not apply, distinguishing fact from opinion, and indicating whether arguments are relevant or irrelevant. See Box 8.1 (page 107) for a summary of strengths and limitations of these types of items.

Rules for Writing True–False Items

The purpose of a true–false item, as with all item types, is to distinguish between those who have and those who have not achieved the intended learning outcome. Achievers should be able to select the correct alternative without difficulty, while nonachievers

BOX 8.1 ● *True–False Items*

Strengths

1. The item is useful for outcomes where there are only two possible alternatives (e.g., fact or opinion, valid or invalid).

2. Less demand is placed on reading ability than in multiple-choice items.

3. A relatively large number of items can be answered in a typical testing period.

4. Complex outcomes can be measured when used with interpretive exercises.

5. Scoring is easy, objective, and reliable.

6. Little space is needed for a large number of questions.

Limitations

1. It is difficult to write items beyond the knowledge level that are free from ambiguity.

2. Marking an item false provides no evidence that the student knows what is correct.

3. No diagnostic information is provided by the incorrect answers.

4. Scores are more influenced by guessing than with any other item type. (There is a 50–50 chance of guessing the correct answer.)

should find the incorrect alternative at least as attractive as the correct one. The rules for writing true–false items are directed toward this end.

1.   Include only one central idea in each statement. The main point of the item should be in a prominent position in the statement. The true–false decision should not depend on some subordinate point or trivial detail. The use of several ideas in each statement should generally be avoided because these tend to be confusing and the answer is more apt to be influenced by reading ability than by the intended outcome.

EXAMPLE

Poor: T   *F   The true–false item, which is favoured by test experts, is also called an alternative-response item.

Better: *T   F   The true–false item is also called an alternative-response item.

The "poor" example must be marked false because many test experts do not favour the true–false item. Such subordinate points are easily overlooked when reading the item. If the point is important, it should be included as the main idea in a separate item.

2.   Keep the statement short and use simple vocabulary and sentence structure. A short, simple statement will increase the likelihood that the point of the item is clear. All students should be able to grasp what the statement is saying. Passing or failing the item should depend solely on whether a student has achieved the necessary knowledge.

EXAMPLE

Poor: *T   F   The true–false item is more subject to guessing but it should be used in place of a multiple-choice item, if well constructed, when there is a dearth of distracters that are plausible.

Better: *T   F   The true–false item should be used in place of a multiple-choice item when only two alternatives are possible.

Long, involved statements like the "poor" version tend to contaminate the achievement measure with a measure of reading comprehension. A basic rule of item writing is to focus on the intended function of the item and remove all irrelevant influences.

3.   Word the statement so precisely that it can unequivocally be judged true or false. True statements should be true under all circumstances and yet free of qualifiers ("may," "possible," and so on), which might provide clues. This requires the use of precise words and the avoidance of such vague terms as "seldom," "frequently," and "often." The same care must, of course, also be given to false statements so that their falsity is not too readily apparent from differences in wording. At first glance, this seems like a simple rule to follow but it causes frequent problems.

EXAMPLE

Poor: T   *F   Lengthening a test will increase its reliability.

Better: *T   F   Lengthening a test by adding items like those in the test will increase its reliability.

The "poor" version of this item must be marked false because it is not true under all conditions. For example, if items are added to the test that all students fail, reliability would not be changed. However, the "poor" version would not be a good item to use in a test because it requires students to mark a very important principle of measurement false. We could say "usually will increase," but the qualifier would encourage those who are uninformed to mark it true and they would receive an unearned point. The "better" version has no such "giveaway" to the answer. In fact, an uninformed student might think that adding similar items to a test of low reliability could not possibly increase reliability—but it does. This example illustrates the great care needed in phrasing statements so that they are unequivocally true but do not contain "giveaways" to the answer.

4.   Use negative statements sparingly and avoid double negatives. The "no" and/or "not" in negative statements are frequently overlooked and they are read as positive statements. Thus, negative statements should be used only when the learning outcome requires them (e.g., in avoiding a harmful practice), and then the negative words should be emphasized by underlining or by use of capital letters. Statements including double negatives tend to be so confusing that they should be restated in positive form.

EXAMPLE

Poor: *T   F   Correction-for-guessing is *not* a practice that should *never* be used in testing.

Better: *T   F   Correction-for-guessing is a practice that should sometimes be used in testing.

The double negatives in the "poor" version introduce sufficient ambiguity to cause the item to be a measure of reading comprehension. The "better" version clearly states the same idea in positive form.

5.   Statements of opinion should be attributed to some source unless used to distinguish facts from opinion. A statement of opinion is not true or false by itself, and it is poor instructional practice to have students respond to it as if it were a factual statement. Obviously, the only way students could mark such an item correctly would be to agree with the opinion of the item writer. It is much more defensible to attribute the item to some source, such as an individual or organization. It then becomes a measure of how well the student knows the beliefs or values of that individual or organization.

EXAMPLE

Poor: T   F   Testing should play a major role in the teaching–learning process.

Better: *T   F   Cameron believes that testing should play a major role in the teaching–learning process.

In some cases, it is useful to use a series of opinion statements that pertain to the same individual or organization. This permits a more comprehensive measure of how well the student understands a belief or value system.

EXAMPLE

Would the author of your textbook agree or disagree with the following statements? Circle A for agree, D for disagree.

*A   D   1. The first step in achievement testing is to state the intended learning outcomes in performance terms.

A   *D   2. True–false tests are superior to multiple-choice tests for measuring achievement.

Using about 10 items like those listed here would provide a fairly good indication of the students' grasp of the author's point of view. Items like this are useful for measuring how well students understand a textbook without requiring them to agree with the opinions expressed. It is desirable, of course, to select opinion statements that are shared by many experts in the area.

Another valuable use of opinion statements is to ask students to distinguish between statements of fact and statements of opinion. This is an important outcome in its own right and is a basic part of critical thinking.

EXAMPLE

Read each of the following statements and circle F if it is a *fact* or circle O if it is an *opinion*.

*F   O   1. The true–false item is a selection-type item.

F   *O   2. The true–false item is difficult to construct.

F   *O   3. The true–false item encourages student guessing.

*F   O   4. The true–false item can be scored objectively.

In addition to illustrating the use of opinion statements in test items, the last two examples illustrate variations from the typical true–false format. These are more logically called *alternative-response* items.

6.   When cause–effect relationships are being measured, use only true propositions. The true–false item can be used to measure the "ability to identify cause–effect relationships" and this is an important aspect of understanding. When used for this purpose, both propositions should be true and only the relationship judged true or false.

EXAMPLE

Poor:	T	*F	True–false items are classified as objective items	*because*	students must supply the answer.
Better:	T	*F	True–false items are classified as objective items	*because*	there are only two possible answers.

The "poor" version is false because of the second part of the statement. With true–false items, students must *select* the answer rather than *supply* it. However, some students may mark this item false because they think the first part of the statement is incorrect. Thus, they receive one point because they *do not know* that true–false items are classified as objective items. Obviously, an item does not function as intended if misinformation can result in the correct answer. The problem with the "poor" version is that all three elements are permitted to vary (part one, part two, and the relationship between them) and it is impossible to tell what part the student is responding to when the item is marked false. In the "better" version both parts of the statement are true and the students must simply decide if the second part explains why the first part is true. In this case it does not, so it is marked false. Typically, a series of items like this is preceded by directions that make clear that only the relationship between the two parts of each statement is to be judged true or false.

7. Avoid extraneous clues to the answer. There are a number of *specific determiners* that provide verbal clues to the truth or falsity of an item. Statements that include such absolutes as "always," "never," "all," "none," and "only" tend to be false; statements with qualifiers such as "usually," "may," and "sometimes" tend to be true. Either these verbal clues must be eliminated from the statements, or their use must be balanced between true items and false items.

EXAMPLE

Poor:	T	*F	A statement of opinion should never be used in a true–false item.
Poor:	*T	F	A statement of opinion may be used in a true–false item.
Better:	*T	F	A statement of opinion, by itself, cannot be marked true or false.

The length and complexity of the statement might also provide a clue. True statements tend to be longer and more complex than false ones because of their need for qualifiers. Thus, a special effort should be made to equalize true and false statements in these respects.

A tendency to use a disproportionate number of true statements, or false statements, might also be detected and used as a clue. Having approximately, but not exactly, equal numbers of each seems to be the best solution. When assembling the test, it is, of course, also necessary to avoid placing the correct answers in some discernible pattern (for instance, T, F, T, F). Random placement will eliminate this possible clue.

8. **Base items on introductory material to measure more complex learning outcomes.** True–false or alternative-response items are frequently used in interpreting written materials, tables, graphs, maps, or pictures. The use of introductory material makes it possible to measure various types of complex learning outcomes. These item types will be illustrated in the section on interpretive exercises later in this chapter

Matching Items

The matching item is simply a variation of the multiple-choice form, but is much faster to construct and takes much less space. The matching format consists of a series of stems, called *premises,* and a series of alternative answers, called *responses.* These are arranged in columns with directions that set the rules for matching. Matching questions are especially suitable when testing knowledge of vocabulary.

EXAMPLE

Directions: Column A contains a list of living things we have been studying. On the line to the left of each name, write the letter of the category in Column B that best fits the name. Each category in Column B may be used once, more than once, or not at all.

Column A

1. _____ Honey bee

2. _____ Robin

3. _____ Dog

4. _____ Rabbit

5. _____ Salmon

6. _____ House fly

7. _____ Penguin

8. _____ Whale

Column B

A. Bird

B. Fish

C. Insect

D. Mammal

See Box 8.2 for the strengths and limitations of matching items.

Vocabulary is the most common use of this type of test question, but the items must be homogeneous. If there are not enough meaningful items, use multiple choice.

Rules for Writing Matching Items

A good matching item should function the same as a series of multiple-choice items. As each premise is considered, all of the responses should serve as plausible alternatives. The rules for item writing are directed toward this end.

1. **Include only homogeneous material in each matching item.** In our earlier example of a matching item, we included *only* types of living beings and possible categories. Similarly, an item might include *only* authors and their works, inventors and their inventions, scientists and their discoveries, or historical events and their dates. This

BOX 8.2 • *Matching Items*

Strengths
1. A compact and efficient form is provided where the same set of responses fits a series of item stems (i.e., premises).
2. Reading and response time is short.
3. Many questions can be asked in little space.
4. Scoring is easy, objective, and reliable.

Limitations
1. This item type is largely restricted to simple knowledge outcomes based on association.
2. It may be difficult to construct items that contain a sufficient number of homogeneous responses.
3. Susceptibility to irrelevant clues is greater than in other item types.

homogeneity is necessary if all responses are to serve as plausible alternatives (see earlier example).

2. Keep the lists of items short and place the brief responses on the right. A short list of items (say fewer than 10) will save reading time, make it easier for the student to locate the answer, and increase the likelihood that the responses will be homogeneous and plausible. Placing the brief responses on the right also saves reading time.

3. Use a larger, or smaller, number of responses than premises, and permit the responses to be used more than once. Both an uneven match and the possibility of using each response more than once reduces the guessing factor. As we noted earlier, proper use of the matching form requires that *all responses be plausible alternatives for each premise.* This, of course, dictates that each response be eligible for use more than once.

4. Place the responses in alphabetical or numerical order. This will make selection of the responses easier and avoid possible clues due to placement.

5. Specify in the directions the basis for matching and indicate that each response may be used once, more than once, or not at all. This will clarify the task for all students and prevent any misunderstanding. Take care, however, not to make the directions too long and involved. The previous example illustrates adequate detail for directions.

6. Put all of the matching item on the same page. This will prevent the distraction of flipping pages back and forth and prevent students from overlooking responses on another page.

The Interpretive Exercise

Complex learning outcomes can frequently be more effectively measured by basing a series of test items on a common selection of introductory material. This may be a paragraph, a table, a chart, a graph, a map, or a picture. The test items that follow the introductory material may be designed to call forth any type of intellectual ability or skill that can be measured objectively. This type of exercise is commonly called an *interpretive exercise*, and both multiple-choice items and alternative-response items are widely used to measure interpretation of the introductory material.

The following example illustrates the use of multiple-choice items. Note that this item type makes it possible to measure a variety of learning outcomes with the same selection of introductory material. In this particular case, Item 1 measures the *ability to recognize unstated assumptions*, Item 2 the *ability to identify the meaning of a term*, and Item 3 the *ability to identify relationships*.

EXAMPLE

Directions: Read the following comments a teacher made about testing. Then answer the questions that follow by circling the letter of the best answer.

"Students go to school to learn, not to take tests. In addition, tests cannot be used to indicate a student's absolute level of learning. All tests can do is rank students in order of achievement, and this relative ranking is influenced by guessing, bluffing, and the subjective opinions of the teacher doing the scoring. The teaching-learning process would benefit if we did away with tests and depended on student self-evaluation."

1. Which one of the following unstated assumptions is this teacher making?
    A. Students go to school to learn.
    B. Teachers use essay tests primarily.
    *C. Tests make no contribution to learning.
    D. Tests do not indicate a student's absolute level of learning.

2. Which one of the following types of tests is this teacher primarily talking about?
    A. Diagnostic test
    B. Formative test
    C. Pretest
    *D. Summative test

3. Which one of the following propositions is most essential to the final conclusion?
    *A. Effective self-evaluation does not require the use of tests.
    B. Tests place students in rank order only.
    C. Tests scores are influenced by factors other than achievement.
    D. Students do not go to school to take tests.

The next example uses a modified version of the alternative-response form. This is frequently called a *key-type* item because a common set of alternatives is used in responding to each question. Note that the key-type item is devoted entirely to the measurement of one learning outcome. In this example, the item measures the *ability to recognize warranted and unwarranted inferences*.

EXAMPLE

Directions: Paragraph A contains a description of the testing practices of Mr. Smith, a high school teacher. Read the description and each of the statements that follow it. Mark each statement to indicate the type of INFERENCE that can be drawn about it from the material in the paragraph. Place the appropriate letter in front of each statement using the following KEY:
T—if the statement may be INFERRED as TRUE.
F—if the statement may be INFERRED as FALSE.
N—if NO INFERENCE may be drawn about it from the paragraph.

Paragraph A

Approximately one week before a test is to be given, Mr. Smith carefully goes through the textbook and constructs multiple-choice items based on the material in the book. He always uses the exact wording of the textbook for the correct answer so that there will be no question concerning its correctness. He is careful to include some test items from each chapter. After the test is given, he lists the scores from high to low on the blackboard and tells each student his or her score. He does not return the test papers to the students, but he offers to answer any questions they might have about the test. He puts the items from each test into a test file, which he is building for future use.

Statements on Paragraph A

(T)	1.	Mr. Smith's tests measure a limited range of learning outcomes.
(F)	2.	Some of Mr. Smith's test items measure at the understanding level.
(N)	3.	Mr. Smith's tests measure a balanced sample of subject matter.
(N)	4.	Mr. Smith uses the type of test item that is best for his purpose.
(T)	5.	Students can determine where they rank in the distribution of scores on Mr. Smith's tests.
(F)	6.	Mr. Smith's testing practices are likely to motivate students to overcome their weaknesses.

Key-type items are fairly easy to develop and can be directly related to specific learning outcomes. The key categories can, of course, be reused by simply changing the introductory material and the statements. Thus, they provide a standard framework for test preparation. Other common key categories include the following: (1) the argument is relevant, irrelevant, or neither; (2) the statement is supported by the evidence, refuted by the evidence, or neither; (3) the assumption is necessary or unnecessary; and (4) the conclusion is valid, invalid, or its validity cannot be determined. Although such standard key categories should not be applied in a perfunctory manner, they can provide guidelines to simplify the construction of the interpretive exercise. See Box 8.3 for strengths and limitations.

BOX 8.3 • *Interpretive Exercises*

Strengths

1. An efficient means of measuring the interpretation of printed information in various forms (e.g., written, charts, graphs, maps, pictures) is provided.

2. More meaningful complex learning outcomes can be measured than with the single-item format.

3. The use of introductory material provides a common basis for responding.

4. Scoring is easy, objective, and reliable.

Limitations

1. It is difficult to construct effective items.

2. Written material is highly dependent on reading skill.

3. This item type is highly subject to extraneous clues.

4. It is ineffective in measuring the ability to originate, organize, and express ideas.

Rules for Constructing Interpretive Exercises

The effectiveness of interpretive exercises, such as those illustrated earlier, depends on the care with which the introductory material is selected and the skill with which the dependent items are prepared. The following rules provide guidelines for preparing high-quality exercises of this type.

1. **Select introductory material that is relevant to the learning outcomes to be measured.** The introductory material may take many forms: written material, table, chart, graph, map, picture, or cartoon. In some cases the interpretation of the introductory material is an important learning outcome in its own right, as in the "interpretation of a weather map" or "the interpretation of a line graph." Here the nature of the introductory material is clearly prescribed by the intended outcome. In other cases, however, the introductory material simply provides the means for measuring other important outcomes. The "ability to distinguish between valid and invalid conclusions," for example, may be measured with different types of introductory material. In this instance we should select the type of material that provides the most direct measure of the learning outcome, is familiar to the examinees, and places the least demand on reading ability. For young children, this means that pictorial materials should typically be favoured.

2. **Select introductory material that is new to the examinees.** Although the form of the material should be familiar to the examinees, the specific content used in an exercise should be new to them. Thus, if they are asked to identify relationships shown in a graph, the type of graph should be familiar but the specific data in the graph must be new. If the data were the same as that presented in the classroom or described in the textbook, the exercise would measure nothing more than the simple recall of information. To measure complex outcomes, some novelty is necessary. How much depends on the specific nature of the intended outcome.

In some cases it is possible to locate introductory material that is new to the examinees by reviewing sources that are not readily available to them. Then it is simply a matter of adapting the material for testing purposes. In other cases it is necessary to prepare completely new material (i.e., write a paragraph, construct a graph, make a map, or draw a picture). In either case further revision will probably be needed when the dependent test items are being prepared. The process is essentially a circular one, with the writing of items requiring some changes in the introductory material and changes there providing ideas for new items. In carrying out this process of adapting and revising the material, be careful not to introduce so much novelty that the exercise no longer provides a valid measure of the intended learning outcome.

3. **Keep the introductory material brief and readable.** It is inefficient for both the test maker and the test taker to use extended introductory material and only one or two test items. If the introductory material is in written form, excessively long selections will also create problems for individuals with inadequate reading skills. Ideally, it should be a brief, concise selection that contains enough ideas for several relevant test items. Material of this type can frequently be obtained from summaries, digests, and other condensed forms of written material. In some cases pictures or diagrams may provide the most concise summary of the material. As noted earlier, we should always favour the type of material that places the least demand on reading ability.

4.   Construct test items that call forth the type of performance specified in the learning outcome. To measure the intended interpretation of the introductory material adequately requires careful phrasing of the questions and special attention to two important cautions. First, *the answer to an item should not be given directly in the material* since some mental process beyond "recognition of a stated fact" is required in measures of intellectual skills. Second, *it should not be possible to answer the question without the introductory material.* If an item can be answered on the basis of general knowledge, it is not measuring the ability to interpret the material in the exercise. A good check on this type of error is to cover the introductory material and attempt to answer the questions without it.

5.   Follow the rules of effective item writing that pertain to the type of objective item used. All of the rules for constructing the various types of objective test items discussed in Chapters 6 and 7 are applicable to the construction of items used in interpretive exercises. Even greater care must be taken to avoid extraneous clues, however, since items in interpretive exercises seem especially prone to such clues and they tend to be more difficult to detect in these items. If the introductory material includes illustrations, for example, special attention should be directed to such things as the size, shape, and position of objects as possible extraneous clues. These are frequently overlooked by the test maker, who is concentrating on the intricacies of the mental response required, but not by the unprepared student, who is frantically searching for any solution to the problem.

The greatest help in constructing interpretive exercises is to review a wide range of sample exercises that use different types of introductory material and different forms of dependent test items. For locating illustrative exercises, see the list of references at the end of the chapter.

Special Considerations

While true–false and matching questions do not present specific problems, interpretive questions might. Students have to read a selection presenting a hypothetical situation, and then answer questions about what *might* be true or what *might* occur under certain conditions. Students who have difficulty reading—or who do not understand the concept of hypothetical situations—may find this type of item difficult. Interpretive questions may be made optional for ESL or special needs students, or such sections may be done orally, if reading is the problem. They should certainly be encouraged to attempt the question, and an assistant should be provided, but if the item is too difficult it should be omitted for these students.

Summary of Points

1. While multiple choice is the most powerful selection format, other types take less time to prepare and may be almost as powerful.
2. The true–false or alternative-response item is appropriate when there are only two possible alternatives.

3. The true–false item is used primarily to measure knowledge of specific facts, although there are some notable exceptions.

4. Each true–false statement should contain only one central idea, be concisely stated, be free of clues and irrelevant sources of difficulty, and have an answer on which experts would agree.

5. Modifications of the true–false item are especially useful for measuring the ability to "distinguish between fact and opinion" and "identify cause–effect relations."

6. Modifications of the true–false item can be used in interpretive exercises to measure various types of complex learning outcomes.

7. The matching item is a variation of the multiple-choice form and is appropriate when it provides a more compact and efficient means of measuring the same achievement.

8. The matching item consists of a list of *premises* and a list of the *responses* to be related to the premises.

9. A good matching item is based on homogeneous material, contains a brief list of premises and an uneven number of responses (more or less) that can be used more than once, and has the brief responses in the right-hand column.

10. The directions for a matching item should indicate the basis for matching and that each response can be used more than once or not at all.

11. The interpretive exercise consists of a series of selection-type items based on some type of introductory material (e.g., paragraph, table, chart, graph, map, or picture).

12. The interpretive exercise uses both multiple-choice and alternative-response items to measure a variety of complex learning outcomes.

13. The introductory material used in an interpretive exercise must be relevant to the outcomes to be measured, new to examinees, at the proper reading level, and as brief as possible.

14. The test items used in an interpretive exercise should call for the intended type of interpretation, and the answers to the items should be dependent on the introductory material.

15. The test items used in an interpretive exercise should be in harmony with the rules for constructing that item type.

Learning Exercises

1. Marking a false statement false does not guarantee that the student knows what is true. How would you handle this problem?

2. Under what conditions is it preferable to use a matching item rather than some other item type? When should matching items be avoided?

3. In a subject area in which you plan to teach, construct an interpretive exercise. Pair and share with two other students. Which exercise is the most difficult of the three? Why? Is that satisfactory, or not?

References and Additional Reading

Carey, L.M. (2001). *Measuring and Evaluating School Learning*, 3rd ed. Boston: Allyn and Bacon.

Linn, R.L., and Gronlund, N.E. (2000). *Measurement and Assessment in Teaching*, 8th ed. Upper Saddle River, NJ: Merrill/Prentice-Hall.

Mehrens, W.A., and Lehmann, I.J. (1991). *Measurement and Evaluation in Education and Psychology*, 4th ed. New York: Holt, Rinehart and Winston.

Oosterhoff, A.C. (1999). *Developing and Using Classroom Assessments*, 2nd ed. Upper Saddle River, NJ: Prentice-Hall.

Weblinks

Extended Matching Questions
http://scholar.lib.vt.edu/ejournals/JVME/V20-3/wilson.html

How to Write True–False Questions
http://www.edu.uleth.ca/courses/ed3604/contf/wrttf/wrttf.html

True–False Questions
http://www.edu.uleth.ca/courses/ed3604/contf/whntf/whntf.html

9

Writing Supply Items: Short Answer and Essay

This chapter will enable you to:

1. Describe the strengths and limitations of short-answer items.
2. Distinguish between well stated and poorly stated short-answer items.
3. Identify and correct faults in poorly stated short-answer items.
4. Match short-answer items to intended learning outcomes.
5. Construct short-answer items that are well stated, relevant to important learning outcomes, and free of defects.
6. Describe the strengths and limitations of essay questions.
7. Distinguish between restricted-response and extended-response essay questions.
8. Describe the strengths and limitations of essay questions.
9. Write essay questions that present a clear task, are relevant to important learning outcomes, and provide guidelines for scoring.
10. Score essay answers more effectively.

As noted in Chapters 7 and 8, selection-type items can be designed to measure a variety of learning outcomes, ranging from simple to complex. They tend to be favoured in achievement tests because they provide (1) greater control of the type of response students can make, (2) broader sampling of achievement, and (3) quicker and more objective scoring. Despite these advantages, supply-type items can also play an important role in measuring achievement.

Supply-type items require students to produce the answer. This may be a single-word or a several-page response. Although the length of response ranges along a continuum, supply-type items are typically divided into (1) short-answer items, (2) restricted-response essay, and (3) extended-response essay (see Figure 9.1).

FIGURE 9.1 • Supply-type items arranged along a "control of response" continuum and a list of learning outcomes typically measured by each item type.

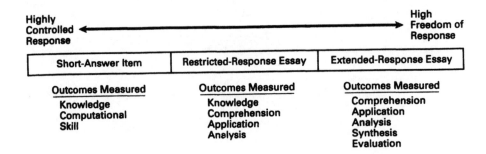

Short-Answer Items

The short-answer (or completion) item requires the examinee to supply the appropriate words, numbers, or symbols to answer a question or complete a statement.

EXAMPLE

What are the incorrect responses in a multiple-choice item called? *(distracters)*
The incorrect responses in a multiple-choice item are called *(distracters)*.

This item type also includes computational problems and any other simple item form that requires supplying the answer rather than selecting it. Except for its use in computational problems, the short-answer item is used primarily to measure simple knowledge outcomes.

The short-answer item appears to be easy to write and use, but there are two major problems in constructing short-answer items. First, it is extremely difficult to phrase the question or incomplete statement so that only one answer is correct. In the example we have noted, for instance, a student might respond with any one of a number of answers that could be defended as appropriate. The student might write "incorrect alternatives," "wrong answers," "inappropriate options," "decoys," "foils," or some other equally descriptive response. Second, there is the problem of spelling. If credit is given only when the answer is spelled correctly, the poor spellers will be prevented from showing their true level of achievement and the test scores will become an uninterpretable mixture of knowledge and spelling skill. On the other hand, if attempts are made to ignore spelling during the scoring process, there is still the problem of deciding whether a badly spelled word represents the intended answer. This, of course, introduces an element of subjectivity that tends to make the scores less dependable as measures of achievement. See Box 9.1 (page 121) for strengths and limitations.

Due to these weaknesses, the short-answer item should be reserved for those special situations where supplying the answer is a necessary part of the learning outcome to be measured; for example, where the intent is to have students *recall* the information, where computational problems are used, or where a selection-type item would make the answer obvious. In these situations, the use of the short-answer item can be defended despite its shortcomings.

BOX 9.1 • *Short-Answer Items*

Strengths
1. It is easy to write test items.
2. Guessing is less likely than in selection-type items.
3. This item type is well suited to computational problems and other learning outcomes where supplying the answer is important.
4. A broad range of knowledge outcomes can be measured.

Limitations
1. It is difficult to phrase statements so that only one answer is correct.
2. Scoring is contaminated by spelling ability.
3. Scoring is more time consuming than for selection-type items.
4. This item type is not very adaptable to measuring complex learning outcomes.

Rules For Writing Short-Answer Items

1. State the item so that only a single, brief answer is possible. This requires great skill in phrasing and the use of precise terms. What appears to be a simple, clear question to the test maker can frequently be answered in many different ways, as we noted with the previous sample item. It helps to review the item with this rule in mind and revise as needed.

2. Start with a direct question and switch to an incomplete statement only when greater conciseness is possible by doing so. The use of a direct question increases the likelihood that the problem will be stated clearly and that only one answer will be appropriate. Also, incomplete statements tend to be less ambiguous when they are based on problems that were first stated in question form.

EXAMPLE

What is another name for true–false items? *(alternative-response items)*
True–false items are also called *(alternative-response items)*.

Usually, questions are better than sentence completion, as questions tend to make the item clearer, especially to younger students.

3. It is best to leave only one blank and it should relate to the main point of the statement. Leaving several blanks to be filled in is often confusing and the answer to one blank may depend on the answer in another.

EXAMPLE

Poor: In terms of type of response, the (matching) item is most like the *(multiple-choice)* item.

Better: In terms of type of response, which item is most like the matching item? *(multiple-choice)*.

In the "poor" version, a number of different responses would have to be given credit, such as "short answer" and "essay," and "true–false" and "multiple-choice." Obviously, the item would not function as originally intended.

It is also important to avoid asking students to respond to unimportant or minor aspects of a statement. Focus on the main idea of the item and leave a blank only for the key response.

4.   Place the blanks at the end of the statement. This permits the student to read the complete problem before coming to the blank to be filled. With this procedure, confusion and rereading of the item is avoided and scoring is simplified. Constructing incomplete statements with blanks at the end is more easily accomplished when the item is first stated as a direct question, as suggested earlier. In some cases, it may be a matter of rewording the item and changing the response to be made.

EXAMPLE

Poor: (Reliability) is likely to increase when a test is lengthened.

Better: When a test is lengthened, reliability is likely to *(increase)*.

With this particular item, the "better" version also provides a more clearly focused item. The "poor" version could be answered by "validity," "time for testing," "fatigue," and other unintended but clearly correct responses. This again illustrates the great care needed in phrasing short-answer items.

5.   Avoid extraneous clues to the answer. One of the most common clues in short-answer items is the length of the blank. If a long blank is used for a long word and a short blank for a short word, this is obviously a clue. Thus, all blanks should be uniform in length. Another common clue is the use of the indefinite article "a" or "an" just before the blank. It sometimes gives away the answer, or at least rules out some possible incorrect answers.

EXAMPLE

Poor: The supply-type item used to measure the ability to organize and integrate material is called an *(essay item)*.

Better: What are supply-type items used to measure the ability to organize and integrate material called? *(essay items)*.

The "poor" version rules out "short-answer item," the only other supply-type item, because it does not follow the article "an." One solution is to include both articles, using "a(an)." Another solution is to eliminate the article by switching to plural.

6.   For numerical answers, indicate the degree of precision expected and the units in which they are to be expressed. Indicating the degree of precision (e.g., to the nearest whole number) will clarify the task for students and prevent them from spending more time on an item than is required. Indicating the units in which to express the answer will aid scoring by providing a more uniform set of responses (e.g., minutes rather than fractions of an hour). When the learning outcome requires knowing the type of unit in common use and the degree of precision expected, this rule must then be disregarded.

Essay Questions

The most notable characteristic of the essay question is the freedom of response it provides. As with the short-answer item, students must produce their own answers. With the essay question, however, they are free to decide how to approach the problem, what factual information to use, how to organize the answer, and what degree of emphasis to give each aspect of the response. Thus, the essay question is especially useful for measuring the ability to organize, integrate, and express ideas. These are the types of performance for which selection-type items and short-answer items are so inadequate.

In deciding when and how to use essay questions, it may be desirable to compare their relative merits with those of selection-type items, as shown in Table 9.1. As can be seen in the table, both item types are efficient for certain purposes and inefficient for others. It is also apparent that the two types tend to complement each other in terms of the types of learning outcomes measured and the effect they are most likely to have on learning. Thus, it is not a matter of using *either* selection-type items or essay questions, but rather *when* should *each* be used. Tests may frequently require both types in order to obtain adequate coverage of the intended learning outcomes.

TABLE 9.1 • *Summary Comparison of Selection-Type Items and Essay Questions*

	Selection-Type Items	Essay Questions
Learning Outcomes Measured	Good for measuring outcomes at the knowledge, comprehension, and application levels of learning; inadequate for organizing and expressing ideas.	Inefficient for knowledge outcomes; best for ability to organize, integrate, and express ideas.
Sampling of Content	The use of a large number of items results in broad coverage, which makes representative sampling of content feasible.	The use of a small number of items limits coverage, which makes representative sampling of content infeasible.
Preparation of Items	Preparation of good items is difficult and time consuming.	Preparation of good items is difficult but easier than with selection-type items.
Scoring	Objective, simple, and highly reliable.	Subjective, difficult, and less reliable.
Factors Distorting Scores	Reading ability and guessing.	Writing ability and bluffing.
Probable Effect on Learning	Encourages students to remember, interpret, and use the ideas of others.	Encourages students to organize, integrate, and express their own ideas.

Types of Essay Questions

The freedom of response permitted by essay questions varies considerably. Students may be required to give a brief and precise response, or they may be given great freedom in determining the form and scope of their answers. Questions of the first type are commonly called *restricted-response questions*, and those of the second type are called *extended-response questions*. This is an arbitrary but convenient pair of categories for classifying essay questions.

Restricted-Response Questions. The restricted-response question places strict limits on the answer to be given. The boundaries of the subject matter to be considered are usually narrowly defined by the problem, and the specific form of the answer is also commonly indicated (by words such as "list," "define," and "give reasons"). In some cases the response is limited further by the use of introductory material or by the use of special directions.

EXAMPLE

Describe the relative merits of selection-type test items and essay questions for measuring learning outcomes at the comprehension level. Confine your answer to one page.

EXAMPLE

Ms Singh, a ninth-grade science teacher, wants to measure her students' "ability to interpret scientific data" with a paper and pencil test.
1. Describe the steps that Ms Singh should follow.
2. Give reasons to justify each step.

Restricting the form and scope of the answers to essay questions has both advantages and disadvantages. Such questions can be prepared more easily, related more directly to specific learning outcomes, and scored more easily. On the other hand, they provide little opportunity for the students to demonstrate their abilities to organize, to integrate, and to develop essentially new patterns of response. The imposed limitations make restricted-response items especially useful for measuring learning outcomes at the comprehension, application, and analysis levels of learning. They are of relatively little value for measuring outcomes at the synthesis and evaluation levels. At these levels, the extended-response question provides the more appropriate measure.

Extended-Response Questions. The extended-response question gives students almost unlimited freedom to determine the form and scope of their responses. Although in some instances rather rigid practical limits may be imposed, such as time limits or page limits, restrictions on the material to be included in the answer and on the form of response are held to a minimum. Students must be given sufficient freedom to demonstrate skills of synthesis and evaluation, and just enough control to assure that the intended intellectual skills and abilities will be called forth by the question. Thus, the amount of structure will vary from item to item depending on the learning outcomes being measured, but the stress will always be on providing as much freedom as the situation permits.

EXAMPLE

Synthesis Outcome: For a course that you are teaching or expect to teach, prepare a complete plan for assessing student achievement. Be sure to include the procedures you would follow, the instruments you would use, and the reasons for your choices.

EXAMPLE

Evaluation Outcome: (The student is given a complete achievement test that includes errors or flaws in the directions, in the test items, and in the arrangement of the items.) Write a critical evaluation of this test using as evaluative criteria the rules and standards for test construction described in your textbook. Include a detailed analysis of the test's strengths and weaknesses and an evaluation of its overall quality and probable effectiveness.

The extended-response question provides for the creative integration of ideas, the overall evaluation of materials, and a broad approach to problem solving. These are all important learning outcomes and ones that cannot be measured by other types of test items. The biggest problem, of course, is to evaluate the answers with sufficient reliability to provide a useful measure of learning. This is a difficult and time-consuming task, but the importance of the outcomes would seem to justify the additional care and effort required (see Box 9.2).

Rules for Writing Essay Questions

The construction of clear, unambiguous essay questions that call forth the desired responses is a much more difficult task than is commonly presumed. The following rules will not make the task any easier, but their application will result in essay items of higher quality.

1. **Use essay questions to measure complex learning outcomes only.** Most knowledge outcomes profit little from being measured by essay questions. These outcomes can

BOX 9.2 • *Essay Questions*

Strengths
1. The highest-level learning outcomes (analysis, synthesis, evaluation) can be measured.
2. Preparation time is less than that for selection-type items.
3. The integration and application of ideas is emphasized.

Limitations
1. There is a brief and therefore possibly inadequate sampling of achievement due to time needed for answering each question.
2. It is difficult to relate to intended learning outcomes because of freedom to select, organize, and express ideas.
3. Scores are raised by writing skill and bluffing, and lowered by poor handwriting, misspelling, and grammatical errors.
4. Scoring is time consuming, subjective, and tends to be unreliable.

---

usually be measured more effectively by objective items that lack the sampling and scoring problems that essay questions introduce. There may be a few exceptions, as when supplying the answer is a basic part of the learning outcome, but for most knowledge outcomes essay questions simply provide a less reliable measure with no compensating benefits.

At the comprehension, application, and analysis levels of learning, both objective tests and essay tests are useful. Even here, though, the objective test would seem to have priority, the essay test being reserved for those situations that require the student to *give* reasons, *explain* relationships, *describe* data, *formulate* conclusions, or in some other way produce the appropriate answer. Where supplying the answer is vital, a properly constructed restricted-response question is likely to be most appropriate.

At the synthesis and evaluation levels of learning, both the objective test and the restricted-response test have only limited value. These tests may be used to measure some specific aspects of the total process, but the production of a complete work (such as a plan of operation) or an overall evaluation of a work (for instance, an evaluation of a novel or an experiment) requires the use of extended-response questions. It is at this level that the essay form contributes most uniquely.

2.   **Relate the questions as directly as possible to the learning outcomes being measured.** Essay questions will not measure complex learning outcomes unless they are carefully constructed to do so. Each question should be specifically designed to measure one or more well defined outcomes. Thus, the place to start, as is the case with objective items, is with a precise description of the performance to be measured. This will help determine both the content and form of the item and will aid in the phrasing of it.

The restricted-response item is related quite easily to a specific learning outcome because it is so highly structured. The limited response expected from the student also makes it possible for the test maker to phrase the question so that its intent is communicated clearly to the student. The extended-response item, however, requires greater freedom of response and typically involves a number of learning outcomes. This makes it more difficult to relate the question to the intended outcomes and to indicate the nature of the desired answer through the phrasing of the question. If the task is prescribed too rigidly in the question, the students' freedom to select, organize, and present the answer is apt to be infringed upon. One practical solution is to indicate to the students the criteria to be used in evaluating the answer. For example, a parenthetical statement such as the following might be added: "Your answer will be evaluated in terms of its comprehensiveness, the relevance of its arguments, the appropriateness of its examples, and the skill with which it is organized." This clarifies the task to the students without limiting their freedom, and makes the item easier to relate to clearly defined learning outcomes.

3.   **Formulate questions that present a clear task to be performed.** Phrasing an essay question so that the desired response is obtained is no simple matter. Selecting precise terms and carefully phrasing and rephrasing the question with the desired response in mind will help clarify the task for the student. Since essay questions are to be used as a measure of complex learning outcomes, avoid starting such questions with "who," "what," "when," "where," "name," and "list." These terms tend to limit the response to knowledge outcomes. Complex achievement is most apt to be called forth by such words as "why," "describe," "explain," "compare," "relate," "contrast," "interpret," "analyze," "criticize," and "evaluate." The specific terminology to be used will be determined largely by the specific behaviour described in the learning outcome to be measured (see Table 9.2 page 128).

TABLE 9.2 • *Types of Complex Outcomes and Related Terms for Writing Essay Questions*

Outcome	Sample Terms
Comparing	compare, classify, describe, distinguish between, explain, outline, summarize
Interpreting	convert, draw, estimate, illustrate, interpret, restate, summarize, translate
Inferring	derive, draw, estimate, extend, extrapolate, predict, propose, relate
Applying	arrange, compute, describe, demonstrate, illustrate, rearrange, relate, summarize
Analyzing	break down, describe, diagram, differentiate, divide, list, outline, separate
Creating	compose, design, devise, draw, formulate, make up, present, propose
Synthesizing	arrange, combine, construct, design, rearrange, regroup, relate, write
Generalizing	construct, develop, explain, formulate, generate, make, propose, state
Evaluating	appraise, criticize, defend, describe, evaluate, explain, judge, write

Check the phrasing of an essay question by writing a model answer, or by formulating a mental answer to the question, and if possible, having a colleague write an answer. This helps the test maker detect any ambiguity in the question, aids in determining the approximate time needed by the student to develop a satisfactory answer, and provides a rough check on the mental processes required. This procedure is most feasible with the restricted-response item, the answer to which is more limited and more closely prescribed.

4.   Do not permit a choice of questions unless the learning outcome requires it. In most tests of achievement, it is best to have all students answer the same questions. If they are permitted to write on only a fraction of the questions, such as three out of five, their answers cannot be evaluated on a comparative basis. Also, since the students will tend to choose those questions they are best prepared to answer, their responses will provide a sample of their achievement that is less representative than that obtained without optional questions. As we noted earlier, one of the major limitations of the essay test is the limited and unrepresentative sampling it provides. Giving students a choice among questions simply complicates the sampling problem further and introduces greater distortion into the test results.

In some situations the use of optional questions might be defensible. For example, if the essay is to be used as a measure of writing *skill* only, some choice of topics on which to write may be desirable. This might also be the case if the essay is used to measure some aspects of creativity, or if the students have pursued individual interests through independent study. Even for these special uses, however, great caution must be exercised in the use of optional questions. The ability to organize, integrate, and express ideas is determined in part by the complexity of the content involved. Thus, an indeterminate amount of contamination can be expected when optional questions are used.

5.   Provide ample time for answering and suggest a time limit on each question. Since essay questions are designed most frequently to measure intellectual skills and abilities, time must be allowed for thinking as well as for writing. Thus, generous time limits should be provided. For example, rather than expecting students to write on several essay questions during one class period, it might be better to have them focus on one or two questions. There seems to be a tendency for teachers to include so many questions in a single essay test that a high score is as much a measure of writing speed as of achievement. This is probably an attempt to overcome the problem of limited sampling, but it tends to be an undesirable solution. In measuring complex achievement, it is better to use fewer questions and to improve the sample by more frequent testing.

Informing students of the appropriate amount of time they should spend on each question will help them use their time more efficiently; ideally, it will also provide a more adequate sample of their achievement. If the length of the answer is not clearly defined by the problem, as in some extended-response questions, it might also be desirable to indicate page limits. Anything that will clarify the form and scope of the task without interfering with the measurement of the intended outcomes is likely to contribute to more effective measurement.

Rules for Scoring Essay Answers

As we noted earlier, one of the major limitations of the essay test is the subjectivity of the scoring. That is, the feelings of the scorers are likely to enter into the judgments they make concerning the quality of the answers. This may be a personal bias toward the writer of the essay, toward certain areas of content or styles of writing, or toward shortcomings in such extraneous areas as legibility, spelling, and grammar. These biases, of course, distort the results of a measure of achievement and tend to lower their reliability.

The following rules are designed to minimize the subjectivity of the scoring and to provide as uniform a standard of scoring from one student to another as possible. These rules will be most effective, of course, when the questions have been carefully prepared in accordance with the rules for construction.

1.   Evaluate answers to essay questions in terms of the learning outcomes being measured. The essay test, like the objective test, is used to obtain evidence concerning the extent to which clearly defined learning outcomes have been achieved. Thus, the desired student performance specified in these outcomes should serve as a guide both for constructing the questions and for evaluating the answers. If a question is designed to measure "the ability to explain cause–effect relations," for example, then the answer should be evaluated in terms of how adequately the student *explains the particular cause–effect relations presented in the question*. All other factors—such as interesting but extraneous factual information, style of writing, and errors in spelling and grammar—should be ignored (to the extent possible) during the evaluation. In some cases separate scores may be given for spelling or writing ability, but these should not be allowed to contaminate the scores that represent the degree of achievement of the intended learning outcomes.

2.   Score restricted-response answers by the point method, using a model answer as a guide. Scoring with the aid of a previously prepared scoring key is possible with the restricted-response item because of the limitations placed on the answer. The procedure involves writing a model answer to each question and determining the number of points to be assigned to it and to the parts within it. The distribution of points within an answer must, of course, take into account all scorable units indicated in the learning outcomes being measured. For example, points may be assigned to the relevance of the examples used and to the organization of the answer, as well as to the content of the answer, if these are legitimate aspects of the learning outcome. As indicated earlier, it is usually desirable to make clear to the student at the time of testing the basis on which each answer will be judged (content, organization, and so on). (Scoring keys will be discussed at length in the next chapter.)

3.   Grade extended-response answers by the rating method, using defined criteria as a guide. Extended-response items allow so much freedom in answering that the preparation of a model answer is frequently impossible. Thus, the test maker usually *grades* each answer by judging its quality in terms of a previously determined set of criteria, rather than *scoring* it point by point with a scoring key. The criteria for judging the quality of an answer are determined by the nature of the question, and thus, by the learning outcomes being measured. If students were asked to "describe a complete plan for preparing an achievement test," for example, the criteria would include such things as (1) the completeness of the plan (e.g., whether it included a statement of objectives, a set of specifications, and the appropriate types of items), (2) the clarity and accuracy with which each step was described, (3) the adequacy of the justification for each step, and (4) the degree to which the various parts of the plan were properly integrated.

Typically, the criteria for evaluating an answer are used to establish about five levels of quality. Then as the answer to a question is read, it is assigned a letter grade or a number from 1 to 5, which designates the reader's rating. One grade may be assigned on the basis of the overall quality of the answer (holistic scoring), or a separate judgment may be made on the basis of each criterion (analytic scoring, or scoring by scoring key). The latter procedure provides the most useful information for diagnosing and improving learning and should be used wherever possible. (These concepts will be discussed in greater detail in the next chapter.)

More uniform standards of grading can usually be obtained by reading the answers to each question twice. During the first reading, the papers should be tentatively sorted into five piles, ranging from high to low in quality. The second reading can then serve the purpose of checking the uniformity of the answers in each pile and making any necessary shifts in rating. Beware of student bluffing (see Box 9.3).

4.   Evaluate all of the students' answers to one question before proceeding to the next question. Scoring or grading essay tests question by question, rather than student by student, makes it possible to maintain a more uniform standard for judging the answers to each question. This procedure also helps offset the *halo effect* in grading. When all of the answers on one paper are read together, the grader's impression of the paper as a whole is apt to influence the grades assigned to the individual answers. Grading question by question prevents the formation of this overall impression of a student's paper. Each answer is more apt to be judged on its own merits when it is read and compared with other answers to the same question than when it is read and compared with other answers by the same student.

5.   Evaluate answers to essay questions without knowing the identity of the writer. This is another attempt to control personal bias during scoring. Answers to essay questions should be evaluated in terms of what is written, not in terms of what is known

BOX 9.3 • *Student Bluffing and Scoring Essays*

Students can obtain higher scores on essay questions by clever bluffing. Although this requires skill in writing and some knowledge of the topic, credit should not be given unless the question is specifically answered. Some common types of bluffing are listed below.

1. Student repeats the question in statement form (slightly paraphrased) and tells how important the topic is (e.g., "The role of assessment in teaching is extremely important. It is hard to imagine effective instruction without it, etc.").

2. Student writes on a well known topic and fits it to the question. For example, if students were asked to compare testing and performance assessment, a student who knows testing well but knows little about performance assessment might describe testing in considerable detail and frequently state that performance assessment is much superior for evaluating the type of learning measured by the test.

3. Student liberally sprinkles the answer with basic concepts, whether they are understood or not. For example, if students were asked to write about any assessment technique, the importance of "validity" and "reliability" might be mentioned frequently.

4. Student includes the teacher's basic beliefs wherever possible (e.g., "The intended learning outcomes must be stated in performance terms before this type of test is constructed or selected").

Bluffing is most effective where plans have not been made for careful scoring of the answers.

about the writers from other contacts with them. The best way to prevent prior knowledge from biasing our judgment is to evaluate each answer without knowing the identity of the writer. This can be done by having the students write their names on the back of the paper or by using code numbers in place of names.

6. **Whenever possible, have two or more persons grade each answer.** The best way to check on the reliability of the scoring of essay answers is to obtain two or more independent judgments. Although this may not be a feasible practice for routine classroom testing, it might be done periodically with a fellow teacher (one who is equally competent in the area). Obtaining two or more independent ratings becomes especially vital where the results are to be used for important and irreversible decisions, such as in the selection of students for further training or for special awards. Here, the pooled ratings of several competent persons may be needed to attain a level of reliability that is commensurate with the significance of the decision being made.

Special Considerations

In some ways, essay questions present fewer problems than do other test items, as the question can be altered to fit the capabilities of the student. Usually an essay question can be easily reworded so the special needs student will be able to attempt it with some chance of success. If there are three essay-style questions on a test, it should not take long to reword them to suit the student; this would take far less time than it would to rewrite 10 multiple-choice questions.

When rewording essay questions, the task can be made less explicit, the number of criteria can be reduced, or the level of analysis and explanation can be simplified. For instance, a question on a unit test about the Industrial Revolution might say: "Explain the statement: "The distilleries of New England and the cotton mills of England were more responsible for slavery than were the plantations of the South." In your answer, consider dates for the start of slavery in the southern states, the start of the triangle trade route, and the abolition of slavery in various parts of the world."

An adapted question for a special needs student might be: "Discuss the triangle trade route and slavery." The task is much less structured, and responses would be difficult to mark, but when it is for only one or two students the challenge is not insurmountable.

Summary of Points

1. Use supply-type items whenever producing the answer is an essential element in the learning outcome (e.g., *defines* terms, instead of *identifies* meaning of terms).
2. Supply-type items include short-answer items, restricted-response essay, and extended-response essay.
3. The short-answer item can be answered by a word, number, symbol, or brief phrase.
4. The short-answer item is limited primarily to measuring simple knowledge outcomes.
5. Each short-answer item should be so carefully written that there is only one possible answer, the entire item can be read before coming to the answer space, and there are no extraneous clues to the answer.
6. In scoring short-answer items, give credit for all correct answers and score for spelling separately.
7. Essay questions are most useful to measuring the ability to organize, integrate, and express ideas.
8. Essay questions are inefficient for measuring knowledge outcomes because they provide limited sampling, are influenced by extraneous factors (e.g., writing skills, bluffing, grammar, spelling, handwriting), and scoring is subjective and unreliable.
9. Restricted-response essay questions can be more easily written and scored, but due to limitations on the responses they are less useful for measuring the higher-level outcomes (e.g., integration of diverse material).
10. Extended-response essay questions provide the freedom to select, organize, and express ideas in the manner that seems most appropriate; therefore, they are especially useful for measuring such outcomes.
11. Essay questions should be written to measure complex learning outcomes, to present a clear task, and to contain only those restrictions needed to call forth the intended response and provide for adequate scoring.
12. Essay answers should be scored by focusing on the intended response, by using a model answer or set of criteria as a guide, by scoring question by question,

and by ignoring the writer's identity. Be wary of student bluffing. If an important decision is to be based on the results, two or more competent scores should be used.

Learning Exercises

1. Choose a grade level or subject area in which you hope to teach, and identify three learning outcomes that could best be measured with essay questions. Construct two essay questions for each learning outcome.

2. Critique the following essay questions, and if necessary restate them so that they meet the criteria of a good essay question.
   (a) Discuss the CPR and its influence on Canada.
   (b) Should the government spend more on environmental protection?
   (c) What do you think of our system of government?

3. For each of the following, would it be more appropriate to use an extended-response question or a restricted-response question?
   (a) Compare two provinces.
   (b) Describe the procedure for using a dictionary.
   (c) Discuss the advantages of magnetometers versus prospecting on the ground.
   (d) Evaluate a short story.

References and Additional Reading

Linn, R.L., and Gronlund, N.E. (2000). *Measurement and Assessment in Teaching*, 8th ed. Upper Saddle River, NJ: Merrill/Prentice-Hall.

McMillan, J.H. (2001). *Classroom Assessments: Principles and Practices for Effective Instruction*, 2nd ed. Boston: Allyn and Bacon.

Osterhoff, A.C. (2001). *Classroom Applications of Educational Measurement*, 3rd ed. Upper Saddle River, NJ: Merrill/Prentice-Hall.

Stiggins, R.J. (2001). *Student-Involved Classroom Assessment*, 3rd ed. Upper Saddle River, NJ: Merrill/Prentice-Hall.

Weblinks

Essays: Making the Marking Criteria Explicit
Research into what students think is important in essays and what markers think.
http://ctiwebct.york.ac.uk/LTSNPsych/Specialist/Norton/essays1.htm

Marking Essays: A Guide to Undergraduate Grades in Sociology
Excellent scoring descriptors from a British university.
http://www.essex.ac.uk/sociology/undergraduate/u_grades.htm#key=

Marking Student Work on the Computer
An interesting site with clear instructions for using computers to help mark student essays.
http://www.aitech.ac.jp/~iteslj/Articles/Holmes-ComputerMarking/

10

Assessing Achievement Through Product and Performance

This chapter will enable you to:

1. Describe how product and performance assessments differ from paper and pencil testing.
2. Identify the strengths and limitation of product and performance assessments.
3. Write intended outcomes for product and performance assessment.
4. Distinguish between restricted and extended product and performance assessment.
5. Describe the general procedure for making a product or performance assessment.
6. Prepare a plan for arranging, observing, recording, and evaluating a product or performance task.
7. Construct a checklist that is well stated, relevant, and easy to use.
8. Construct a rating scale that is well stated, relevant, and easy to use.
9. Construct a scoring key that accurately describes the criteria and weights.
10. Construct a holistic scoring rubric.

It is popular at the moment to divide assessment techniques into paper and pencil tests and "performance" assessment—"performance" assessment including products and skills. This text has chosen to treat these two areas separately, on the grounds that products and performances are quite different, and so should be discussed separately. This chapter will deal first with general principles common to both, then with products, and then with performance assessment.

With regard to the amount of space devoted to these topics, traditional assessment texts concentrate on paper and pencil testing, and add product and performance assessments as things to be carried out when paper and pencil tests are not sufficient. This text has spent considerable time on how to compose paper and pencil tests, but only because there is a lot to consider, not because they are more important than product and performance assessments (see Box 10.1).

BOX 10.1 • *Assessments of Skills and Products*

Strengths

1. Can evaluate complex learning outcomes and skills that cannot be evaluated with traditional paper and pencil tests.

2. Provides a more natural, direct, and complete evaluation of some types of reasoning, oral, and physical skills.

3. Provides greater motivation for students by clarifying goals and making learning more meaningful.

4. Encourages the application of learning to real-life situations.

Limitations

1. Requires considerable time and effort to use.

2. Judgment and scoring performance is subjective, burdensome, and typically has low reliability.

3. Evaluation must frequently be done individually, rather than in groups.

Components of Product and Performance Skills

Although the focus in this chapter is on the assessment of product and performance skills, it is important to note that there are several components that must be considered before and during the assessment.

In assessing writing ability, for example, we are concerned with knowledge of vocabulary, grammar, and similar basic elements needed for effective writing, as well as interests and attitudes that support good writing. When assessing the ability to prepare a report, we are concerned with the ability to create a thesis statement, research skills, organization, and other elements that go into making a good report. In assessing laboratory skills, we are concerned with the student's knowing the names and uses of the equipment and the procedures to be followed, as well as having an attitude of care in handling the equipment and making accurate measurements. The knowledge components can be measured by tests before the skill is evaluated or made a part of the evaluation. The affective component is typically made a part of the skill assessment (e.g., handles equipment in a careful manner, follows all safety precautions in operating the machine). In any event, all components of the product or performance must be considered when planning for the assessment.

Stating Objectives for Product and Performance Assessment

In planning for instruction, the objectives for product and performance assessment should be developed at the same time as the objectives are being prepared for the testable learning outcomes. The same two-step procedure of stating the general objectives first and then defining them with a list of specific learning outcomes is followed. A list of objectives for a test construction unit, for example, could be stated as follows.

1. Prepares a table of specifications for an achievement test.

   1.1 Writes a clear description of the achievement domain to be tested.

   1.2 States the intended learning outcomes in performance terms.

   1.3 Lists the content areas to be covered by the test.

   1.4 Constructs a twofold table of specifications that indicates the proportion of items to be devoted to each learning outcome and each area of content.

   1.5 Checks the table of specifications with the achievement domain, to be certain the test measures a representative sample of the desired achievement.

All these outcomes will be assessed in the product, which can take any of a number of forms. The most efficient product for the above outcomes would be an outline for a unit of study, with the outcomes to be tested highlighted; a twofold table attached; and a brief concordance tying the table to the unit outline.

Statements such as these clarify what is involved in preparing a table of specifications and what the final product should be like. An evaluation can be made by using the statements as they are and adding a rating scale to each item to indicate degree of success, or by developing more specific criteria in each area (e.g., Comprehensive description of achievement domain, Intended learning outcomes are clearly stated). In either case the objectives set the stage for the assessment by focusing attention on what is to be assessed (see Box 10.2).

Restricted and Extended Product and Performance Tasks

Product and performance tasks may be restricted to fit a specific and limited skill (e.g., measuring humidity) or extended to a comprehensive performance that includes numerous specific skills (e.g., predicting weather). Although this dichotomy is somewhat arbitrary, it is useful in planning assessments. In some cases, it may be desirable to assess specific skills before putting them together in a more complex product or performance. In other cases, it may be desirable to use restricted product or performance

---

BOX 10.2 • *Writing Objectives for Skills and Products*

1. State each general objective so that it clearly describes the skill or product to be assessed.

2. List specific outcomes for each objective that are most relevant to a successful performance or a satisfactory product.

3. List enough specific outcomes to clarify what is meant by an effective product or performance.

4. State the specific outcomes in terms of observable dimensions of the skill or product.

5. State the specific outcomes so that they are clear to students.

tasks to diagnose problems in performing a complex task. For example, students having difficulty with laboratory procedures might benefit from a restricted assessment of measurement skills, and students having difficulty constructing a wood or metal product might need a restricted assessment of how to use a particular tool. Although our major focus is the overall performance, assessing restricted aspects of it can serve as guides for its improvement. This is another example of how teaching and assessment work together to improve learning.

Restricted product and performance tasks are typically highly restricted and limited in scope, as shown in the following examples.

EXAMPLES

Write a one-page report describing a field trip.
Give a one-minute speech on a given topic.
Read aloud a brief selection of poetry.
Construct a graph from a given set of data.
Demonstrate how to use a measuring instrument.

By limiting the scope of the task, it is easier to focus the observation and to judge the response. It should be recognized, however, that a series of restricted tasks do not provide sufficient evidence of a comprehensive performance. For that, we need more extended tasks that integrate the specific skills into a complex pattern of movements or the production of a high-quality product.

Extended product and performance tasks are typically less structured and broader in scope, as illustrated in the following examples.

EXAMPLES

Design and conduct an experiment.
Design and build a wood or metal product.
Write a short story.
Repair a malfunctioning motor.
Paint a picture.
Demonstrate a physical or musical performance.

Extended product and performance assessments typically give students greater freedom in selecting and carrying out the tasks and greater opportunity for self-assessment and self-improvement. Student–teacher discussions of the ongoing performance and the final results should focus on both the quality of the product or performance and the development of the students' independent learning skills.

Steps in Preparing Product and Performance Assessments

Effective assessments are most likely to result when a systematic approach is used. The following procedural steps outline the main factors to consider when making product or performance assessments.

1. Specifying the performance outcomes.
2. Selecting the focus of the assessment (procedure, product, or both).

3. Selecting an appropriate degree of realism.

4. Selecting the performance situation.

5. Selecting the method of observing, recording, and scoring.

Having discussed issues common to both products and performances, we will now turn to those aspects that differ, and will start by discussing product assessment.

Specifying the Outcomes for Products

If the intended learning outcomes have been prespecified for the instruction, it is simply a matter of selecting those that require the use of product assessment. If outcomes are not available, they should be identified and defined for the areas to be assessed. Restricted outcomes commonly use verbs such as *identify, construct,* and *demonstrate* (and their synonyms). A brief description of these verbs and some illustrative objectives for restricted performance outcomes are shown in Table 10.1.

Extended Product Outcomes

The extended product task may require students to seek information from a variety of sources beyond those provided by the task itself. They may need to use the library, make observations, collect and analyze data in an experiment, conduct a survey, or use a computer or other types of equipment. They may have to identify which aspects of the task are most relevant. The process or procedures that they use may be observed and be an important part of the assessment, but the most important measure of success is the product itself. The product that is produced may take a variety of forms (e.g., the construction and presentation of graphs or tables, the use of photographs or drawings, or the construction of physical models). Products may be developed over the course of several days and include opportunities for revision or modification. This freedom enables students to demonstrate their ability to select, organize, integrate, and evaluate information and ideas. However, extended tasks often mean loss of efficiency, possible loss of breadth of coverage of the content domain, and greater difficulty in rating performance.

TABLE 10.1 • *Typical Action Verbs and Illustrative Instructional Objectives for Restricted Product Outcomes*

Action Verbs	Illustrative Instructional Objectives
CONSTRUCT: Makes a product to fit a given set of specifications (typical verbs: construct, assemble, build, design, draw, make, prepare)	Draw a diagram for an electrical circuit. Design a pattern for making a dress. Prepare a circle graph. Construct a weather map. Prepare an experimental design.
WRITE: Prepares a written product to meet given specifications (typical verbs: write, prepare, create, compare and contrast)	Write a sonnet. Prepare a report. Create an annotated bibliography. Compare and contrast two short stories.

If the task is carefully thought out, it can include the advantages of both limited and extended tasks. For instance, the 1991 British Columbia Science Assessment at Grade 4 is shown in Box 10.3. As can be seen, this task requires students to do simple observations, to measure and record the outcomes of floating three wooden blocks in different liquids, to draw conclusions, and to make predictions. In this example, the manipulations, observations, and measurements are relatively simple, but these basic skills are critical in many settings and are not well assessed in a purely paper and pencil assessment. In this case, the students' performance (the act) was assessed through the product (the answers to the questions).

The effective use of product assessments requires careful attention to task selection and to the ways products will be scored. We need to take care in the identification of the complex skills we want to measure, in the construction of tasks that will require students to demonstrate those skills, and in the evaluation of the resulting product. Without careful attention to these aspects of the assessment, it is unlikely that the effort will yield adequately reliable or valid measures of the complex skills that are being sought. For assessing more complex outcomes, extended products are used. These are discussed in the next sections.

Defining the Extended Product

One of the most common extended products is the *project,* which is typically a number of products incorporated in a single assignment. The project can be designed to include a combination of academic, communication, thinking, and related skills that result in a complex performance, product, or problem-solving activity. Ideally, it involves multiple outcomes and criteria for each, as well as student participation in all phases of the project, including its assessment (see Box 10.4 page 139).

To illustrate the use of projects in assessment, we will focus on a problem-solving type of project. Typically, an unstructured problem (like those in the real world) is used so that there is no simple or single solution. This increases the complexity of the problem and provides for greater focus on higher-level learning outcomes (e.g., analysis, synthesis, evaluation). It also provides for the assessment of a greater range of skills useful later in life (e.g., locating resources, writing, speaking, self-assessment).

BOX 10.3 • *Hands-On Assessment Task*

Station: Floating Wood

Objectives

1. Students observe how three wooden blocks (same size and shape, different woods) float in water.

2. Students observe how two of the blocks float in salt water.

3. Students predict what will happen to the third block in salt water.

4. Students explain their predictions.

Source: British Columbia Assessment of Science 1991, Ministry of Education, Victoria, BC

BOX 10.4 • *Characteristics of a Good Student Project*

1. It focuses on multiple learning outcomes.
2. It includes the integration of understandings, skills, and strategies.
3. It is concerned with problems and activities that relate to out-of-school life.
4. It involves the active participation of students in all phases of the project.
5. It provides for student self-assessment and independent learning.
6. It requires skills that are generalizable to similar situations.
7. It is feasible within the constraints of the students' present knowledge, time limits, and available resources and equipment.
8. It is both challenging and motivating to students.
9. It is fair and doable by all students.
10. It provides for collaboration between the students and the teacher.

A common outline for a problem-solving project includes the following items.

1. Establishing criteria and standards.
2. Selecting and stating the problem.
3. Locating and selecting resources.
4. Writing the report.
5. Designing and completing a research study or making a product.
6. Orally presenting and defending the project.

Each of these steps is guided by the teacher and involves considerable student–teacher collaboration.

Establishing Criteria and Standards

Because of the multiple outcomes expected from a project, criteria must be established in many areas; for example, for each of the major areas of problem selection, research skills, report writing, product design and construction, and oral presentation. Throughout these areas, or as separate categories, criteria must also be established for level of thinking shown and general problem-solving skills. These criteria may be developed by the teacher or they may be cooperatively prepared with the students. The latter procedure tends to provide greater understanding of the criteria by students and tends to be more motivating. The final list of criteria should be checked against the instructional objectives to be sure they are in agreement.

Standards that describe levels of success on each criterion should be set at the same time as the criteria are prepared. These may be stated for use in scoring keys, holistic scoring rubrics, or may be included as part of a rating scale to be used in evaluating the project.

Selecting and Stating the Problem

Students should be free to select a problem that interests them, but the selection may require considerable help from the teacher. Many students are in the "tell me what to do" mode, and one or two conferences may be needed to help them think about possible problems to study. In helping students select a problem, it is important to keep in mind how suitable the problem is for the student. Is it too difficult or too easy for the student? Does it provide an opportunity for new learning, or is it one the student has already studied? Will the problem be motivating to the student or one that is done grudgingly? Will the problem provide significant learning experiences that are in harmony with the intended learning outcomes? These and similar concerns will aid in helping the student select an appropriate and worthwhile problem to study.

Students also typically need help in phrasing the problem so that it is clear, objective, and realistic. Stating the problem in question form usually provides the crux of the problem most effectively. For example, changing "Study of the Environment" to "How Can We Improve the Environment?" helps provide a focus on a major problem. From here it is possible to go to more specific statements, such as "How Can We Improve the Air or Water?" Asking students to put their topics in question form forces them to pose problems. It is then just a matter of helping them refine the statements until they are clear and realistic.

If criteria for selecting and stating a problem have been developed beforehand, as should be done, they can be stated in evaluation form and serve as an aid in the process. They can also, of course, provide a basis for later assessment of the project. Criteria such as the following can be combined with other project criteria and used as a basis for a rating scale.

1. Selects and states a realistic problem.

    1.1. Is the problem in harmony with the student's present knowledge and skill?

    1.2. Does the problem provide opportunities for the student to learn new knowledge and skills?

    1.3. Does the problem provide opportunities for assessing cognitive and communication skills?

    1.4. Does the problem relate to real-world situations?

    1.5. Does the problem have more than one possible solution?

    1.6. Is the problem stated clearly?

    1.7. Is the statement of the problem free from bias and distortion?

In stating the criteria, it is important that they be understandable to the students. This can be accomplished by having the students help develop the criteria. If the problem requires teacher-prepared criteria, they can be presented to the students for clarification and rewording as needed. In any event, criteria should be clear to students and available to them at the beginning of the project. This will provide a focus for doing the project and a guide for self-assessment and peer assessment later.

Locating and Selecting Resources

After stating the problem clearly, the student is expected to go to reference books and other sources to gather information. Other sources might include interviews with knowledgeable people in the community (e.g., banker, accountant, doctor, scientist), observation of a process (e.g., council meeting, trial, bakery operation), or writing a letter to a

Member of Parliament requesting information. The point is, students are expected to obtain information from any source that can provide help with the problem—as we do in real life.

This phase of the project might include criteria similar to the following.

2. Selects appropriate resource material.

    2.1. Has a variety of resources been selected?

    2.2. Is the resource material relevant to the problem?

    2.3. Do the resources provide various possible solutions to the problem?

    2.4. Does the resource material include evidence supporting the suggested solutions?

    2.5. Is there enough resource material to provide for valid conclusions?

Writing the Report

The written report provides an opportunity for students to combine ideas from various sources, analyze and interpret the findings, and summarize and draw conclusions. The criteria for judging the report should be used as a guide for writing it. The written report provides an important means of assessing higher-order thinking skills and, thus, they should be reflected in the criteria.

The following list illustrates how criteria might be stated for the written report.

3. Writes a clear and effective report.

    3.1. Has the problem been clearly stated?

    3.2. Have the study procedures been adequately described?

    3.3. Has the material from various sources been analyzed, compared, and evaluated?

    3.4. Have the findings been integrated into a well organized report?

    3.5. Have the findings been supported by adequate and relevant information?

    3.6. Does the summary include the main points?

    3.7. Are the conclusions in harmony with the findings and the limits of the study?

    3.8. Does the report exhibit good reasoning ability?

The specific nature of the criteria will, of course, be influenced by the content, instructional objectives, and level of the instruction. Emphasis on reasoning ability might require more specific criteria on the quality of the questions raised, the relevance of the arguments, and distinctions between supported and unsupported statements. Emphasis on communication skills might call for criteria on the clarity of the writing, grammar, and spelling. At lower grades, the criteria would, of course, need to be modified to fit the age level of the students. Our illustrative criteria are general and simply show how the intended learning outcomes might be stated so that they are most useful for instruction, learning, and assessment. If properly stated, they can be easily converted to a rating scale by adding numbers from 1 to 4, representing different levels of performance, as shown later in the section on Preparing a Rating Scale and in Box 10.5.

BOX 10.5 • *Sample Rating Scale Form for a Project*

Directions: Rate each item by circling the appropriate number. The numbers represent the following values: 4—excellent; 3—good; 2—satisfactory, 1—weak (needs modification).

Selecting and Stating the Problem

4 3 2 1 (a) Is the problem in harmony with the student's present knowledge and skill?

4 3 2 1 (b) (add others)

Locating and Selecting Resources

4 3 2 1 (a) Has a variety of resources been selected?

4 3 2 1 (b) (add others)

Writing the Report

4 3 2 1 (a) Has the problem been clearly stated?

4 3 2 1 (b) (add others)

Conducting a Research Study

4 3 2 1 (a) Have proper procedures been followed?

4 3 2 1 (b) (add others)

Building a Product

4 3 2 1 (a) Did the product match the specifications?

4 3 2 1 (b) (add others)

Oral Presentation of Project

4 3 2 1 (a) Did the oral presentation reflect understanding of the problem studied?

4 3 2 1 (b) (add others)

In any event, the student should be aware of the completed list of criteria before writing this report, and use the criteria to evaluate the report and then to revise it as needed. It is helpful for the teacher to evaluate the report and compare the ratings with those of the student in a conference before the student revises the report. Peer evaluations may, of course, also be used.

Designing and Completing a Research Study or Making a Product

In some cases, the written report may serve as a basis for a research study. In others, the written report may serve as a basis for constructing a product. This might be a map, poster, chart, graph, model, or some other type of exhibit illustrating the findings, or it might be a wood or metal product, as in the vocational area. In the latter case, the focus of the project may be on designing and constructing the product, but the study phase is still important. For a woodworking project, for example, the study phase may involve a comparison of different types of wood, various construction procedures, or a history of the product (e.g., making a replica of an antique chair). The study phase provides for the combining of academic and vocational skills in carrying out the project and increases the opportunity for including higher-level thinking skills in the project.

Criteria for assessing the research or product should be stated in the same manner as those listed earlier. The specific nature of the criteria for a research study will depend on the type of problem being studied. However, some general criteria should be considered, such as the use of proper procedures, control of variables, selection and use of equipment, accuracy of measurements, adequacy of interpretation of results, and validity of conclusions. Adapting these and similar criteria to the specific research project and phrasing them in terms the students can understand provides a sound basis for conducting the research and for its later assessment.

The criteria for a product will depend on the type of product that is being constructed and its relation to the written report. If an exhibit, such as a graph or poster, is being constructed as part of the project, for example, the criteria will include how well it illustrates the findings, its ease of interpretation, and the like. For a woodworking project, the criteria might be concerned with both the procedure (e.g., selection of tools and materials, use of tools and machines, etc.) and the product (e.g., appearance, meeting specifications, and functioning properly). As indicated earlier, the criteria should be known to students before starting on the construction project. It is also helpful to put the criteria in rating form (as illustrated later in the chapter) to clarify how they will be used in the assessment.

Orally Presenting and Defending the Project

Upon completion of the project, it may be desirable to have each student describe the procedures and findings to a group of students, parents, or members of the community. The nature of the group depends on the purpose of the assessment, the type of project, and how the school is organized.

The final presentation gives the student practice in public speaking and in defending his or her work. This, of course, also provides another opportunity to evaluate higher-order thinking skills through use of questions that require the student to defend the procedures, findings, and products of the project. As with other phases of the project, evaluation of the presentation is guided by a set of criteria developed at the beginning of the project and fully shared with the students.

The expanded project described here includes multiple outcomes, such as research skills, writing skills, speaking skills, thinking skills, self-assessment skills, and, in some cases, vocational skills. The specific nature of such a project will, of course, vary with the area of instruction and the purpose of the project. It is helpful to review descriptions of how this and other types of expanded product assessments are functioning in the schools. The list of references at the end of the chapter provides numerous descriptions and examples of product assessment in action.

Marking Products

There are a number of factors to consider when marking products. The discussion on advantages and problems associated with products mentioned some of the difficulties with marking: it is subjective, time consuming, and unless done conscientiously, may not help the student improve. Further, the more complex the product, the more difficult the assessment. However, many of the problems can be overcome by means of suitable scoring methods. This section looks at the two categories of marking products: analytic and holistic scoring.

Analytic Scoring

Scoring keys are the major type of **analytic scoring** (i.e., when we want a judgment on each criterion by which the performance or product is to be judged). In evaluating writing skill, for example, such things as organization, vocabulary, style, ideas, and mechanics might be judged separately. The scoring key then becomes an instrument for directing observation to these criteria and provides a convenient means of recording and scoring our judgments.

Analytic Scoring Keys

An analytic scoring key consists of two parts: a list of criteria, and the possible scores, or **weights,** for each one. Such scoring keys are easy to make up, and have the advantage of providing students with feedback about their strengths and weaknesses. They are therefore ideal for formative assessment, where the emphasis is on improving student performance rather than on deciding student grades. Analytic scoring keys enable a teacher to focus on specific characteristics of a product at a time. The separation of characteristics such as writing mechanics from the quality of the essay content can be especially useful. Separate scores for characteristics such as these provide the student with clearer feedback about the strengths and weaknesses of the response.

Analytic scores for writing skills may consist of just two broad categories—such as "rhetorical effectiveness" and "conventions," or "content quality" and "mechanics." Sometimes, finer distinctions are useful. A scoring key for an essay on French literature, for instance, might have several categories, corresponding to the course objectives:

1. Ideas
2. Organization
3. Word choice
4. Sentence construction
5. Conventions

Further, markers and students can be guided by differing weights for the criteria. For instance, if the teacher thought that all of the above criteria were of equal value, he or she would give each the same weight. If the essay were worth 25 marks, each criterion would have a weight of 5. If the teacher thought the criteria were of different importance, the weighting would reflect that differing importance. In that case, the key might look like this:

Ideas	9
Organization	5
Word choice	3
Sentence construction	5
Conventions	3
TOTAL	25

In this case, the teacher has been stressing the content of the material taught, so the ideas are weighted heavily. Organization and sentence construction have also been stressed, so their weighting reflects that.

Analytic scoring keys do not take long to construct, and provide the teacher and student with a guide to the importance of each criterion relative to the others. Students can assist in the formulation of the key, which gives them a sense of ownership and focuses their attention even more. If the students write out the scoring key and submit it as part of the product (on the back of an essay, for instance), the teacher knows they are aware of each element, and marking time is saved because the teacher does not have to write out the key for each product.

Scoring keys do, however, have some drawbacks. First, they tend to have less inter-rater reliability than other scoring guides. Because there is no descriptor of what students must do to attain a mark for each criterion, different markers may interpret the requirements differently, and award different marks for similar performances. For this reason, such scoring keys are not commonly used when tests are marked by a number of markers, such as with large-scale testing. Under classroom conditions, however, that is not a problem.

Secondly, each question must be worth a fairly large number of marks. Each criterion should be weighted at least 2, and 3 is better. That means that a scoring key with 4 criteria will be worth a minimum of 12 marks, and if there is to be a differentiated weighting the value will be at least 15. Again, in a classroom situation this is of no consequence, but in large-scale testing it might not be possible.

In summation, analytic scoring keys are an excellent choice for the classroom teacher who wishes to emphasize some criteria, and who wishes to communicate to his or her students their strengths and weaknesses.

Analytic Scoring Rubrics

The analytic scoring rubric shares the basic form of the scoring key in a more elaborate form. Along with the list of criteria and weight for each criterion, there is a descriptor that tells what the student must do to obtain marks. These rubrics are very popular at the present time, and can be found virtually everywhere. They have the advantages of the analytic scoring key, with the added advantage that they are likely to provide more inter-rater reliability. For this reason they are widely used by educational jurisdictions such as provinces in wide-scale testing, where student exams are marked by a number of markers. The disadvantage, of course, is that they take a considerable amount of time to prepare, and are therefore less useful to the classroom teacher. A simple scoring key might take two minutes to prepare, while a rubric that does the same thing might take two hours.

Holistic Scoring

Holistic scoring is based on an overall impression of the product rather than a consideration of the individual elements. The global judgment is made by assigning a numerical score to the product as a whole. Typically, between 4 and 8 points are used, and an even number of points is favoured to avoid a "middle dumping ground." Evaluation consists of quickly examining the product and assigning the number that matches the general impression of the product. In the case of writing assessment, for example, the reader will read each writing sample quickly for overall impression and place it in one of the piles ranging from 4 to 1. It is assumed that good writing is more than a sum of the individual elements that go into writing, and that holistic scoring will capture this total impression of the work.

Holistic scoring can be guided by scoring rubrics that clarify what each level of quality is like. A holistic scoring rubric for writing is shown in Box 10.6. These descriptions of each level do not provide for analysis of the product but simply list the criteria to keep in mind when making the overall judgment. Another way to clarify the meaning of each score level for a product is to use a *product scale or reference set.* This consists of a series of sample products that represent various degrees of quality. In writing assessment, for example, a writing sample representing each level of quality from 4 to 1 is created and each writing product is compared to the sample models and assigned the number of the sample it matches most closely. Product scales are especially useful where the quality of the product is difficult to define (e.g., art, creative writing).

For most instructional purposes, both holistic and analytic scoring are useful. One gives the global judgment of the product and the other provides diagnostic information useful for improving performance. Where both are used, the global judgment should be made first so some specific element does not distort the general impression of the product.

Improving Product Assessments

Product assessments can provide useful information concerning student achievement, but they are subject to all of the errors of observation and judgment, such as personal bias, generosity error (tendency to overrate), and halo effect (judging individual characteristics in terms of a general impression). Thus, if product assessments are to provide valid information, special care must be taken to improve the objectivity, reliability, and

---

BOX 10.6 • *Sample Scoring Rubric for Writing*

4— Interesting throughout
   Flows smoothly, good transitions
   Well organized for topic
   Good use of mechanics and sentence structure
3— Interesting most of the time
   Flows smoothly but some poor transitions
   Organized but some weaknesses
   Minor mechanical errors
2— Interest lowered by lapses in focus
   Flow is interrupted by many poor transitions
   Organization weak, strays from topic
   Some serious mechanical errors
1— No clear focus
   Jerky and rambling
   Poorly organized
   Many mechanical errors and weak sentence structure

meaningfulness of the results. The guidelines listed in Box 10.7 enumerate ways to improve the usefulness of product assessments.

Minimizing Excess Help and Cheating

There are two topics to be discussed in this section—excess help, and cheating. Some would say they are the same topic, differing only in degree. Others would say they are qualitatively different, rather than quantitatively. We take the position that they are quite different, because the teacher's responses to them have to be different.

Too Much Help for Elementary Students

This is not typically a problem at the primary level. Primary teachers do not assign many tasks to be done at home, and even when they do they can judge whether the child performed the task independently, based on work performed in class. At the intermediate level, however, a considerable proportion of the students' work is done out of class, and the teacher might not be able to judge the amount of assistance received.

We encourage children to solicit their parents' help with schoolwork, for a variety of reasons. At what point does that help go too far? At what point does it become counterproductive? This text is concerned with assessment. The aim of assessment is to find out what students know and what they can do, in part so we can help them improve. If parents or older siblings or friends do the work, however, what have we learned about the student who was supposed to do it? Nothing.

So the key here is the intent of the assignment. If the assignment is designed to teach the child how to do something, then help is not at all out of line. In fact, it is probably a good thing, as it ties home and school together, allows parents to model work habits, and has all the other advantages that come from parental involvement in their child's schooling. On the other hand, if the intent is to find out whether the child can do something, to ascertain whether he or she possesses certain skills, help is not a good thing. The easiest way to solve the problem is to communicate with parents.

BOX 10.7 • *Improving Product Assessments*

1. Specify the intended outcomes in observable terms and describe the use to be made of the results.
2. Limit the observable dimensions of the product to a reasonable number.
3. Provide clear, definite criteria for judging the product.
4. Use a scoring procedure that is appropriate for the use to be made of the results (e.g., holistic for global evaluation, analytic for diagnostic purposes).
5. Inform students of the method and criteria to be used in evaluating the performance.
6. Supplement and verify performance assessments with other evidence of achievement.
7. Take steps to ensure assistance is appropriate.

At the start of the year, send home a letter explaining that you will be having the students do a certain amount of work at home. Some of this work will be intended to teach the students how to do the task, or to practise it, while other assignments will be aimed at showing you (the teacher) whether the students have attained a certain level of performance. Explain that each assignment will be described in an assignment sheet that will explain the purpose, provide a scoring key, and tell parents how much help is appropriate. There will still be some parents who will help their children when you have asked them not to, but they will be in the minority. (By the way, the students should copy the assignment from the board, rather than the teacher photocopying it. It's cheaper, and the students will have a clearer idea of what is expected if they write it out.)

Cheating

At the secondary level, the problem is likely to be different. Intermediate students and parents may not know how much help is appropriate. Secondary students should realize that anything being marked is supposed to be the work of the student, and any help beyond a very small amount is inappropriate. In extreme cases, excess reliance on outside assistance is called *plagiarism* or cheating.

You can combat plagiarism or cheating in several ways. First, explain what plagiarism is. Tell students how to cite other people's work in their writing, and how to prepare a bibliography. Then, tell them that for each assignment you will inform them how much help is appropriate. Send home the same sort of communication described above.

Have the students copy out the assignment sheet and take it home. Have parents sign the sheet to indicate they have seen it. This not only tells parents how much help is appropriate, but it tells them what their children are doing in school. Students are more likely to keep up with the work when their parents know what is assigned. Many schools have students carry notebooks in which assignments are recorded, along with other communications to parents.

You can further lessen the problem (and the problem of students who get other students to do their work) by having a certain amount of work done in class. It is sometimes difficult to find time for students to do assignments in class time, and often resources are required that are not available in class, but preliminary work can be done, outlines prepared, and so on. Further, you might assign part of a period when students actually write two or three paragraphs so you can see them do it. You can also insist that rough work be turned in with the final copy, or you can ask to see work in progress on a regular basis, and award marks for intermediate steps. In the case of students who work on a word processor, you can ask that they save their drafts on a disk so you can see the writing process. Finally, Box 10.8 (page 149) offers some suggestions regarding plagiarism and the Internet.

Elements of Performance

What is a performance? It is a situation where the student (or a group of students) does something while the marker watches. We will discuss requirements of structuring performances later, but the most important element is that students must know what they are expected to do, and must know they are being judged, so they can put forth their best effort.

BOX 10.8 • *Plagiarism and the Internet*

The Internet has made plagiarism a much greater problem than it used to be. When the only source of information was the printed word, it was possible for teachers to make a reasonably accurate guess as to the probable source of an assignment that was clearly superior to a student's normal output. Most students simply copied verbatim from whatever source they had chosen, and the writing style alone gave them away.

Unfortunately, the Internet has many sites that offer, both free and at a price, papers on a great variety of topics, many written in a style that would be typical of a secondary school student.

1. The best defence is to assign specific topics rather than giving students wide choices. If the assignment is "Write 1000 words about the Riel Rebellion," students will be able to find papers on the Internet that fit this description. If the assignment is "Write 1000 words on the role of the CPR in the Riel Rebellion," students will find it considerably more difficult to obtain a ready-made paper.
2. Check for original author identification clues. Follow up with a Web search for a personal homepage and the Web site(s) of the organization(s) with which the author is affiliated.
3. Check for original source identification clues. Follow up with a Web search for the original source.
4. Identify unusual keywords or unique phrases and search for them with one of the large search engines such as Hotbot or Infoseek.
5. Look at original text of sources listed in the bibliography.
6. Browse these Web sites:
   Free Papers! (www.freepapers.com)
   School Sucks (www.schoolsucks.com)
   Other People's Papers (www.oppapers.com)
   Absolutely Free Online Essays (www.freeessay.com)
   Free Termpapers (www.realpapers.com)
   Helpful Sites for Term Papers (www.studyworld.com/term_paper_links.htm)
   Evil House of Cheat (www.cheathouse.com)
   Research Papers Online A+ (www.ezwrite.com)
   A1 Termpaper (www.a-1termpaper.com)
   Genius Papers (www.geniuspapers.com)

Source: Adapted from Cut-and-Paste Plagiarism: Preventing, Detecting and Tracking Online Plagiarism, by Lisa Hinchliffe http://alexia.lis.uiuc.edu/~janicke/plagiary.html.

As with product-based assessments, performance-based assessments are often referred to as "authentic assessments," and the earlier discussion applies here as well. There is one more thing to say on that subject associated with performance-based assessment, however: the more "authentic" the circumstances surrounding a performance, the less reliable (and therefore the less valid) the performance will be. That seems to be counter to common sense: if the aim of school is to prepare students for the real world, and if "authentic" means "as close to real world conditions as possible," it would seem to be logical that the more "authentic" the task, the more valid it would be. The problem is, however, that in the real world circumstances change. No matter how hard we try, no two performances will take place under exactly the same conditions, so students will be judged under different conditions each time they perform, which puts reliability into question. Furthermore, different students will have to perform under different conditions, which is unfair. Still, we have no other way to judge certain learning outcomes, so the best we can do is to make conditions as similar as possible.

"Hands-on" performance tasks that require students to manipulate objects, measure outcomes, and observe results of experimental manipulations are sometimes essential to capture the full array of skills needed to perform "authentic" tasks. This is obvious in the case of a driving test or a performance test for a dentist, but it may also be true in science and other areas. Research has shown that computer simulations of tasks in science sometimes may be good substitutes for actual hands-on performance of the task, but in other instances even high-fidelity simulations may have relatively poor relationships to hands-on performance. Poor relationships between simulations and actual hands-on performance occur most commonly when the manipulation of an apparatus (e.g., mixing a compound or taking a measurement) is an integral part of the task.

Performances are important in many different areas of study. For example, science courses are concerned with laboratory skills, English and foreign-language courses are concerned with communication skills, and skill outcomes are emphasized heavily in art and music courses, industrial education, business education, agricultural education, home economics courses, and physical education. Thus, in most instructional areas performance assessment is essential. Although tests and products can tell us whether students know what to do in a particular situation, more direct assessments are needed to evaluate their actual performance skills. Box 10.9 points out some strengths and weaknesses of performance assessment.

BOX 10.9 • *Performance Assessments*

Strengths
1. Can evaluate complex learning outcomes and skills that cannot be evaluated with traditional paper and pencil tests.
2. Provide a more natural, direct, and complete evaluation of some types of reasoning, oral, and physical skills.
3. Provide greater motivation for students by clarifying goals and making learning more meaningful.
4. Encourage the application of learning to real-life situations.
5. Students often enjoy performing and watching performances, which are a welcome change in the classroom routine.

Limitations
1. Require considerable time and effort to use.
2. Judgment and scoring performance is subjective, burdensome, and typically has low reliability.
3. Evaluation must frequently be done individually, rather than in groups.
4. Evaluation is difficult, as performance is of a transitory nature.
5. Performance is by nature unfair, for a variety of reasons.
6. Many students are shy, or have negative feelings about performing.

Specifying the Performance Outcomes

As with products, If the intended learning outcomes have been prespecified for the instruction, it is simply a matter of selecting those that require the use of performance assessment. If performance outcomes are not available, they should be identified and defined for the areas of performance to be assessed. Restricted performance outcomes commonly use verbs such as *identify, construct,* and *demonstrate* (and their synonyms). A brief description of these verbs and some illustrative objectives for restricted performance outcomes are shown in Table 10.2.

The following examples illustrate realistic sets of tasks for performance assessments.

Demonstrates Skill in Oral Reporting

1. Stands in a natural manner.
2. Maintains good eye contact.
3. Uses appropriate facial expressions.
4. Uses gestures effectively.
5. Speaks clearly and with good volume.
6. Speaks at an appropriate rate.
7. Presents ideas in an organized manner.
8. Uses appropriate language.
9. Maintains interest of the group.

TABLE 10.2 • *Typical Action Verbs and Illustrative Instructional Objectives for Performance Outcomes*

Action Verbs	Illustrative Instructional Objectives
IDENTIFY: Selects the correct objects, part of the object, procedure, or property (typical verbs: identify, locate, select, touch, pick up, mark, describe)	Select the proper tool. Identify the parts of a typewriter. Choose correct laboratory equipment. Select the most relevant statistical procedure. Locate an automobile malfunction. Identify a musical selection. Identify the experimental equipment needed. Identify a specimen under the microscope.
DEMONSTRATE: Performs a set of operations or procedures (typical verbs: demonstrate, drive, measure, operate, perform, repair, set up)	Drive an automobile. Measure the volume of a liquid. Operate a filmstrip projector. Perform a modern dance step. Repair a malfunctioning TV set. Set up laboratory equipment. Demonstrate taking a patient's temperature. Demonstrate the procedure for tuning an automobile.

Repairs a Malfunctioning Motor

1. Identifies the nature of the malfunction.
2. Identifies the system causing the malfunction.
3. Selects the tests to be made.
4. Conducts the tests in proper sequence.
5. Locates the malfunctioning component.
6. Replaces or repairs the component.
7. Removes and replaces parts in proper sequence.
8. Uses proper tools in a correct manner.
9. Follows safety precautions throughout procedure.

In some cases, the order in which the performance tasks are listed is unimportant, as illustrated by the first example. In other performance assessments, the sequence of steps provides a systematic approach to be followed. In these cases, as illustrated by the second example, placing the tasks in proper sequence will make it easier to observe and record the performance and to note errors in procedure.

Extended performance outcomes typically involve multiple instructional objectives, and it is important to consider all of them when designing a study. A research project, for example, might include intended learning outcomes as follows:

1. Designs and conducts an experiment.
2. Writes an accurate account of the study.
3. States valid conclusions.
4. Writes a critique of the procedure and findings.
5. Presents and defends the study in class.

These outcomes would need to be defined in more specific terms, like the two described earlier, but stating the general objectives first and then specifying them in more detail provides a useful procedure. In defining each major outcome, it may be desirable to divide some in two (e.g., Designs an experiment, Conducts an experiment). In other cases, some may be combined. For example "States valid conclusions" may be included as part of "Writes an accurate account of the study." In any event, the final list should provide a major list of the intended learning outcomes, each clearly specified by descriptions of what students can do to demonstrate achievement of the outcomes. More detailed descriptions of how to state intended learning outcomes and define them in performance terms can be found in Gronlund (2000).

Selecting the Focus of the Assessment

Performance assessment focuses on the procedure as opposed to the product. The nature of the performance frequently dictates where the emphasis should be placed, but in some cases there are also other considerations. Those types of performance that don't result in a product (e.g., speaking, reading aloud, physical skills, musical performance) require that the performance be evaluated in progress.

In other cases, both procedure and product are important aspects of a performance. For example, skill in locating and correcting a malfunction in a television set involves following a systematic procedure (rather than using trial and error) in addition to producing a properly repaired set. Frequently, procedure is emphasized during the early stages of learning and products later, after the procedural steps have been mastered.

In assessing typing skill, for example, proper use of the "touch system" would be evaluated at the beginning of instruction, but later evaluation would focus on the neatness and accuracy of the typed material and the speed with which it was produced. Similarly, in such areas as cooking, woodworking, and painting, correct procedure is likely to be stressed during the early stages of instruction and the quality of the product later. Procedure evaluation may also be used during later stages of instruction, of course, in order to detect errors in procedure that might account for an inferior product.

In general, focus the performance assessment on the procedure when:

1. there is no product, or product evaluation is infeasible (e.g., unavailable or too costly).

2. the procedure is orderly and directly observable.

3. correct procedure is crucial to later success.

4. analysis of procedural steps can aid in improving a product.

Where both the procedure and the product are observable, the emphasis given to each will depend on the skill being assessed and the stage of skill development. However, when the procedure has been sufficiently mastered, product evaluation is favoured because it typically provides a more objective basis for judgment, it can be done at a convenient time, and judgments can be rechecked if necessary.

Performance assessment should be focused on the product when:

1. different procedures can result in equally good products (e.g., writing a theme).

2. the procedure is not available for observation (e.g., take-home work).

3. the procedural steps have been mastered.

4. the product has qualities that can be clearly identified and judged.

Selecting an Appropriate Degree of Realism

Performance assessment in instructional settings typically falls somewhere between the usual paper and pencil test and performance in real-life situations. Although we can't expect to duplicate the natural situation in which the learning will later be used, we can strive for performance assessments that approximate real-world conditions. This, then, is another dimension to consider in preparing performance assessments. How much "realism" can we incorporate into our assessment? The more the better, of course, but authenticity is a matter of degree.

The presence of varying degrees of realism in a performance assessment can be illustrated by the simple example of applying arithmetic skills to the practical problem of determining correct change while shopping in a store (adapted from Fitzpatrick and Morrison, 1971). A simulation of this situation might range from the use of a story problem (low realism) to an actual purchase in a storelike situation (high realism). The various problem situations that might be contrived for this performance measure are shown in Figure 10.1. It should be noted that even though solving a story problem is relatively low in realism, it simulates the criterion situation to a greater degree than simply asking students to subtract 69 from 100. Thus, even with paper and pencil testing it is frequently possible to increase the degree of realism to a point where the results are useful in assessing performance outcomes.

The degree of realism selected for a particular situation depends on a number of factors. First, the nature of the instructional objectives must be considered. Acceptable performance in paper and pencil applications of skill, or in other measures with a low degree of realism, might be all that the instruction is intended to achieve. This is frequently the case with introductory courses that are to be followed by more advanced courses emphasizing applied performance. Second, the sequence of instruction within a particular course may indicate that it would be desirable to measure paper and pencil applications before "hands-on" performance is attempted. Locating the source of a malfunction on a diagram, for example, might precede working with actual equipment. Third, numerous practical constraints—such as time, cost, availability of equipment, and difficulties in administering and scoring—may limit the degree of realism that can be obtained. Fourth, the task itself may restrict the degree of realism in a test situation. In testing first aid skills, for example, it would be infeasible (and undesirable) to use actual patients with wounds, broken bones, and other physical conditions needed for realistic assessment. Thus, although we should strive for as high a degree of realism as the performance outcomes dictate, it is frequently necessary to make compromises in preparing performance assessments.

FIGURE 10.1 • Illustration of various degrees of realism in measuring the ability to determine correct change while making a purchase in a store.

Low realism	Have students solve this story problem: "If you bought a toy for 69¢ and you gave the clerk $1.00, how much change would you get?"
	Demonstrate the problem situation with actual money and ask each student to judge whether the change is correct.
	Pair off the students, give them actual money, and have them role-play the problem situation.
High realism	Set up a mock toy store and have each student demonstrate the "purchase" of a toy with actual money.

Selecting the Performance Situation

Performance assessments can be classified by the type of situation or setting being used. The following classification system closely approximates the degree of realism present in the situation and includes the following types: (1) paper and pencil performance, (2) identification test, (3) structured performance test, (4) simulated performance, (5) work sample, and (6) extended research project. Although these categories overlap to some degree, they are useful for describing and illustrating the various approaches used in performance assessment.

Paper and Pencil Performance

Paper and pencil performance differs from the more traditional paper and pencil test by placing greater emphasis on the application of knowledge and skill in a simulated setting. These paper and pencil applications might result in desired terminal learning outcomes, or they might serve as an intermediate step to performance that involves a higher degree of realism (for example, the actual use of equipment).

In many cases, paper and pencil performance might simply provide a first step toward hands-on performance. For example, before using a particular measuring instrument, such as a micrometer, it might be desirable to have students read various settings from pictures of the scale. Although the ability to read the scale is not a sufficient condition for accurate measurement, it is a necessary one. In this instance, paper and pencil performance would be favoured because it is a more convenient method of testing a group of students. Using paper and pencil performance as a precursor to hands-on performance might be favoured for other reasons. For example, if the performance is complicated and the equipment is expensive, demonstrating competence on paper and pencil situations could avoid subsequent accidents or damage to equipment.

Similarly, in the health sciences, skill in diagnosing and prescribing for hypothetical patients could avoid later harm to real patients.

Identification Test

The identification test includes a wide variety of situations representing various degrees of realism. In some cases, a student may be asked simply to identify a tool or piece of equipment and to indicate its function. A more complex situation might present the student with a particular performance task (e.g., locating a short in an electrical circuit) and ask him or her to identify the tools, equipment, and procedures needed in performing the task. An even more complex type of identification test might involve listening to the operation of a malfunctioning machine (such as an automobile motor, a drill, or a lathe) and, from the sound, identifying the most probable cause of the malfunction.

Although identification tests are widely used in industrial education, they are by no means limited to that area. The biology teacher might have students identify specimens that are placed at various stations around the room, or identify the equipment and procedures needed to conduct a particular experiment. Similarly, chemistry students might be asked to identify "unknown" substances, foreign-language students to identify correct pronunciation, mathematics students to identify correct problem-solving procedures,

English students to identify the "best expression" to be used in writing, and social studies students to identify various leadership roles as they are acted out in a group. Identifying correct procedures is also important, of course, in art, music, physical education, and such vocational areas as agriculture, business education, and home economics.

The identification test is sometimes used as an *indirect* measure of performance skill. The experienced plumber, for example, is expected to have a broader knowledge of the tools and equipment used in plumbing than is the inexperienced plumber. Thus, a tool identification test might be used to eliminate the least skilled in a group of applicants for a position as a plumber. More commonly, the identification test is used as an instructional device to prepare students for actual performance in real or simulated situations.

Structured Performance Test

A structured performance test provides for an assessment under standard, controlled conditions. It might involve such things as making prescribed measurements, adjusting a microscope, following safety procedures in starting a machine, or locating a malfunction in electronic equipment. The performance situation is structured and presented in a manner that requires all individuals to respond to the same set of tasks.

The construction of a structured performance test follows somewhat the same pattern used in constructing other types of achievement tests but there are some added complexities. The test situation can seldom be fully controlled and standardized, it typically takes more time to prepare and administer, and it is frequently more difficult to score. To increase the likelihood that the test situation will be standard for all individuals, instructions should be used that describe the test situation, the required performance, and the conditions under which the performance is to be demonstrated. Instructions for locating a malfunction in electronic equipment, for example, would typically include the following:

1. Nature and purpose of the test.
2. Equipment and tools provided.
3. Testing procedure:
    a. Type and condition of equipment.
    b. Description of required performance.
    c. Time limits and other conditions.
4. Method of judging performance.

When using performance tests, it may be desirable to set performance standards that indicate the minimum level of acceptable performance. These might be concerned with accuracy (e.g., measure temperature *to the nearest two-tenths of a degree*), the proper sequencing of steps (e.g., adjust a microscope *following the proper sequence of steps*), total compliance with rules (e.g., check *all safety guards* before starting a machine), or speed of performance (e.g., locate a malfunction in electronic equipment *in three minutes*). Some common **standards** for judging performance are shown in Box 10.10 (page 158).

Performance standards are, of course, frequently used in combination. A particular performance may require correct form, accuracy, and speed. How much weight to give to each depends on the stage of instruction as well as the nature of the performance. In

BOX 10.10 • *Some Common Standards for Judging Performance*

Type	Examples
Rate	Solve 10 addition problems in two minutes.
	Type 40 words per minute.
Error	Make no more than two errors per typed page.
	Count to 20 in Spanish without error.
Time	Set up laboratory equipment in five minutes.
	Locate an equipment malfunction in three minutes.
Precision	Measure a line within one-eighth of an inch.
	Read a thermometer within two-tenths of a degree.
Quantity	Complete 20 laboratory experiments.
	Locate 15 relevant references.
Quality (rating)	Write a neat, well spaced business letter.
	Demonstrate correct form in diving.
Percentage Correct	Solve 85 percent of the math problems.
	Spell 90 percent of the words in the word list correctly.
Steps Required	Diagnose a motor malfunction in five steps.
	Locate a computer error using the proper sequence of steps.
Use of Material	Build a bookcase with less than 10 percent waste.
	Cut out a dress pattern with less than 10 percent waste.
Safety	Check all safety guards before operating a machine.
	Drive an automobile without breaking any safety rules.

assessing laboratory measurement skills, for example, correct procedure and accuracy might be stressed early in the instruction, and concern about speed of performance delayed until the later stages of instruction. The particular situation might also influence the importance of the dimension. In evaluating typing skill, for example, speed might be stressed in typing routine business letters, whereas accuracy would be emphasized in typing statistical tables for economic reports.

Simulated Performance

Simulated performance is an attempt to match the performance in a real situation—either in whole or in part. In physical education, for example, swinging a bat at an imaginary ball, shadow boxing, and demonstrating various swimming or tennis strokes are simulated performances. In science, vocational, and business courses, skill activities are frequently designed to simulate portions of actual job performance. In mathematics, the use of computers in solving lifelike problems represents simulated performance. Similarly, in social studies, student role-playing of a jury trial, a city council meeting, or a job interview provides the instructor with opportunities to evaluate the simulated performance of an assigned task. In some cases, specially designed equipment is used for instructional and assessment purposes. In both driver training and flight training, for example, students are frequently trained and tested on simulators. Such simulators may prevent personal injury or damage to expensive equipment during the early stages of skill development. Simulators are also used in various types of vocational training programs.

In some situations, simulated performance testing might be used as the final assessment of a performance skill. This would be the case in assessing students' laboratory performance in chemistry, for example. In many situations, however, skill in a simulated setting simply indicates readiness to attempt actual performance. The student in driver training who has demonstrated driving skill in the simulator, for example, is now ready to apply his or her skill in the actual operation of an automobile.

Work Sample

The work sample requires the student to perform actual tasks that are representative of the total performance to be measured. The sample tasks typically include the most crucial elements of the total performance and are performed under controlled conditions. In being tested for automobile driving skill, for example, the student is required to drive over a standard course that includes the most common problem situations likely to be encountered in normal driving. The performance on the standard course is then used as evidence of the ability to drive an automobile under typical operating conditions.

Performance assessments in business education and industrial education are frequently of the work-sample type. When students are required to take and transcribe shorthand notes from dictation, type a business letter, or operate a computer to analyze business data, a work-sample assessment is being employed. Similarly, in industrial education, a work-sample approach is being used when students are required to complete a metalworking or woodworking project that includes all of the steps likely to be encountered in an actual job situation (steps such as designing, ordering materials, and constructing). Still other examples are the operation of machinery, the repair of equipment, and the performance of job-oriented laboratory tasks. The work-sample approach to assessing performance is widely used in occupations involving performance skills, and many of these situations can be duplicated in the school setting.

Selecting the Method of Observing, Recording, and Scoring

When assessing performances, some type of guided observation and method of recording and scoring the results is needed. Commonly used procedures include (1) systematic observation and anecdotal records, (2) checklists, and (3) rating scales.

Systematic Observation and Anecdotal Records

Observing students in natural settings is one of the most common methods of assessing performance outcomes. Unfortunately, the observations are typically unsystematic and frequently no record is made of the observation. For minor performance tasks that are easily corrected, like how to hold a paintbrush or how to label a graph, informal observation may be all that is needed. For more comprehensive performance situations, however, the observations should be systematic and typically some record of the observation should be made. This will enhance the observations' objectivity, meaningfulness, and usefulness at a later date.

Observations are frequently guided by checklists or rating scales, but there is some advantage in making and recording less structured observations. For example, noting how students approach a task, how persistent they are in completing it, and how carefully they work has significance for evaluating their success in performing the task. Similarly, one student may need assistance on every step of the performance, while another student completes the task early and turns to help others. These important aspects of performance are apt to be overlooked by more structured observational devices but can be described in anecdotal records.

An **anecdotal record** is a brief description of some significant event. It typically includes the observed behaviour, the setting in which it occurred, and a separate interpretation of the event. Although keeping anecdotal records can be time consuming, the task can be kept manageable by limiting the records to certain types of behaviour (e.g., safety) and to those individuals needing the most help (e.g., slow, careless). The records are likely to be most useful when (1) they focus on meaningful incidents, (2) they are recorded soon after the incident, (3) they contain enough information to be understandable later, and (4) the observed incident and its interpretation are kept separate. What is desired is a brief, objective, self-sufficient description of a meaningful incident and a separate interpretation (if needed) of what the incident means. As these records of events accumulate for a particular individual, a typical pattern of behaviour is obtained.

Checklists

The **checklist** is basically a list of measurable dimensions of a performance or product, with a place to record a simple "yes" or "no" judgment. If a checklist were used to evaluate a set of procedures, for example, the steps to be followed might be placed in sequential order on the form; the observer would then simply check whether each action was taken or not taken. A checklist for evaluating a product typically contains a list of the dimensions that characterize a good product (size, colour, shape, and so on), and a place to check whether each desired characteristic is present or absent. Thus, the checklist simply directs attention to the elements to be observed and provides a convenient means of recording judgments.

Construction of a checklist for performance assessment involves the following steps.

1. List the procedural steps or product characteristics to be evaluated.
2. Add common errors to the list, if such is useful in diagnosing poor performance.
3. Arrange the list in some logical order (e.g., sequence of steps).
4. Provide instructions and a place for checking each item.
5. Add a place for comments at the bottom of the form, if needed.

Rating Scales

The rating scale is similar to the checklist and serves somewhat the same purpose in judging procedures and products. The main difference is that the rating scale provides an opportunity to mark the degree to which an element is present instead of using the simple "present–absent" judgment. The scale for rating is typically based on the frequency with which an action is performed (e.g., always, sometimes, never), the general quality of a performance (e.g., outstanding, above average, average, below average), or a set of descriptive phrases that indicate degrees of acceptable performance (e.g., completes task quickly, slow in completing task, cannot complete task without help). Like the checklist, the rating scale directs attention to the dimensions to be observed and provides a convenient form on which to record the judgments.

A sample rating scale for evaluating both procedures and product is shown in Figure 10.2. Although this numerical rating scale uses fixed alternatives, the same scale items could be described by descriptive phrases that vary from item to item.

In this case, each rated item would be arranged as follows:

(a) Plan for the project

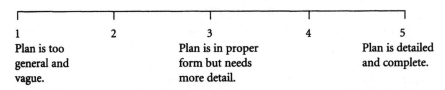

A space for comments might also be added under each item, or at the bottom of each set of items, to provide a place for clarifying the ratings or describing how to improve performance.

FIGURE 10.2 • Rating scale of a woodworking project.

Directions: Rate each of the following items by circling the appropriate number. The numbers represent the following values: 5—outstanding; 4—above average; 3—average; 2—below average; 1—unsatisfactory.

Procedure Rating Scale
How effective was the student's performance in each of the following areas?

5 4 3 2 1   (a)   Preparing a detailed plan for the project.
5 4 3 2 1   (b)   Determining the amount of material needed.
5 4 3 2 1   (c)   Selecting the proper tools.
5 4 3 2 1   (d)   Following the correct procedure for each operation.
5 4 3 2 1   (e)   Using tools properly and skillfully.
5 4 3 2 1   (f)   Using materials without unnecessary spoilage.
5 4 3 2 1   (g)   Completing the work within a reasonable amount of time.

Product Rating Scale
To what extent does the product meet the following criteria?

5 4 3 2 1   (a)   The product appears neat and well constructed.
5 4 3 2 1   (b)   The dimensions match the original plan.
5 4 3 2 1   (c)   The finish meets specifications.
5 4 3 2 1   (d)   The joints and parts fit properly.
5 4 3 2 1   (e)   The materials were used effectively.

The construction of a rating scale for performance assessment typically includes the following steps.

1. List the procedural steps or product characteristics to be evaluated.

2. Select the number of points to use on the scale and define them by descriptive terms or phrases.

3. Arrange the items on the rating scale so that they are easy to use.

4. Provide clear, brief instructions that tell the rater how to mark items on the scale.

5. Provide a place for comments, if needed for diagnostic or instructional purposes.

Analytic Versus Holistic Scoring

The discussion on analytic and holistic scoring earlier in this chapter applies to performance assessment as well, but there are some important differences. Scoring rubrics (i.e., scoring guides) for a psychomotor skill are shown in Box 10.11. These descriptions of each level do not provide for analysis of the performance, but simply list the criteria to keep in mind when making the overall judgment.

Again, for most instructional purposes, both holistic and analytic scoring are useful: one gives the global judgment of the performance, and the other provides diagnostic information useful for improving performance. Where both are used, the global judgment should be made first so some specific element does not distort the general impression of the product. As with product assessment, scoring keys have the advantage of being easy to construct, and of telling the student exactly what his or her strengths and weaknesses are.

BOX 10.11 • *General Scoring Rubric for a Psychomotor Skill*

Excellent	Uses procedure rapidly and skillfully. Explains function of each step in procedure. Modifies procedure to fit changing conditions.
Good	Uses procedure correctly but with some hesitation. Gives general explanation of steps in procedure. Modifies procedure but needs some instructor guidance.
Acceptaable	Uses procedure correctly but is slow and clumsy. Explanation of procedure is limited. Modifies procedures but only after demonstration by instructor.
Inadequate	Fails to use procedure correctly. Explanation of procedure shows lack of understanding. Uses trial and error in adjusting procedure.

Improving Performance Assessments

Performance assessments can provide useful information concerning student achievement, but they are subject to all of the errors of observation and judgment—such as personal bias, generosity error (tendency to overrate), and halo effect (judging individual characteristics in terms of a general impression). Thus, if performance assessments are to provide valid information, special care must be taken to improve the objectivity, reliability, and meaningfulness of the results. The guidelines listed in Box 10.12 enumerate ways to improve the usefulness of performance assessments.

Special Considerations

Adapting product assignments for special needs students is generally easier than adapting tests. As the product does not have to be the same for all students, the special needs student can be assigned a task within his or her capability. The requirements can be made less complex, the length shorter, or an entirely different task can be assigned. As always, the time to make the decision is in the planning stages, when the parents and student (if appropriate) can be consulted.

Performances are particularly important with regard to special needs students, because they are carried out in view of the other students. The teacher should take every opportunity to include the special needs student in class activities, but there are some things special needs students simply cannot do and should not be asked to do. On the other hand, just because the student cannot perform as well as others does not mean he

---

BOX 10.12 • *Improving Performance Assessments*

1. Specify the intended performance outcomes in observable terms and describe the use to be made of the results.
2. Limit the observable dimensions of the performance to a reasonable number.
3. Provide clear, definite criteria for judging the procedure or product.
4. Select the performance setting that provides the most relevant and realistic situation.
5. If a structured performance situation is used, provide clear and complete instructions.
6. Be as objective as possible in observing, judging, and recording the performance.
7. Observe the performance under various conditions and use multiple observations whenever possible.
8. Make a record as soon as possible after an observation.
9. Use evaluation forms that are clear, relevant, and easy to use.
10. Use a scoring procedure that is appropriate for the use to be made of the results (e.g., holistic for global evaluation, analytic for diagnostic purposes).
11. Inform students of the method and criteria to be used in evaluating the performance.
12. Supplement and verify performance assessments with other evidence of achievement.

or she should be excluded. Talk to the parents and, if appropriate, to the student before making a decision.

If the student is to perform, will the requirements or method of measurement be changed? Will students' peer assessment be different?

Perhaps the most important consideration with regard to special needs students and performances is the need for all students to accept their differences. This is, of course, important at all times, but especially so when the special needs student is performing in front of the class. Teachers must prepare the students at the beginning of the year, or when a special needs student is enrolled in the class, and shortly before the performance takes place as well.

If it is not deemed appropriate that the student perform in front of the class, can it be done after school or at lunch hour, in front of a smaller group? Would the support of another student help?

Summary of Points

1. Product and performance assessments provide direct evidence of valued learning outcomes that cannot be adequately assessed by traditional paper and pencil testing, but they are time consuming to use and require greater use of judgment in scoring.

2. Product and performance tasks contain knowledge and affective components as well as the skill component. All three components must be considered when planning these assessments.

3. Writing objectives involves stating each general objective so that it describes a skill and then defining it by a list of specific outcomes that are relevant, clarify an effective product or performance, and are stated in observable terms that are easily understood by students.

4. Restricted product and performance tasks are highly structured and limited in scope (e.g., construct a graph). Extended product and performance tasks are typically less well structured and broad in scope (e.g., design and conduct an experiment).

5. The first step in product and performance assessment is to specify the intended outcome.

6. Performance and product assessment may focus on a procedure (e.g., giving a speech), or both a procedure and a product (e.g., using tools properly in building a bookcase).

7. In some cases, it may be desirable to emphasize procedure evaluation during the early stages of instruction (e.g., touch system in typing) and product evaluation later (typed letter).

8. There are varying degrees of realism in product and performance assessment, and the aim is to obtain as high a degree of realism as possible within the various constraints (e.g., time, cost, availability of equipment).

9. Paper and pencil assessment is useful as a terminal measure in many areas (e.g., writing, drawing, problem solving) and can serve as a first step toward hands-on performance in others (e.g., procedure for repairing an automobile engine).

10. The identification test is typically concerned with identifying the tools, equipment, and procedures needed for a performance task and serves as an *indirect* measure of performance, or as an instructional device to prepare students for actual performance.

11. A structured performance test provides for an assessment under standard, controlled conditions (e.g., locating a malfunction in electronic equipment). The tools, equipment, conditions, and standards of performance are all carefully prescribed.

12. Performance assessment based on simulated performance (e.g., driver's training simulator) and the work sample (e.g., analyze business data on a computer) has a high degree of realism. Many performance skills in laboratory courses, business education, and industrial education can be evaluated at this level.

13. Observing students in natural settings and keeping anecdotal records can aid in evaluating aspects of performance that are likely to be overlooked by more structured methods (e.g., work habits).

14. Rating scales allow for analytic scoring and direct attention to the performance dimensions to be observed, and provide a convenient form on which to record the judgments.

15. Holistic scoring rubrics and product scales are especially useful where global judgments are being made (e.g., debates, playing a sport).

16. Improving performance assessments involves making clear what is to be observed, how it is to be observed, how the observations are to be recorded, and how the results are to be scored and used. In addition, any procedure that contributes to more objective observations and records will aid in increasing the reliability and meaningfulness of the results.

Learning Exercises

1. In an area in which you are teaching or plan to teach, identify several learning outcomes that can best be measured with product-based assessment tasks. For each learning outcome, construct two tasks.

2. Construct a scoring key for one of the following that would be useful for assessing the product.
   (a) Constructing a map, chart, or graph.
   (b) Writing a personal or business letter.
   (c) Writing a theme, poem, or short story.
   (d) Making a drawing or painting.
   (e) Making a product in home economics.
   (f) Making a product in industrial education.

3. Explain the relative advantages of a holistic descriptor and a scoring key. When would you use one or the other for judging a performance?

References and Additional Reading

Arter, J., and McTighe, J. (2001). *Scoring Rubrics in the Classroom*. Thousand Oaks, CA: Corwin Press.

British Columbia Assessment of Science 1991. Ministry of Education. Victoria, BC

Chase, C.I. (1999). *Contemporary Assessment for Educators*. New York: Longman.

Fitzpatrick, R., and Morrison, E.J. (1971). "Performance and Product Evaluation," Chapter 9 in R.L. Thorndike (ed.), *Educational Measurement*, 2nd ed. Washington, DC: American Council on Education.

Gronlund, N.E. (2000). *How to Write and Use Instructional Objectives*, 6th ed. Upper Saddle River, NJ: Merrill/Prentice-Hall.

Linn, R.L., and Gronlund, N.E. (2000). *Measurement and Assessment in Teaching*, 8th ed. Upper Saddle River, NJ: Merrill/Prentice-Hall.

Oosterhoff, A.C. (2001). *Classroom Applications of Educational Measurement*, 3rd ed. Upper Saddle River, NJ: Merrill/Prentice-Hall.

Weblinks

Assessment of Written Products
This site presents a good discussion of various methods of marking products.
http://www.writeenvironment.com/AssessmentOfWrittenProducts.html

Chemical Structure Drawing and Marking on the Web
This site shows how to mark a product (drawings of chemical structures) that is hard to quantify.
http://science.uniserve.edu.au/workshop/chemit/ridley.html

Landmark Ad
Marking scheme for a complex student product assignment.
http://www.tensigma.org/product_pdfs/pa.ss.all.pdf

Fitness and Skill Testing
Physical education assessment.
http://www.sportschallenge.iinet.net.au/fitness.html

Oregon State Scoring Guide: Speaking
http://www.ode.state.or.us/asmt/resource/scorguides/speakingofficialscoringguide benchmarks123cim.pdf

11

Portfolio Assessment

This chapter will enable you to:

1. Describe the advantages and difficulties of using a portfolio as a means of assessment.
2. Distinguish between a developmental portfolio and a showcase portfolio.
3. List the types of portfolio entries that should be considered in your teaching area.
4. Describe the factors to consider in planning a portfolio.
5. Describe a procedure for getting started in the use of a portfolio in the classroom.
6. Prepare a scoring key for the structural evaluation of a portfolio in your teaching area.
7. Prepare a scoring key for evaluating a student's learning progress as shown in a portfolio in your teaching area.
8. Prepare a holistic scoring rubric for evaluating a student's final level of performance as shown in a portfolio, in your teaching area.

Between 1990 and 2000, portfolios became important means of assessment in many schools. In some schools and districts, they are used as a basic—or sole—method of product assessment. In others, they provide another useful tool in the teacher's assessment kit. A portfolio is a collection of student work that has been selected and organized to show student learning progress (developmental portfolio) or to show samples of the student's best work (showcase portfolio). A common practice is to use the developmental portfolio throughout an instructional program and the showcase portfolio at the end. Thus, the showcase portfolio provides a collection of work that indicates the student's final level of performance. Some schools have used the showcase portfolio as a basis for high school graduation. In the United States, some states have used them on a statewide basis as a means of assessing performance in basic skills. In 2002, British Columbia made portfolios mandatory for secondary school graduation. Our focus will be on **portfolio assessment** in the classroom instructional program.

The assessment value of portfolios is found in the variety of types of evidence that are available for judging student products. They typically include various types of independent work (e.g., writing samples, drawings, research reports, computer worksheets, projects) as well as assessment results in the form of written comments, checklists, rating scales, test scores, and conference reports. The assessment data is also likely to include the student's self-assessments, peer assessments, and teacher assessments. See Box 11.1 for what portfolios can show.

Students play an active role in selecting the entries and maintaining the portfolio. This provides for another important item to be included in a portfolio—that is, the student's reflections on such things as why the entry was chosen, what it illustrates, what was learned, and what might be done to improve performance. These written reflections cause students to focus on the learning process, the changes taking place, and the growth in their learning.

The active participation of students in selecting entries for the portfolio helps them focus on the criteria of successful performance, and their reflections on the criteria provide a basis for developing critical thought and deeper understanding. The criteria also make students aware of their responsibility to participate fully in the learning process, an important step toward becoming independent learners.

Advantages of Using Classroom Portfolios

Portfolios have a number of specific advantages as a means of assessing classroom learning.

1. Learning progress over time can be clearly shown (e.g., changes in writing, thinking, or research skills).

2. Focus on students' best work provides a positive influence on learning (e.g., best writing samples, best examples of reasoning and problem solving).

3. Comparing current work to past work provides greater motivation than comparison to the work of others (e.g., growth in knowledge and skills).

4. Self-assessment skills are increased due to the student selection of best samples of work (e.g., focus is on criteria of good performance).

BOX 11.1 • *What a Student Portfolio Can Show*

1. Learning progress over time.
2. Student's current best work.
3. Comparison of best work to past work.
4. Development of self-assessment skills.
5. Development of reflective learning.
6. Individual's level and pace of work.
7. Clear evidence of learning to parents and others.
8. The amount of teacher–student collaboration involved.

5. Reflective learning is encouraged as students are asked to comment on each portfolio entry (e.g., Why do you consider this your best work?)

6. Portfolios provide for adjustment to individual differences (e.g., students work at their own levels but work toward common goals).

7. Portfolios provide for clear communication of learning progress to students, parents, and others (e.g., work samples obtained at different times can be shown and compared).

8. Use of portfolios increases teacher–student collaboration in the teaching–learning–assessment process.

Problems With Portfolios

Despite the numerous advantages of using portfolios, they are time consuming to maintain and use. Assisting students in the selection of portfolio entries, providing feedback on the students' work, and periodically reviewing the students' learning progress requires considerable student–teacher conference time. A simple collection of samples of student work put into a file does not constitute a portfolio. Much greater care is required in the development of a portfolio that will be useful in instruction and assessment.

In the past year or two, portfolios have fallen out of favour to some extent, partly because too much was expected of them. Portfolios, it was thought by many, would solve many assessment problems, especially in the United States, where teachers were searching for replacements for paper and pencil testing. In fact, while portfolios did solve some problems, they created new ones, and many teachers went back to the methods they had used in the past. This was also true in Canada, where product assessment (which is, of course, the basis for portfolios) has always been an important part of assessment. Specific difficulties include the following.

1. The portfolio has to be maintained. In the case of most elementary (and many secondary) students, the teacher has to do this, or there will be no portfolio after the first month.

2. The portfolio has to be stored safely. If storage space is at a premium in the classroom, that might be difficult.

3. Once completed, the portfolio has to be marked. If the mark is simply the sum of the work in the portfolio—work that was marked as it was collected—this would seem to be a duplication of effort.

4. If the portfolio is to be used to show parents what the student has done, some sort of explanation has to take place.

Planning for the Use of Portfolios

To increase the portfolio's value as an instructional and assessment tool, think carefully about the following major considerations when planning for the use of portfolios in the classroom:

1. Purpose of the portfolio.

2. Types of entries to include.

3. Guidelines for selecting and evaluating the entries.
4. Maintaining and using the portfolio.
5. Evaluating the portfolio.

Each of these will be discussed in turn.

Purpose of the Portfolio

The main purpose of the classroom portfolio, as with any method of assessment, is to improve student learning. As noted earlier, it provides unique contributions to this goal by showing actual samples of student work, providing for comparisons of work in different areas and progress over time, providing opportunities for students to evaluate their own work and reflect on it, conveying clear evidence of learning to all interested persons, and increasing students' participation in the learning process.

Although the main purpose of the assessment portfolio is to improve student learning, a secondary purpose is to help students become responsible for their own learning. This means students actively participate in selecting the samples to be included in the portfolios, in assessing the quality of entries, in reflecting on what was learned and how to improve performance, in maintaining the portfolio, and in evaluating it. All of this is done under the guidance of the teacher, of course, but there should be a weaning away of control as students become increasingly capable of independent learning.

In some schools, the students have limited opportunity to participate because of the requirements set by the department, school, or district. All a teacher can do in these cases, obviously, is to provide the students with as much freedom of choice as is allowed by the constraints. For example, if the nature of the task and the criteria for the assessment are predetermined, provide students with a limited choice of tasks within that framework.

Portfolios may be set up for more specific purposes than the assessment portfolio we have been discussing. For example, a portfolio may be used to showcase only the student's best work for use in grading, accountability, or placement in permanent school records. A portfolio may be limited to evidence that shows the development of student self-assessment skills and growth toward becoming an independent learner. A portfolio may be limited to the development of research skills only. We have been stressing the comprehensive use of portfolios in assessing student learning, but portfolios can serve a variety of purposes. Thus, it is important to be clear about the purpose of the portfolio. This will help answer the following basic questions.

1. What understandings and skills should result from the use of the portfolio?
2. What types of performance tasks are best for providing the needed evidence?
3. Who are the users of the portfolio and how will they use it?

Types of Entries To Include

The selection of entries for the portfolio is guided by the purpose, the intended learning outcomes, and the use to be made of the results. If the portfolio is limited to a specific area such as writing skill, the entries might be limited to one type of writing (e.g., narrative) or include different types of writing tasks (e.g., letters, essays, poetry). The entries might also include writing on different topics or in specific content areas (e.g., scientific writing). Both the first draft of the writing and later revisions might also be included. The specific types of entries will depend on the goals of instruction, how the information is to be used in the instructional programs, and with whom the information will be shared.

A more comprehensive portfolio will include samples of various types of student work, depending on the area of instruction. In math, for example, entries might include samples of problem solving, written explanations of how to solve problems, mathematical charts and graphs, and computer printouts of problem solving. Science entries might include examples of experimental studies, laboratory skills, evidence of conceptual understandings, student-designed projects, and field studies. The types of entries to include will, of course, vary with the purpose of the portfolio, the grade level, the instructional objectives, and any school requirements concerning the nature of the portfolio.

As noted earlier, each entry should be accompanied by the student's reflections on the entry, possibly written on a brief form with spaces for answering questions like, What did I do? What did I learn? How would I improve it? Such questions cause students to think about their learning and their need to take responsibility for it.

In addition to the other entries, portfolios should also include test scores, checklists, rating scales, and other types of relevant data used for assessing learning (see Box 11.2).

Guidelines for Selecting and Evaluating the Entries

The portfolio should not be a repository for all of the student's work. If this is done, it becomes too cumbersome and unmanageable. Its content should be a sample of the student's best work, or latest work in progress, in selected areas. The areas may be determined by the teacher or by school requirements. In any event, the selection and evaluation of the portfolio entries should be determined by guidelines such as the following.

1. Entries should be in harmony with the goals of instruction and the use to be made of the portfolio (e.g., to improve learning, for use in parent–teacher conferences, as part of a schoolwide assessment).

2. Entries should provide a variety of types of evidence (e.g., written, oral, exhibits, projects).

3. Entries should be selected in terms of the criteria to be used in judging them.

BOX 11.2 • *What Types of Entries Should Be Included*

1. Entries selected by students (e.g., work samples, writing samples, drawings, performance tasks, projects, assessment results).

2. Student reflections on the entries:

    2.1 Why was this entry selected?
    2.2 What was done to accomplish it?
    2.3 What was learned from it?
    2.4 What changes would improve it?

4. Entries should be selected by students, or at least they should be involved in the process.

5. Entries should be complex enough to allow for students' self-evaluations and their reflections on the learning that resulted.

6. Entries should be started early in the instructional program, the better to show growth in learning.

7. Entries should be evaluated by using the criteria and standards established for the performance tasks.

The procedure for developing criteria for evaluating the portfolio entries is the same here as for any product task, like those discussed in Chapter 10. The criteria should specify the types of performance we are willing to accept as evidence of a quality product, and the standards should identify the various levels of acceptable performance. These are then used in preparing scoring keys or holistic scoring rubrics to be used in the assessments.

The criteria can aid students in selecting, preparing, and evaluating the samples to be entered in the portfolio by focusing their attention on the elements to be included in the product. In working on a problem-solving project, for example, criteria like those discussed in the last chapter make clear to the students that the project requires a realistic problem, the selection and use of various resources, a written report, the preparation of an exhibit, and an oral report to a group. The specific criteria in each area make clear how the project will be judged and thus provide direction for student learning. Within the framework provided by the criteria, the students are still free to select a problem that interests them.

Our discussion makes clear why the criteria and standards must be shared with students at the beginning of the instruction. They provide guidelines for the preparation of the portfolio entries, for the students' self-assessments and reflections, and for the final assessment of the performance.

Maintaining and Using the Portfolios

The portfolio entries are typically placed in file folders or notebooks and stored in a cabinet. As noted earlier, it is important to keep the portfolio entries down to a manageable number, so that they can be arranged in an orderly and useful manner. A hodgepodge collection of material is apt to defeat the purpose of using portfolios. Arranging the entries by sections and placing a table of contents in front of the file makes it easier to maintain the file and to locate material when evaluating learning progress or reporting to parents. Each entry should be dated and labelled before placing it in the file.

Students should actively participate in the maintenance of the portfolio. It is a collection of their work, so they should aid in setting the guidelines for what goes into the portfolio, selecting the portfolio samples, and evaluating the progress reflected in the samples of work. Unless a student is an active participant, he or she is likely to feel that it is not a personal portfolio.

The portfolio is to be reviewed periodically during a student–teacher conference. Here, student and teacher can view the content together, compare evaluations, and discuss strengths in learning progress and areas where improvement is needed. The portfolio is also used in parent–teacher conferences to demonstrate and discuss student achievement. There is no better way to make clear to parents what a student is learning than by the use of actual samples of student work.

If portfolios have not been used in the school before, one might start on a small scale. A safe approach is to start with one specific area, such as writing, drawing, problem solving, laboratory work, or some other relevant learning activity. This makes it possible to practise the procedure with a limited and clearly defined task. The goals and criteria can be more easily specified, the nature of the entries is more readily identifiable, and the entire process is more manageable. Once experience is obtained in helping students select entries, evaluate and reflect on their work, and maintain the portfolio, other content and skills can be added.

The specific nature of the portfolio entries varies so widely from one instructional area to another and one level of instruction to another that it is wise to consult some of the numerous references on portfolio design and use before getting started. Especially useful are those illustrating the criteria, forms, and procedures used in specific content areas. The references at the end of this chapter provide a sample of helpful resource material.

Evaluating the Portfolio

As noted earlier, criteria for each performance task that is to serve as an entry should be clearly specified beforehand, as is done with any performance assessment. The criteria provide guidelines for preparing and evaluating the entry and should be shared with students early in the process. They are typically converted to rating scales or other scoring rubrics that can be used in self-assessment, peer assessment, and teacher assessment. The specification of criteria and their use in task assessment have been discussed and illustrated earlier and need not be repeated here. In addition to these specific performance assessments, however, there is a need to evaluate the portfolio structure and the students' overall performance.

Evaluating the Portfolio Structure

The criteria for evaluating the structure of the portfolio should clarify the main features of an effective portfolio. Although these will vary somewhat with the content and level of instruction, some general criteria should apply to all portfolios. The list in Box 11.3 (page 173) includes some of main ones to be considered.

General criteria such as these provide guidelines both for developing a portfolio and for detecting shortcomings in its makeup. Criteria for evaluating a portfolio in a given content area could be made more specific and content oriented. For example, in a science course, item 2 might be stated as, "Does the portfolio provide evidence of understandings, laboratory skills, and research skills?" Thus, the general criteria can serve as a guide for developing a more content-relevant set of criteria.

Evaluating the Student's Overall Portfolio Performance

In addition to the evaluation of individual samples as they are entered in the portfolio, there is a need to evaluate the student's overall performance. Criteria concerning the

BOX 11.3 • *General Criteria for Evaluating the Portfolio's Structure*

1. Has the purpose of the portfolio been clearly stated?
2. Does the portfolio provide evidence of various types of student learning?
3. Does the portfolio include evidence of complex learning in realistic settings?
4. Does the portfolio include enough entries in each area to make valid judgments?
5. Does the portfolio include students' self-evaluations and their reflections on what was learned?
6. Does the portfolio enable one to determine learning progress and current level of learning?
7. Does the portfolio provide clear evidence of learning to users of the portfolio?
8. Does the portfolio provide for student participation and responsibility?
9. Does the portfolio provide guidelines for the student participation?
10. Does the portfolio present the entries in a well organized and useful manner?
11. Does the portfolio include assessments based on clearly stated criteria of successful performance?
12. Does the portfolio provide for greater interaction between instruction and assessment?

improvement in performance during the year and the final level of performance can provide the basis for a rating scale or holistic scoring rubric.

Evaluating Student Improvement. For evaluating a student's improvement over the school year, a scoring key is typically favoured because it can focus attention on the student's strengths and weaknesses. A scoring key based on general criteria is shown in Box 11.4. Note that all criteria in the example have been given equal weight: if certain criteria are deemed to be more important than others, they should be weighted more.

The items in our illustrative scoring key are, obviously, very general but they illustrate the types of items to consider when preparing this form of assessment instrument. The specific items to include would be determined by the instructional area, the intended learning outcomes of the instruction, and the purpose of the portfolio. A set of items for a writing portfolio, for example, would focus on the improvement of specific writing skills (e.g., word choice, sentence structure, organization, flow of ideas, etc.). A language arts portfolio would not only include specific items on writing skills but also on reading skills, reading comprehension, and speaking and listening skills. In addition to the specific items needed to fit the nature of the instruction, however, some of the general criteria still should be considered. Growth in self-assessment skills, reflective skills, and independent learning should be of interest in all areas of instruction.

The unique advantage of the portfolio in assessing student growth is that the entries over the school year provide sequential evidence of changes in student performance that can be examined and re-examined, if needed, when judging the degree of improvement. The scoring key simply provides a convenient place to record the judgments. As with the assessment of individual entries, the students can also use the scoring key to rate their own overall improvement and, if desired, compare it to the teacher's ratings.

BOX 11.4 • *Portfolio Ratings of Student Improvement*

Directions: Rate each of the following items by circling the appropriate number. The numbers represent the following values: 4—outstanding progress; 3—good progress; 2—satisfactory progress; 1—unsatisfactory progress.

To what extent does the student show improvement in:

4	3	2	1	Understanding of concepts
4	3	2	1	Application of information
4	3	2	1	Reasoning ability
4	3	2	1	Writing skills
4	3	2	1	Speaking skills
4	3	2	1	Problem-solving skills
4	3	2	1	Performance skills
4	3	2	1	Computational skills
4	3	2	1	Computer skills
4	3	2	1	Self-assessment skills
4	3	2	1	Reflection skills
4	3	2	1	Work-study skills
4	3	2	1	Independent learning

Evaluating the Student's Final Level of Performance. For an evaluation of the student's final level of performance, a holistic scoring rubric is preferred. Here we are interested in an overall impression of each student's terminal performance. If the portfolio is focused on one limited area of instruction, such as narrative writing, a single scoring rubric may suffice. However, for most courses of instruction, several scoring rubrics would be needed. In science, for example, separate scoring rubrics for understanding science concepts, application of concepts and methods, scientific research skills, and process skills may be needed. In math, separate scoring rubrics for conceptual understanding, problem solving, reasoning ability, and using math in communications might be needed.

The preparation of scoring rubrics for an overall evaluation of a student's final level of performance is time consuming but the following outline of steps should help.

   1. **Prepare a list of criteria for each scoring rubric to be prepared.** A review of the instructional objectives and the criteria used for portfolio entries should help here. For overall assessment of a student's final level of performance in the portfolio, however, there is a problem of selecting a limited number of criteria. A list of six or fewer is desirable so that the scoring rubric does not become too cumbersome. This means focusing on the most important criteria for judging the quality of the performance. A common procedure is to state the criteria you think are most important and then consult the literature to get help on how to combine them into a list of major criteria.

   2. **Select the number of categories of performance to be used.** A good procedure is to start with four categories and expand it to six or eight if finer distinctions are needed. It is frequently difficult to describe more than four discrete levels of performance. A guide for preparing holistic scoring rubrics, using four categories, is presented in Box 11.5 (page 175). The commonly used category labels and the frequently used terms

for stating criteria were gleaned from currently used scoring rubrics in various content areas. The lists are not meant to be exhaustive and should not be used in a perfunctory manner, but they should be helpful in getting started.

3. Adapt scoring rubrics from published sources. The literature on portfolios and scoring rubrics provides numerous examples of scoring rubrics in various areas of instruction that might be adapted for use in an overall evaluation of student performance. Because of the difficulty of preparing holistic scoring rubrics, selecting those rubrics that seem most appropriate and then adapting them by modifying the criteria to fit your particular instructional situation and type of portfolio can provide a good way to start. When completed, check to be sure they are appropriate for your use.

4. Check your prepared scoring rubrics to see if they work as intended. When you have completed the sets of scoring rubrics, try them out by evaluating students' sample portfolios. This will help you determine if the criteria focus on the most important areas of performance and provide clear distinctions between the various levels of performance. At this point you might just need some fine-tuning.

Special Considerations

Portfolios can be very useful for special needs students. Because the portfolio is unique to each student, it matters not that the special needs student is not doing the same work

BOX 11.5 • *Guide for Preparing Holistic Scoring Rubrics*

Level Number	Category Labels	Frequently Used Terms When Stating Criteria	
4	Exemplary	Sophisticated	Thorough
	Superior	Extensive	Deep
	Distinguished	Comprehensive	Elegant
	Excellent	Unique	Perceptive
		Clear	Efficient
3	Satisfactory	Appropriate	Mostly
	Adequate	Consistent	Clear
	Competent	Relevant	Accurate
	Good	Acceptable	Broad
		Detailed	Variety
2	Minimal	Paraphrases	Inconsistent
	Borderline	Shallow	Incomplete
	Marginal	Limited	Basic
	Fair	Weak	Minor
		Minimal	Conventional
1	Unsatisfactory	Trivial	Incoherent
	Inadequate	Unclear	Lacks
	Incomplete	Vague	Disorganized
	Poor	General	Irrelevant
		Inaccurate	Superficial

as are other students. The portfolio will contain whatever the student has produced. For ESL students, the portfolio can serve as a record of learning English, a record that can be kept as a family document for generations to come. For students with an IEP, the portfolio can provide evidence that the objectives of the IEP are being met. Students will require help with the portfolio, perhaps more help than other students will need, but it is time well spent. In fact, even if you decide not to have all students keep portfolios when you become a teacher, you may well have special needs students keep one.

Summary of Points

1. A portfolio is a collection of student work that has been selected and organized to show learning progress (developmental portfolio) or to show the student's best work (showcase portfolio).
2. Both types of portfolios are useful in the classroom—the developmental to show student growth during the school year, and the showcase to indicate final level of learning.
3. The assessment value of portfolios is found in the vast array of evidence of learning they provide, the actual use of students' samples of work, the active participation of students in selecting entries and maintaining the portfolio, and the variety of types of assessment data included.
4. The specific advantages of using a portfolio in the classroom are that it shows actual samples of student work, provides for comparisons of work in different areas and growth over time, provides students with an opportunity to evaluate and reflect on their work, provides clear evidence of learning to all interested persons, and provides for increased participation of students in the teaching–learning–assessment process.
5. Problems with portfolios include the need for teachers to supervise the collection and storage, marking, and storage space.
6. Planning for the use of portfolios involves determining their purpose, the types of entries to include, the guidelines for selecting and evaluating the entries, the procedures for maintaining and using the portfolio, and the criteria for an overall evaluation of the portfolio.
7. Although the main purpose of using a portfolio is to improve student learning, a secondary purpose is to encourage students to participate more actively in the learning process and become more responsible for their own learning. This is an important step in students' becoming independent learners.
8. The structural evaluation of a portfolio can be accomplished by considering a series of questions concerning its makeup, organization, and content.
9. The overall evaluation of student progress shown in the portfolio can be determined by a rating scale that focuses on the learning outcomes being assessed by the portfolio.
10. The final level of student performance can best be determined by holistic scoring rubrics for each of the major areas of instruction included in the portfolio.

Learning Exercises

1. Suppose you were designing a portfolio for this assessment class.
    (a) What are two purposes that might be served by a portfolio for this class?
    (b) In what ways would the portfolio need to be different for these two purposes?
    (c) Specify guidelines for inclusion of six entries in the portfolio.
    (d) Describe scoring guidelines for one of the six entries and for obtaining an overall portfolio score.
    (e) Discuss the advantages and disadvantages of using a portfolio for the two purposes you identified.

2. Obtain, if possible, examples of one or more student portfolios and guidelines used by the student's teacher to specify how students should construct their portfolios. Review and evaluate the portfolio of work using either the evaluation criteria provided by the teacher or, if there are none, criteria that you specify. Analyze the strengths and weaknesses of the portfolio guidelines.

3. Find a person who has a portfolio to be used in the real world (an artist, a model, a designer, an architect). Discuss the contents with the owner, and prepare a presentation for the class, explaining the rationale for the contents.

References and Additional Reading

Arter, J., and McTighe, J. (2001). *Scoring Rubrics in the Classroom.* Thousand Oaks, CA: Corwin Press.

Cole, D.J., Ryan, C.W., Kick, F., and Mathies, B.K. (2000). *Portfolios Across the Curriculum and Beyond,* 2nd ed. Thousand Oaks, CA: Corwin Press.

Johnson, B. (1996). *Performance Assessment Handbook: Volume 1, Portfolios and Socratic Seminars* (Princeton, NJ: Eye on Education.

Linn, R.L., and Gronlund, N.E. (2000). *Measurement and Assessment in Teaching,* 8th ed. Upper Saddle River, NJ: Merrill/Prentice-Hall.

McMillan, J.H. (2001). *Classroom Assessment: Principles and Practices for Effective Instruction,* 2nd ed. Boston: Allyn and Bacon.

Weblinks

Portfolios for Assessment and Instruction
Provides framework for development and use of portfolios in instruction and assessment.
http://ericae.net/db/edo/ED388890htm

Writing Portfolios at the Elementary Level: A Study of Methods for Writing
Assessment provides examples of scoring rubrics.
http://www.cse.ucla.edu/

The Evolution of a Portfolio Program: The Impact and Quality of the Vermont Program in the Second Year
Describes the Vermont experience with portfolios.
http://www.cse.ucla.edu/

12

Grading and Reporting

This chapter will enable you to:

1. Distinguish between absolute grading and relative grading.
2. Describe how to select a proper frame of reference, or standard, for assigning grades.
3. Explain why learning ability, improvement, and effort provide a poor basis for grading.
4. Describe and defend the grading system you would use in your area of instruction.
5. Demonstrate how properly to weight components to be included in a grade.
6. Describe a rationale for making the pass–fail decision.
7. Write a statement—to be given to students—that describes your grading procedures.
8. Report learning progress to students and parents.

Grades assigned to student work should represent the extent to which the instructional objectives (i.e., the intended learning outcomes) have been achieved and should be in harmony with the grading policies of the school. Some schools have both clearly defined objectives and grading policies; many schools have neither. With or without the guidance of clear-cut policies and procedures, the assigning of grades is a difficult and frustrating task. It is somewhat easier if valid evidence of achievement has been gathered throughout the course.

Assessment of learning during instruction might include the use of objective and essay tests, ratings, papers, and various types of performance assessment. The problem of grading is that of summarizing this diverse collection of information into a single letter grade or brief report. Because the single letter grade (e.g., A, B, C, D, F) is the most widely used grading system, we shall focus on how best to assign such grades. This involves several important considerations: (1) What frame of reference, or standard, should be used to report level of performance? (2) How should the performance data be combined for grading? (3) What guidelines should be followed to provide the most effective and fair grading system? Each of these will be discussed in turn.

Selecting the Basis for Grading

Letter grades are typically assigned by comparing a student's performance to a prespecified standard of performance (absolute or criterion-referenced grading) or to the performance of the members of a group (relative or norm-referenced grading). In some cases, grades are based on or modified by the learning ability of the student, the amount of improvement shown over a given instructional period, or student effort. As we shall see later, these factors provide an inadequate basis for assigning grades.

Absolute or Standards-Based Grading

A common type of absolute grading is the use of letter grades defined by a 100-point system. Whether assigning grades to an individual set of test scores or as a basis for the final grades in a course, the set of grades might be expressed as one of the following:

		Points	Points	Points
A	=	90–100	95–100	91–100
B	=	80–89	85–94	86–90
C	=	70–79	75–84	81–85
D	=	60–69	65–74	75–80
F	=	below 60	below 65	below 75

In the case of an individual test, this 100-point system might represent the percentage of items correct or the total number of points earned on the test. When used as a final grade, it typically represents a combination of scores from various tests and other assessment results. In any event, it provides an absolute basis for assigning letter grades.

Which set of points provides the best basis for assigning grades? There is no way of knowing. The distribution of points is arbitrary. Whatever distribution is used, however, should be based on the teacher's experience with this and past groups of students, knowledge concerning the difficulty of the intended learning outcomes, the difficulty of the tests and other assessments used, the conditions of learning, and the like. These are all subjective judgments, however, and shifts in the proportion of students getting the letter grade of A or F are difficult to evaluate. Do a larger number of grades of A represent improved instruction and better study habits by students, or easier tests and less rigid grading of papers and projects? Do more failures indicate poor teaching, inadequate study, or assessments that have inadvertently increased in difficulty?

Despite the problem of setting meaningful standards for an absolute grading system, this method is widely used in schools. It is most appropriate in programs where the set of learning tasks has been clearly specified, the standards have been defined in terms of the learning tasks, and the tests and other assessment techniques have been designed for criterion-referenced interpretation. All too frequently, however, absolute grading is based on some hodgepodge of ill-defined achievement results. When the distribution of points does not fit the grading scale, the points are adjusted upward or downward by some obscure formula to get a closer fit. Needless to say, such grades do not provide a meaningful report of the extent to which the intended learning outcomes have been achieved.

Relative or Norm-Based Grading

When assigning grades on a relative basis, the students are typically ranked in order of performance (based on a set of test scores or combined assessment results) and the students ranking highest receive a letter grade of A, the next highest receive a B, and so on. What proportion of students should receive each grade is predetermined and might appear as one of the following:

	Percent of Students	Percent of Students
A	15	10–20
B	25	20–30
C	45	40–50
D	10	10–20
F	5	0–10

The percent of students to be assigned each grade is just as arbitrary as the selection of points for each grade in the absolute grading system. The use of a range of percents (e.g., A = 10–20 percent) should probably be favoured because it makes some allowance for differences in the ability level of the class. It does not make sense to assign an A to 15 percent of both a regular class and a gifted class. Likewise, in an advanced course a larger proportion of A and B grades should be assigned and fewer (if any) F grades because the low-achieving students have been "weeded out" in earlier courses. When these percentages have been set by the school system, one has little choice but to follow the school practice—at least until efforts to change it are successful.

Older measurement books recommended using the normal curve to assign grades. This resulted in the same percent of A and F grades (e.g., 7 percent) and B and D grades (e.g., 38 percent). Although some teachers may still use such a system, its use should be discouraged. Measures of achievement in classroom groups seldom yield normally distributed scores. Also, to maintain the same proportion of grades, especially failures, at different grade levels does not take into account that the student population is becoming increasingly select as the failing students are held back or drop out of school.

The relative grading system requires a reliable ranking of students; thus, it is most meaningful when the achievement measures provide a wide range of scores. This makes it possible to draw the lines between grades with greater assurance that misclassifications will be kept to a minimum. Ideally, of course, the spread of scores should be based on the difficulty and complexity of the material learned. For example, an A should not simply represent more knowledge of factual material, but a higher level of understanding, application, and thinking skills. Thus, although norm-referenced interpretation is being utilized, the real meaning of the grades comes from referring back to the nature of the achievement that each grade represents. See Box 12.1 (page 181) for a summary comparison of absolute and relative grading.

Learning Ability, Improvement, and Effort

In some cases, attempts are made to base grades on achievement in relation to learning ability, the amount of improvement in achievement, or the amount of effort a student puts forth. All of these procedures have problems that distort the meaning of grades.

BOX 12.1 • *Absolute Grading and Relative Grading*

ABSOLUTE GRADING

Strengths

1. Grades can be described directly in terms of student performance, without reference to the performance of others.

2. All students can obtain high grades if mastery outcomes are stressed and instruction is effective.

Limitations

1. Performance standards are set in an arbitrary manner and are difficult to specify and justify.

2. Performance standards tend to vary unintentionally due to variations in test difficulty, assignments, student ability, and instructional effectiveness.

3. Grades can be assigned without clear reference to what has been achieved (but, of course, they should not be).

4. Where teachers assign marks largely on the basis of products and performances rather than tests, student grades can be as much a result of teacher marking behaviour as of student achievement.

RELATIVE GRADING

Strengths

1. Grades can easily be described and interpreted in terms of rank in a group.

2. Grades distinguish among levels of student performance that are useful in making prediction and selection decisions.

3. When there is a limited number of rewards available (scholarships, entry to post-secondary institutions, for instance), relative grading is the only fair way to decide who gets the rewards.

Limitations

1. The percent of students receiving each grade is arbitrarily set.

2. The meaning of a grade varies with the ability of the student group.

3. Grades can be assigned without clear reference to what has been achieved (but, of course, they should not be).

Grading on the basis of *learning ability* has sometimes been used at the elementary level to motivate students with less ability. At first glance, it seems sensible to give a grade of A to students who are achieving all that they are capable of achieving. There are two major problems with this procedure, however. First, it is difficult, if not impossible, to get a dependable measure of learning ability apart from achievement. Both tests have similar type items and measure similar concepts. Second, the meaning of the grades becomes distorted. A low-ability student with average performance might receive an A, whereas a high-ability student with average performance receives a grade of C. Obviously, the grades are no longer very meaningful as indicators of achievement.

This procedure has serious problems for teachers in future years, as they cannot rely on the grades shown on the student's records. Using the amount of *improvement* as a basis for grading also has its problems. For one, the difference scores between measures of achievement over short spans of time are very unreliable. For another, students who score high on the entry test cannot possibly get a high grade because little improvement can be shown. Students who know about this grading procedure ahead of time can, of course, do poorly on the first test and be assured of a fairly good grade. This is not an uncommon practice where grades are based on improvement. Finally, the grades lack meaning as indicators of achievement when increase in achievement becomes more important than level of achievement. For example, a low-achieving student with considerable improvement might receive an A, while a high-achieving student with little improvement receives a B or C. Again, teachers in later years will be handicapped by this procedure.

Grading on the basis of *effort,* or adjusting grades for effort, also distorts the meaning of the results. Low-achieving students who put forth great effort receive higher grades than their achievement warrants and high-achieving students who put forth little effort are likely to receive lower grades than deserved. Although such grading seems to serve a motivational function for low-achieving students, the grades become meaningless as measures of the extent to which students are achieving the intended learning outcomes.

In summary, assigning grades that take into account learning ability, amount of improvement, or effort simply contaminates the grades and distorts their meaning as indicators of student achievement. A letter grade is most useful when it represents achievement—and only achievement. Other factors may be rated separately on a report card, and should be, but they should not be allowed to distort the meaning of the letter grade.

A Combination of Absolute and Relative Grading

Grades should represent the degree to which instructional objectives (i.e., intended learning outcomes) are achieved by students. Some of the objectives of instruction are concerned with minimum essentials that must be mastered if a student is to proceed to the next level of instruction. Other objectives are concerned with learning outcomes that are never fully achieved but toward which students can show varying degrees of progress. The first are called minimal objectives and the second developmental objectives.

Minimal objectives are concerned with the knowledge, skill, and other lower-level learning outcomes that represent the minimum essentials of the course. In order to receive a passing grade, a student must demonstrate that this basic knowledge and skill, which are prerequisite to further learning in the area, have been learned to a satisfactory degree. *Developmental objectives* are concerned with higher-level learning outcomes such as understanding, application, and thinking skills. Although we can identify degrees of progress toward these objectives, we cannot expect ever to achieve them fully. In science, for example, we might expect all students to master basic terms, concepts, and skills, but encourage each student to proceed as far as he or she can in understanding and applying the scientific process and in developing the intellectual skills used by scientists. Similarly, all students in math might be expected to master the fundamental operations, but show wide diversity in problem-solving ability and mathematical reasoning. In all instructional areas there are lower-level objectives that should be mastered by all students and higher-level objectives that provide goals that never can be fully achieved. Thus, with minimal objectives we attempt to obtain a uniformly high level of performance for all students, and with developmental objectives we encourage each stu-dent to strive for maximum development.

As indicated earlier, the pass–fail decision should be based on whether the minimal objectives have been mastered. Students demonstrating that they have achieved the min-imal objectives, and thus have the necessary prerequisites for success at the next level of instruction, should be passed. Those who do not should fail. This requires an *absolute* judgment, not a relative one. Students should not be failed simply because their achieve-ment places them near the bottom of some group. It is the nature of the achievement that is significant.

Above the pass–fail cutoff point, grades should be assigned on a relative basis. This is because students' scores will tend to be spread out in terms of their degree of devel-opment beyond the minimal level. Students cannot be expected to master the more complex learning outcomes described by developmental objectives, but they can show varying degrees of progress toward their attainment. Although it would be ideal to have a scale of achievement ranging from simple to complex so that absolute grading could be used, this is not possible at this time. The best we can do is obtain a spread of student achievement scores in terms of the complexity of the learning outcomes attained and use relative grading. If properly done, a grade of A would represent greater achievement of the higher-level learning outcomes and not simply a high relative position in the group. This would assume, of course, that tests and other assessment techniques would measure a range of achievement from simple to complex, and not just knowledge of fac-tual information and simple skills.

In most cases the province, district, or school will dictate the grading policy, includ-ing the basis on which the grades are to be assigned. Regardless of the system used, it is important to relate the grades back to student achievement so that different grades rep-resent different levels of performance. Letter grades without an achievement referent tend to have little meaning. It is important that all teachers in a school use the same phi-losophy and method for assigning grades. There is plenty of room for individuality in other areas of teaching, but parents and students want consistency in grading.

Combining Data for Grading

Assigning grades typically involves combining results from various types of assessment, including such things as tests, projects, papers, and laboratory work. If each element is to be included in the grade in terms of its relative importance, the data must be com-bined in such a way that proper weights are used. For example, if we want test scores to count for 50 percent, papers 25 percent, and laboratory work 25 percent of the grade, we need a method that will result in grades that reflect this emphasis. The process is sim-plified if all assessment results are converted to numerical scores first. It is then simply a matter of following a systematic procedure of combining scores.

The method of combining scores so that a proper weight is obtained for each ele-ment is not as simple as it seems. A common procedure is simply to add scores togeth-er if they are to have equal weight and to multiply by 2 if an element is to count twice as much as another. This typically will not result in each element receiving its proper weight, even if the highest possible score is the same for all sets of scores. How much influence each element has in a composite score is determined by the spread—or variability—of scores and not the number of total points.

The problem of weighting scores when combining them can best be illustrated with a simple example. Let's assume that we only have two measures of achievement and we want to give them equal weight in a grade. Our two sets of achievement scores have score ranges as follows:

Test scores	20 to 100
Laboratory work	30 to 50

If we simply added together a student's test score and score on laboratory work, the grade the student received would be determined largely by the test score because of its wide spread of scores. This can be shown by comparing two students: one who had the highest test score and lowest laboratory score (Student 1), and one who had the lowest test score and highest laboratory score (Student 2).

	Student 1	**Student 2**
Test score	100	20
Laboratory score	30	50
Composite score	130	70

It is quite obvious from the difference in composite scores that the weightings are not equal.

With sets of scores like those for our test and laboratory work, it is not uncommon for teachers to attempt to give them equal weight by making the top possible scores equal. This can be done, of course, by multiplying the score on laboratory work by 2, making the highest possible score 100 for both measures. Here is how the two composite scores for our hypothetical students would compare under this system:

	Student 1	**Student 2**
Test score	100	20
Laboratory score ($\times 2$)	60	100
Composite score	160	120

Our composite scores make clear that equalizing the maximum possible scores does not provide equal weights either. As noted earlier, the influence a measure has on the composite score depends on the spread, or variability, of scores. Thus, the greater the spread of scores, the larger the contribution to the composite score.

We can give equal weights to our two sets of scores by using the **range** of scores in each set. Because our test scores have a range of 80 (100 − 20) and our laboratory scores have a range of 20 (50 − 30), we must multiply each laboratory score by 4 to equalize the spreads of scores and, thus, give them equal weight in the composite score. Here are the composite scores for our two hypothetical students:

	Student 1	**Student 2**
Test score	100	20
Laboratory score ($\times 4$)	120	200
Composite score	220	220

At last we have a system that gives the two measures equal weight in the composite score. Note that if we wanted to count our test score *twice* as much as the laboratory score, we would multiply it by 2 and the laboratory score by 4. However, if we wanted to have our laboratory score count twice as much as the test score, we would have to multiply each laboratory score by 8. Thus, when we originally multiplied our laboratory scores by 4, we simply adjusted the spread of those scores to match the spread of the test scores. When the two sets of scores have the same range of scores, we can then assign additional weights in terms of their relative importance (see Box 12.2).

The range of scores provides only a rough approximation of score variability, but it is satisfactory for most classroom grading purposes. A more dependable basis for weighting grade components can be obtained with the standard deviation.

Some teachers obtain a composite grade by converting all test scores and other assessments to letter grades, converting the letter grades to numbers (e.g., A = 4, B = 3, C = 2, D = 1, F = 0), and then averaging them for a final grade. When this procedure is followed, information is lost because the data are reduced to only five categories. For example, a student with a high A and high B would receive the same average grade as a student with a low A and a low B. To overcome this problem, pluses and minuses are sometimes added (e.g., A+ = 12, A = 11, A– = 10, B+ = 9, B = 8, B– = 7, etc.). This provides more

---

BOX 12.2 ● *Computing Composite Scores for Grading*

1. Select assessments to be included in the composite score and assign percentages.
2. Record desired weight for each assessment.
3. Equate range of scores by using multiplier.
4. Determine weight to apply to each score by multiplying "desired weight" by "multiplier to equate ranges."

Components		Desired Weight	Range of Scores	Multiplier to Equate Ranges	Weight to Apply to Each Score
1. Test scores	50%	2	20 to 100	1	2 × 1 = 2
2. Laboratory work	25%	1	30 to 50	4	1 × 4 = 4
3. Homework	25%	1	0 to 10	8	1 × 8 = 8

COMPUTING THE COMPOSITE SCORES

Students	Raw Scores			Weighted Scores			Composite
	1	2	3	1(×2)	2(×4)	3(×8)	1(w)+2(w)+3(w)
Nguyen	93	42	8	186	168	64	418
Derek	84	45	10	168	180	80	428
Maria	85	47	7	170	188	56	414
Jonus	95	35	10	190	140	80	410

Note that Derek had the highest composite score but would have had the lowest if the raw scores had simply been added together, or even if the test score had been multiplied by 2 (the desired weight). That is because the measure with the biggest range of scores has the greatest influence on the combined scores unless adjustments are made to equate the spreads of scores. Compare Jonus's raw scores and composite scores to Derek's.

categories but some information is still lost. A better solution is to use numerical scores on all assessments and then combine these numerical scores into a composite score before assigning grades.

Guidelines for Effective and Fair Grading

Assigning grades that provide a valid measure of student achievement, that have a meaning beyond the classroom in which they are given, and that are considered to be fair by students is a difficult but important part of teaching. The following guidelines provide a framework that should help clarify and standardize the task.

1.   **Inform students at the beginning of instruction what grading procedures will be used.** This should include what will be included in the final grade (e.g., tests, projects, laboratory work) and how much weight will be given to each element. It should also include a description, in achievement terms, of what each letter grade represents. A descriptive handout may be helpful.

2.   **Base grades on student achievement, and achievement only.** Grades should represent the extent to which the intended learning outcomes were achieved by students. They should *not* be contaminated by student effort, tardiness, misbehaviour, or other extraneous factors. These can be reported upon separately, but they should not influence the achievement grade. If they are permitted to become a part of the grade, the meaning of the grade as an indicator of achievement is lost.

3.   **Base grades on a wide variety of valid assessment data.** All too frequently, grades are based primarily, if not entirely, on test scores. If grades are to be sound indicators of achievement, all important learning outcomes must be assessed and the results included in the final grade. Evaluations of papers, projects, and laboratory work are not as reliable as objective test scores, but to eliminate them lowers the validity of the grades.

4.   **When combining scores for grading, use a proper weighting technique.** As noted earlier, the influence of a component on the overall grade is determined by the spread, or variability, of the scores. Thus, in combining scores to obtain a composite for assigning grades, be sure the spreads of scores are equalized before weighting and combining them.

5.   **Select an appropriate frame of reference for grading.** If the entire instruction is based on mastery learning, it is necessary to use an *absolute* standard for grading and to define the grades in mastery terms. For conventional classroom instruction, the pass–fail distinction should be described in absolute terms and the grades above that determined by relative position in the group. However, these relative letter grades should have achievement referents representing learning outcomes ranging from simple to complex.

6.   **Review borderline cases by re-examining all achievement evidence.** When setting a cutoff point for each grade, there is typically a student or two just below the cutoff line. Measurement errors alone might be responsible for a student being just below (or above) the line. Also, the composite score may contain a clerical error, or one low test score contributing to the composite score may be due to illness or some other extraneous factor. In any event, it is wise to review the data for borderline cases and make any needed adjustments. When in doubt, fair grading would favour giving the student the higher grade.

Although in this chapter we focused on assigning grades, it does not imply that all student assignments and activities should be graded. Using brief tests, written assignments, and projects as learning tools is frequently more effective if the focus is on detecting and overcoming learning errors rather than on assigning grades. Formative assessment emphasizes this function of assessment results. Whether graded or not, however, all assessments of student achievement should include plans for the effective feedback of results along with suggestions for improving learning. Grading is an important and necessary task in teaching but it is secondary to our main purpose—improving student learning.

Reporting to Students and Parents

The letter grade is typically required for school records, but a more elaborate report is needed for describing achievement to students and parents. One method is to use a reporting system that provides a rating of performance on each of the major learning outcomes of a course of instruction. The example of a Science Performance Report shown in Box 12.3 illustrates a form for this purpose. The report could be made more informative by listing the specific learning outcomes for each major outcome. If the instructional objectives and specific learning outcomes are specified at the beginning of instruction, as they should be, the report form can easily be arranged and shared with students when instruction begins. Just do not make the list so long and cumbersome that it overwhelms students and confuses parents. It may be helpful to have a committee of teachers, students and parents work out a satisfactory report form for your grade level, department, or the entire school.

A comprehensive report form should contain a place for an achievement grade (uncontaminated by effort, tardiness, misbehaviour, or similar factors), a separate grade for effort (if desired), and a list of the intended learning outcomes, work habits, and personal characteristics to be rated. The letter grade is useful as an overall measure of

---

BOX 12.3 • *Science Performance Report*

The circled number indicates the student's level of performance on each of the major learning outcomes being evaluated. The numerical ratings are defined as follows:

4—Outstanding performance.
3—Good performance, some improvement needed.
2—Inadequate performance, needs additional work.
1—Did not achieve the intended outcome.

4	3	2	1	(a)	Knows scientific terms and facts.
4	3	2	1	(b)	Understands science concepts and processes.
4	3	2	1	(c)	Applies science learning to new situation.
4	3	2	1	(d)	Demonstrates reasoning ability.
4	3	2	1	(e)	Demonstrates research skills.
4	3	2	1	(f)	Demonstrates laboratory proficiency.
4	3	2	1	(g)	Solves math problems needed in science.

achievement and is easily recorded for administrative uses. But the ratings of intended learning outcomes and related characteristics provide the most valuable information for improving learning and instruction, and reporting progress to students and parents.

Using a Portfolio

As noted in Chapter 11, there is no better way of reporting student achievement than by using a portfolio. The collected samples of work make clear to students and parents alike what students are learning and how well they are learning it. In conference with students and parents, you can present a summary of the students' achievements and then support it by showing actual samples of the students' work. This provides as comprehensive and complete a report of student achievement as is possible. The conference also provides for two-way communication that permits the student or parent to ask for clarification and to discuss ways to improve performance.

If portfolios are not used in the school, it is still wise to use samples of student work when discussing learning progress and level of achievement with students and parents. Combined with a report form, like the one described earlier, work samples can be very useful in clarifying student achievement.

Special Considerations

Grading is an area of particular concern in relation to special needs students. Some provinces and some school districts have enunciated guidelines to be followed when assigning letter grades to special needs students. In that case, those guidelines will provide direction to teachers. In cases where schools or teachers must devise their own practices, there are three circumstances to be considered.

If the student in question can achieve reasonable success with regard to the work being done, he or she can be graded on the same basis as other students. This may mean that a student is graded along with other students in some subject areas, or in some units of instruction, but not in others. As long as the student and parents know this is the case, the greater the extent to which special needs students can be treated as regular students the better.

If the student has an Individualized Education Plan (IEP), the reporting requirement will be built into the plan. The plan will include specific learning outcomes for the student, and the report will state how well the student is achieving those outcomes. Some jurisdictions have standard forms, some have forms built into each IEP, and others use anecdotal reports and no grades are required. In those cases, writing the report is relatively easy.

If the student does not have an IEP, but cannot possibly meet the standards commonly expected of students at his or her grade level, the reporting challenge is much greater. The first rule is BE CAREFUL. If you have a student who you suspect has some sort of special need, but has not been identified as such, find out why. Do not assume that the system is wrong and you are right. Ask the principal, former teachers, and district personnel before you modify the child's program and formulate reports on the basis of that program.

If you then decide to modify the program, or your reporting process, BE HONEST. Tell the parents what you intend to do and get their approval. When teachers report on a student's achievement, parents assume the grading has been done on the same basis as for other students, and that an A on their child's report is the same as an A on the next door neighbour child's report. If they find out the truth after several years of school they will be most unhappy, or may not believe the teacher who finally faces up to the task of reporting accurately.

Summary of Points

1. Grades should represent achievement of the intended learning outcomes and be uncontaminated by other factors.
2. Grades should be assigned in accordance with the grading policies and procedures of the school.
3. Absolute grading requires predetermined standards based on clearly specified learning tasks and measures designed for criterion-referenced interpretation.
4. If instruction is based on a mastery learning program, absolute grading should be used with defined cutoff points and a stated rationale for the selection of the cutoff points.
5. Relative grading is based on the ranking of individuals in a group, but relative grades should also have content meaning. Higher grades should represent higher levels of understanding, application, thinking skills, and performance skills.
6. Where relative grading is used, the pass–fail decision should still be determined on an absolute basis. The important question is: Does this student have the minimum knowledge and skill needed to succeed at the next level of instruction?
7. A good compromise between absolute and relative grading for use in conventional classroom instruction is a grading system based on minimal objectives (to determine the pass–fail decision) and developmental objectives that spread students out in terms of the difficulty and complexity of the material learned.
8. Basing grades on achievement in relation to learning ability, amount of improvement, or effort will only distort the meaning of grades as measures of achievement.
9. Grades should be based on valid measures of achievement. Validity is built in during the construction of tests and other assessment procedures by designing instruments that measure the intended outcomes of instruction.
10. Grades should be based on a variety of achievement assessments. Test scores should be supplemented by various types of performance assessment that measure the intended outcomes of instruction more directly (e.g., writing samples, laboratory work).
11. Components entering into an overall grade should be adjusted for the spread of scores before weighting them in terms of their importance.
12. Borderline cases should be given the benefit of the doubt and assigned the higher grade, unless a review of the achievement data indicates otherwise.
13. Attitude, effort, misbehaviour, and other nonachievement factors might be rated separately but should not be allowed to influence the achievement grade.

14. Some tests and assessment procedures can be used for learning purposes and need not be assigned a grade (e.g., formative use of learning assessments).
15. Reporting to students and parents involves informing them of the extent to which the intended learning outcomes are being achieved. Both detailed performance reports and portfolios are useful for this purpose.
16. Whatever grading and reporting system is used, the procedures should be made clear to students at the beginning of instruction. A descriptive handout may be useful for this.
17. Special needs students can receive letter grades if they can achieve success in the regular curriculum, the IEP can provide assessment guidelines, or, on a modified program, students can be graded pass–fail or receive letter grades.

Learning Exercises

1. What types of information are most useful in a grading and reporting system designed to support the instructional program of the school? Why?

2. List as many ways as you can think of for improving grading and reporting in schools.

3. Write or obtain two learning outcomes for a mentally handicapped student. Assume he has succeeded in mastering one outcome to a considerable degree, but has done very poorly on the second. Write a report to his parents on the two outcomes. Be sure to specify what a satisfactory performance would entail, and the degree to which the student has met the requirement.

References and Additional Reading

Airasian, P.W. (1997). *Classroom Assessment*, 3rd ed. New York: McGraw-Hill, 1997.

Linn, R.L., and Gronlund, N.E. (2000). *Measurement and Assessment in Teaching*, 8th ed. Upper Saddle River, NJ: Merrill/Prentice-Hall.

McMillan, J.H. (2001). *Classroom Assessment: Principles and Practices for Effective Instruction.*

2nd ed. Upper Saddle River, NJ: Merrill/Prentice-Hall.

Oosterhoff, A.C. (2001). *Classroom Applications of Educational Measurement*, 3rd ed. Upper Saddle River, NJ: Merrill/Prentice-Hall.

Weblinks

Assessment of Our Students
Discusses problems with various methods of grading.
http://thunder1.cudenver.edu//OTE/nn/vol5/5_1.htm

Feedback and Grading
General discussion on various methods.
http://www.osu.edu/education/ftad/Publications/TeachingHandbook/chap-7.html

Grading Students in Inclusive Settings
Addresses the problems of grading special needs students.
http://www.newpaltz.edu/migrant/grading.html

Appendix

Principles for Fair Student Assessment Practices for Education in Canada[1]

The *Principles for Fair Student Assessment Practices for Education in Canada* contains a set of principles and related guidelines generally accepted by professional organizations as indicative of fair assessment practice within the Canadian educational context. Assessments depend on professional judgment; the principles and related guidelines presented in this document identify the issues to consider in exercising this professional judgment and in striving for the fair and equitable assessment of all students.

Assessment is broadly defined in the *Principles* as the process of collecting and interpreting information that can be used (i) to inform students, and their parents/guardians where applicable, about the progress they are making toward attaining the knowledge, skills, attitudes, and behaviours to be learned or acquired, and (ii) to inform the various personnel who make educational decisions (instructional, diagnostic, placement, promotion, graduation, curriculum planning, program development, policy) about students. Principles and related guidelines are set out for both developers and users of assessments. Developers include people who construct assessment methods and people who set policies for particular assessment programs. Users include people who select and administer assessment methods, commission assessment development services, or make decisions on the basis of assessment results and findings. The roles may overlap, as when a teacher or instructor develops and administers an assessment instrument and then scores and interprets the students' responses, or when a ministry or department of education or local school system commissions the development and implementation of an assessment program and scoring services and makes decisions on the basis of the assessment results.

The *Principles for Fair Student Assessment Practices for Education in Canada* is the product of a comprehensive effort to reach consensus on what constitutes sound principles to guide the fair assessment of students. The principles and their related guidelines should be considered neither exhaustive nor mandatory; however, organizations, institutions, and individual professionals who endorse them are committing themselves **to endeavour to follow their intent and spirit** so as to achieve fair and equitable assessments of students.

Organization and Use of the Principles

The principles and their related guidelines are organized in two parts. Part A is directed at assessments carried out by teachers at the elementary and secondary school levels. Part A is also applicable at the post-secondary level with some modifications, particularly with respect to whom assessment results are reported. Part B is directed at standardized assessments developed external to the classroom by commercial test publishers, provincial and territorial ministries and departments of education, and local school jurisdictions.[2]

Five general principles of fair assessment practices are provided in each part. Each principle is followed by a series of guidelines for practice. In the case of Part A where no prior sets of standards for fair practice exist, a brief comment accompanies each guideline to help clarify and illuminate the guideline and its application.

The Joint Advisory Committee recognizes that in the field of assessment some terms are defined or used differently by different groups of people. To maintain as much consistency in terminology as possible, an attempt has been made to employ generic terms in the *Principles*.

A. Classroom Assessments

Part A is directed toward the development and selection of assessment methods and their use in the classroom by teachers. Based on the conceptual framework provided in the *Standards for Teacher Competence in Educational Assessment of Students* (1990), it is organized around five interrelated themes:

    I.   Developing and Choosing Methods for Assessment

    II.   Collecting Assessment Information

    III. Judging and Scoring Student Performance

    IV. Summarizing and Interpreting Results

    V.   Reporting Assessment Findings

The Joint Advisory Committee acknowledges that not all of the guidelines are equally applicable in all circumstances. However, consideration of the full set of principles and guidelines within Part A should help to achieve fairness and equity for the students to be assessed.

I. *Developing and Choosing Methods for Assessment*
Assessment methods should be appropriate for and compatible with the purpose and context of the assessment.

Assessment method is used here to refer to the various strategies and techniques that teachers might use to acquire assessment information. These strategies and techniques include, but are not limited to, observations, text- and curriculum-embedded questions and tests, paper-and-pencil tests, oral questioning, benchmarks or reference sets, interviews, peer- and self-assessments, standardized criterion-referenced and norm-referenced tests, performance assessments, writing samples, exhibitions, portfolio assessment, and project and product assessments. Several labels have been used to describe subsets of these alternatives, with the most common being "direct assessment," "authentic assessment," "performance assessment," and "alternative assessment." However, for the purpose of the *Principles*, the term assessment method has been used to encompass all the strategies and techniques that might be used to collect information from students about their progress toward attaining the knowledge, skills, attitudes, or behaviours to be learned.

    1.   Assessment methods should be developed or chosen so that inferences drawn about the knowledge, skills, attitudes, and behaviours possessed by each student are valid and not open to misinterpretation.

Validity refers to the degree to which inferences drawn from assessment results are meaningful. Therefore, development or selection of assessment methods for collecting information should be clearly linked to the purposes for which inferences and decisions are to be made. For example, to monitor the progress of students as proofreaders and editors of their own work, it is better to assign an actual writing task, to allow time and resources for editing (dictionaries, handbooks, etc.), and to observe students for evidence of proofreading and editing skill as they work than to use a test containing discrete items on usage and grammar that are relatively devoid of context.

2.   Assessment methods should be clearly related to the goals and objectives of instruction, and be compatible with the instructional approaches used.

To enhance validity, assessment methods should be in harmony with the instructional objectives to which they are referenced. Planning an assessment design at the same time as planning instruction will help integrate the two in meaningful ways. Such joint planning provides an overall perspective on the knowledge, skills, attitudes, and behaviours to be learned and assessed, and the contexts in which they will be learned and assessed.

3.   When developing or choosing assessment methods, consideration should be given to the consequences of the decisions to be made in light of the obtained information.

The outcomes of some assessments may be more critical than others. For example, misinterpretation of the level of performance on an end-of-unit test may result in incorrectly holding a student from proceeding to the next instructional unit in a continuous progress situation. In such "high-stake" situations, every effort should be made to ensure the assessment method will yield consistent and valid results. "Low stake" situations, such as determining if a student has correctly completed an in-class assignment, can be less stringent. Low stake assessments are often repeated during the course of a reporting period using a variety of methods. If the results are aggregated to form a summary comment or grade, the summary will have greater consistency and validity than its component elements.

4.   More than one assessment method should be used to ensure comprehensive and consistent indications of student performance.

To obtain a more complete picture or profile of a student's knowledge, skills, attitudes, or behaviours, and to discern consistent patterns and trends, more than one assessment method should be used. Student knowledge might be assessed using completion items; process or reasoning skills might be assessed by observing performance on a relevant task; evaluation skills might be assessed by reflecting upon the discussion with a student about what materials to include in a portfolio. Self-assessment may help to clarify and add meaning to the assessment of a written communication, science project, piece of art work, or an attitude. Use of more than one method will also help minimize inconsistency brought about by different sources of measurement error (for example, poor performance because of an "off-day"; lack of agreement among items included in a test, rating scale, or questionnaire; lack of agreement among observers; instability across time).

5.   Assessment methods should be suited to the backgrounds and prior experiences of students.

Assessment methods should be free from bias brought about by student factors extraneous to the purpose of the assessment. Possible factors to consider include culture, developmental stage, ethnicity, gender, socio-economic background, language, special interests, and special needs. Students' success in answering questions on a test or in an oral quiz, for example, should not be dependent upon prior cultural knowledge, such as understanding an allusion to a cultural tradition or value, unless such knowledge falls within the content domain being assessed. All students should be given the same opportunity to display their strengths.

6.   Content and language that would generally be viewed as sensitive, sexist, or offensive should be avoided.

The vocabulary and problem situation in each test item or performance task should not favour or discriminate against any group of students. Steps should be taken to ensure that stereotyping is not condoned. Language that might be offensive to particular groups of students should be avoided. A judicious use of different roles for males and females and for minorities and the careful use of language should contribute to more effective and, therefore, fairer assessments.

7.   Assessment instruments translated into a second language or transferred from another context or location should be accompanied by evidence that inferences based on these instruments are valid for the intended purpose.

Translation of an assessment instrument from one language to another is a complex and demanding task. Similarly, the adoption or modification of an instrument developed in another country is often not simple and straightforward. Care must be taken to ensure that the results from translated and imported instruments are not misinterpreted or misleading.

II. *Collecting Assessment Information*

Students should be provided with a sufficient opportunity to demonstrate the knowledge, skills, attitudes, or behaviours being assessed.

Assessment information can be collected in a variety of ways (observations, oral questioning, interviews, oral and written reports, paper-and-pencil tests). The guidelines which follow are not all equally applicable to each of these procedures.

1.   Students should be told why assessment information is being collected and how this information will be used.

Students who know the purpose of an assessment are in a position to respond in a manner that will provide information relevant to that purpose. For example, if students know that their participation in a group activity is to be used to assess cooperative skills, they can be encouraged to contribute to the activity. If students know that the purpose of an assessment is to diagnose strengths and weaknesses rather than to assign a grade, they can be encouraged to reveal weaknesses as well as strengths. If the students know that the purpose is to assign a grade, they are well advised to respond in a way that will maximize strength. This is especially true for assessment methods that allow students to make choices, such as with optional writing assignments or research projects.

2.   An assessment procedure should be used under conditions suitable to its purpose and form.

Optimum conditions should be provided for obtaining data from and information about students so as to maximize the validity and consistency of the data and information collected. Common conditions include such things as proper light and ventilation, comfortable room temperature, and freedom from distraction (e.g., movement in and out of the room, noise). Adequate work-space, sufficient materials, and adequate time limits appropriate to the purpose and form of the assessment are also necessary. For example, if the intent is to assess student participation in a small group, adequate work space should be provided for each student group, with sufficient space between sub-groups so that the groups do not interfere with or otherwise influence one another and so that the teacher has the same opportunity to observe and assess each student within each group.

3.   In assessments involving observations, checklists, or rating scales, the number of characteristics to be assessed at one time should be small enough and concretely described so that the observations can be made accurately.

Student behaviours often change so rapidly that it may not be possible simultaneously to observe and record all the behaviour components. In such instances, the number of components to be observed should be reduced and the components should be described as concretely as possible. One way to manage an observation is to divide the behaviour into a series of components and assess each component in sequence. By limiting the number of components assessed at one time, the data and information become more focused, and time is not spent observing later behaviour until prerequisite behaviours are achieved.

4.   The directions provided to students should be clear, complete, and appropriate for the ability, age, and grade level of the students.

Lack of understanding of the assessment task may prevent maximum performance or display of the behaviour called for. In the case of timed assessments, for example, teachers should describe the time limits, explain how students might distribute their time among parts for those assessment instruments with parts, and describe how students should record their responses. For a portfolio assessment, teachers should describe the criteria to be used to select the materials to be included in a portfolio, who will select these materials, and, if more than one person will be involved in the selection process, how the judgments from the different people will be combined. Where appropriate, sample material and practice should be provided to further increase the likelihood that instructions will be understood.

5.   In assessments involving selection items (e.g., true–false, multiple-choice), the directions should encourage students to answer all items without threat of penalty.

A correction formula is sometimes used to discourage "guessing" on selection items. The formula is intended to encourage students to omit items for which they do not know the answer rather than to "guess" the answer. Because research evidence indicates that the benefits expected from the correction are not realized, the use of the formula is discouraged. Students should be encouraged to use whatever partial knowledge they have when choosing their answers, and to answer all items.

6.   When collecting assessment information, interactions with students should be appropriate and consistent.

Care must be taken when collecting assessment information to treat all students fairly. For example, when oral presentations by students are assessed, questioning and probes should be distributed among the students so that all students have the same opportunity to demonstrate their knowledge. While writing a paper-and-pencil test, a student may ask to have an ambiguous item clarified, and, if warranted, the item should be explained to the entire class.

7.   Unanticipated circumstances that interfere with the collection of assessment information should be noted and recorded.

Events such as a fire drill, an unscheduled assembly, or insufficient materials may interfere in the way in which assessment information is collected. Such events should be recorded and subsequently considered when interpreting the information obtained.

8.   A written policy should guide decisions about the use of alternate procedures for collecting assessment information from students with special needs and students whose proficiency in the language of instruction is inadequate for them to respond in the anticipated manner.

It may be necessary to develop alternative assessment procedures to ensure a consistent and valid assessment of those students who, because of special needs or inadequate language, are not able to respond to an assessment method (for example, oral instead of written format, individual instead of group administered, translation into first language, providing additional time). The use of alternate procedures should be guided by a written policy developed by teachers, administrators, and other jurisdictional personnel.

III. *Judging and Scoring Student Performance*
Procedures for judging or scoring student performance should be appropriate for the assessment method used and be consistently applied and monitored.

Judging and scoring refers to the process of determining the quality of a student's performance, the appropriateness of an attitude or behaviour, or the correctness of an answer. Results derived from judging and scoring may be expressed as written or oral comments, ratings, categorizations, letters, numbers, or as some combination of these forms.

1.   Before an assessment method is used, a procedure for scoring should be prepared to guide the process of judging the quality of a performance or product, the appropriateness of an attitude or behaviour, or the correctness of an answer.

To increase consistency and validity, properly developed scoring procedures should be used. Different assessment methods require different forms of scoring. Scoring selection items (true–false, multiple-choice, matching) requires the identification of the correct or, in some instances, best answer. Guides for scoring essays might include factors such as the major points to be included in the "best answer" or models or exemplars corresponding to different levels of performance at different age levels and against which comparisons can be made. Procedures for judging other performances or products might include specification of the characteristics to be rated in performance terms and, to the extent possible, clear descriptions of the different levels of performance or quality of a product.

2.   Before an assessment method is used, students should be told how their responses or the information they provide will be judged or scored.

Informing students prior to the use of an assessment method about the scoring procedures to be followed should help ensure that similar expectations are held by both students and their teachers.

3.   Care should be taken to ensure that results are not influenced by factors that are not relevant to the purpose of the assessment.

Various types of errors occur in scoring, particularly when a degree of subjectivity is involved (e.g., marking essays, rating a performance, judging a debate). For example, if the intent of a written communication is to assess content alone, the scoring should not be influenced by stylistic factors such as vocabulary and sentence structure. Personal bias errors are indicated by a general tendency to rate all students in approximately the same way (e.g., too generously or too severely). Halo effects can occur when a rater's general impression of a student influences the rating of individual characteristics or when a previous rating influences a subsequent rating. Pooled results from two or more independent raters (teachers, other students) will generally produce a more consistent description of student performance than a result obtained from a single rater. In combining results, the personal biases of individual raters tend to cancel one another.

4.   Comments formed as part of scoring should be based on the responses made by the students and in a way that students can understand and use them.

Comments, in oral and written form, are provided to encourage learning and to point out correctable errors or inconsistencies in performance. In addition, comments can be used to clarify a result. Such feedback should be based on evidence pertinent to the learning outcomes being assessed.

5.   Any changes made during scoring should be based upon a demonstrated problem with the initial scoring procedure. The modified procedure should then be used to rescore all previously scored responses.

Anticipating the full range of student responses is a difficult task for several forms of assessment. There is always the danger that unanticipated responses or incidents that are relevant to the purposes of the assessment may be overlooked. Consequently, scoring should be continuously monitored for unanticipated responses and these responses should be taken into proper account.

6.   An appeal process should be described to students at the beginning of each school year or course of instruction that they may use to appeal a result.

Situations may arise where a student believes a result incorrectly reflects his/her level of performance. A procedure by which students can appeal such a situation should be developed and made known to them. This procedure might include, for example, checking for addition or other recording errors or, perhaps, judging or scoring by a second qualified person.

IV. *Summarizing and Interpreting Results*

Procedures for summarizing and interpreting assessment results should yield accurate and informative representations of a student's performance in relation to the goals and objectives of instruction for the reporting period.

Summarizing and interpreting results refers to the procedures used to combine assessment results in the form of summary comments and grades which indicate both a student's level of performance and the valuing of that performance.

1.   Procedures for summarizing and interpreting results for a reporting period should be guided by a written policy.

Summary comments and grades, when interpreted, serve a variety of functions. They inform students of their progress. Parents, teachers, counsellors, and administrators use them to guide learning, determine promotion, identify students for special attention (e.g., honours, remediation), and to help students develop future plans. Comments and grades also provide a basis for reporting to other schools in the case of school transfer and, in the case of senior high school students, post-secondary institutions and prospective employers. They are more likely to serve their many functions and those functions are less likely to be confused if they are guided by a written rationale or policy sensitive to these different needs. This policy should be developed by teachers, school administrators, and other jurisdictional personnel in consultation with representatives of the audiences entitled to receive a report of summary comments and grades.

2. The way in which summary comments and grades are formulated and interpreted should be explained to students and their parents/guardians.

Students and their parents/guardians have the "right-to-know" how student performance is summarized and interpreted. With this information, they can make constructive use of the findings and fully review the assessment procedures followed.

It should be noted that some aspects of summarizing and interpreting are based upon a teacher's best judgment of what is good or appropriate. This judgment is derived from training and experience and may be difficult to describe specifically in advance. In such circumstances, examples might be used to show how summary comments and grades were formulated and interpreted.

3. The individual results used and the process followed in deriving summary comments and grades should be described in sufficient detail so that the meaning of a summary comment or grade is clear.

Summary comments and grades are best interpreted in the light of an adequate description of the results upon which they are based, the relative emphasis given to each result, and the process followed to combine the results. Many assessments conducted during a reporting period are of a formative nature. The intent of these assessments (e.g., informal observations, quizzes, text-and-curriculum embedded questions, oral questioning) is to inform decisions regarding daily learning, and to inform or otherwise refine the instructional sequence. Other assessments are of a summative nature. It is the summative assessments that should be considered when formulating and interpreting summary comments and grades for the reporting period.

4. Combining disparate kinds of results into a single summary should be done cautiously. To the extent possible, achievement, effort, participation, and other behaviours should be graded separately.

A single comment or grade cannot adequately serve all functions. For example, letter grades used to summarize achievement are most meaningful when they represent only achievement. When they include other aspects of student performance such as effort, amount (as opposed to quality) of work completed, neatness, class participation, personal conduct, or punctuality, not only do they lose their meaningfulness as a measure of achievement, but they also suppress information concerning other important aspects of learning and invite inequities. Thus, to more adequately and fairly summarize the different aspects of student performance, letter grades for achievement might be complemented with alternate summary forms (e.g., checklists, written comments) suitable for summarizing results related to these other behaviours.

5.   Summary comments and grades should be based on more than one assessment result so as to ensure adequate sampling of broadly defined learning outcomes.

More than one or two assessments are needed to adequately assess performance in multi-facet areas such as Reading. Under-representation of such broadly defined constructs can be avoided by ensuring that the comments and grades used to summarize performance are based on multiple assessments, each referenced to a particular facet of the construct.

6.   The results used to produce summary comments and grades should be combined in a way that ensures that each result receives its intended emphasis or weight.

When the results of a series of assessments are combined into a summary comment, care should be taken to ensure that the actual emphasis placed on the various results matches the intended emphasis for each student.

When numerical results are combined, attention should be paid to differences in the variability, or spread, of the different sets of results and appropriate account taken where such differences exist. If, for example, a grade is to be formed from a series of paper-and-pencil tests, and if each test is to count equally in the grade, then the variability of each set of scores must be the same.

7.   The basis for interpretation should be carefully described and justified.

Interpretation of the information gathered for a reporting period for a student is a complex and, at times, controversial issue. Such information, whether written or numerical, will be of little interest or use if it is not interpreted against some pertinent and defensible idea of what is good and what is poor. The frame of reference used for interpretation should be in accord with the type of decision to be made. Typical frames of reference are performance in relation to pre-specified standards, performance in relation to peers, performance in relation to aptitude or expected growth, and performance in terms of the amount of improvement or amount learned. If, for example, decisions are to be made as to whether or not a student is ready to move to the next unit in an instructional sequence, interpretations based on pre-specified standards would be most relevant.

8.   Interpretations of assessment results should take account of the backgrounds and learning experiences of the students.

Assessment results should be interpreted in relation to a student's personal and social context. Among the factors to consider are age, ability, gender, language, motivation, opportunity to learn, self-esteem, socio-economic background, special interests, special needs, and "test-taking" skills. Motivation to do school tasks, language capability, or home environment can influence learning of the concepts assessed, for example. Poor reading ability, poorly developed psychomotor or manipulative skills, lack of test-taking skills, anxiety, and low self-esteem can lead to lower scores. Poor performance in an assessment may be attributable to a lack of opportunity to learn because required learning materials and supplies were not available, learning activities were not provided, or inadequate time was allowed for learning. When a student performs poorly, the possibility that one or more factors such as these might have interfered with a student's response or performance should be considered.

9.   Assessment results that will be combined into summary comments and grades should be stored in a way that ensures their accuracy at the time they are summarized and interpreted.

Comments and grades and their interpretations, formulated from a series of related assessments, can be no better than the data and information upon which they are based. Systematic data control minimizes errors which would otherwise be introduced into a student's record or information base, and provides protection of confidentiality.

10. Interpretations of assessment results should be made with due regard for limitations in the assessment methods used, problems encountered in collecting the information and judging or scoring it, and limitations in the basis used for interpretation.

To be valid, interpretations must be based on results determined from assessment methods that are relevant and representative of the performance assessed. Administrative constraints, the presence of measurement error, and the limitations of the frames of reference used for interpretation also need to be accounted for.

V. *Reporting Assessment Findings*

Assessment reports should be clear, accurate, and of practical value to the audiences for whom they are intended.

1. The reporting system for a school or jurisdiction should be guided by a written policy. Elements to consider include such aspects as audiences, medium, format, content, level of detail, frequency, timing, and confidentiality.

The policy to guide the preparation of school reports (e.g., reports of separate assessments; reports for a reporting period) should be developed by teachers, school administrators, and other jurisdictional personnel in consultation with representatives of the audiences entitled to receive a report. Cooperative participation not only leads to more adequate and helpful reporting, but also increases the likelihood that the reports will be understood and used by those for whom they are intended.

2. Written and oral reports should contain a description of the goals and objectives of instruction to which the assessments are referenced.

The goals and objectives that guided instruction should serve as the basis for reporting. A report will be limited by a number of practical considerations, but the central focus should be on the instructional objectives and the types of performance that represent achievement of these objectives.

3. Reports should be complete in their descriptions of strengths and weaknesses of students, so that strengths can be built upon and problem areas addressed.

Reports can be incorrectly slanted towards "faults" in a student or toward giving unqualified praise. Both biases reduce the validity and utility of assessment. Accuracy in reporting strengths and weaknesses helps to reduce systematic error and is essential for stimulating and reinforcing improved performance. Reports should contain the information that will assist and guide students, their parents/guardians, and teachers to take relevant follow-up actions.

4. The reporting system should provide for conferences between teachers and parents/guardians. Whenever it is appropriate, students should participate in these conferences.

Conferences scheduled at regular intervals and, if necessary, upon request provide parents/guardians and, when appropriate, students with an opportunity to discuss assessment procedures, clarify and elaborate their understanding of the assessment results, summary comments and grades, and reports, and, where warranted, to work with teachers to develop relevant follow-up activities or action plans.

5.   An appeal process should be described to students and their parents/guardians at the beginning of each school year or course of instruction that they may use to appeal a report.

Situations may arise where a student and his/her parents/guardian believe the summary comments and grades inaccurately reflect the level of performance of the student. A procedure by which they can appeal such a situation should be developed and made known to them (for example, in a school handbook or newsletter provided to students and their parents/guardians at the beginning of the school year).

6.   Access to assessment information should be governed by a written policy that is consistent with applicable laws and with basic principles of fairness and human rights.

A written policy, developed by teachers, administrators, and other jurisdictional personnel, should be used to guide decisions regarding the release of student assessment information. Assessment information should be available to those people to whom it applies—students and their parents/guardians, and to teachers and other educational personnel obligated by profession to use the information constructively on behalf of students. In addition, assessment information might be made available to others who justify their need for the information (e.g., post-secondary institutions, potential employers, researchers). Issues of informed consent should also be addressed in this policy.

7.   Transfer of assessment information from one school to another should be guided by a written policy with stringent provisions to ensure the maintenance of confidentiality.

To make a student's transition from one school to another as smooth as possible, a clear policy should be prepared indicating the type of information to go with the student and the form in which it will be reported. Such a policy, developed by jurisdictional and ministry personnel, should ensure that the information transferred will be sent by and received by the appropriate person within the "sending" and "receiving" schools respectively.

B. Assessments Produced External to the Classroom

Part B applies to the development and use of standardized assessment methods used in student admissions, placement, certification, and educational diagnosis, and in curriculum and program evaluation. These methods are primarily developed by commercial test publishers, ministries and departments of education, and local school systems.

The principles and accompanying guidelines are organized in terms of four areas:

I.   Developing and Selecting Methods for Assessment

II.   Collecting and Interpreting Assessment Information

III.   Informing Students Being Assessed

IV.   Implementing Mandated Assessment Programs

The first three areas of Part B are adapted from the *Code of Fair Testing Practices for Education* (1988) developed in the United States. The principles and guidelines as modified in these three sections are intended to be consistent with the *Guidelines for Educational and Psychological Testing* (1986) developed in Canada. The fourth area has been added to contain guidelines particularly pertinent for mandated educational assessment and testing programs developed and conducted at the national, provincial, and local levels.

I. *Developing and Selecting Methods for Assessment*

Developers of assessment methods should strive to make them as fair as possible for use with students who have different backgrounds or special needs. Developers should provide the information users need to select methods appropriate to their assessment needs.

Developers should:

1. Define what the assessment method is intended to measure and how it is to be used. Describe the characteristics of the students with which the method may be used.

2. Warn users against common misuses of the assessment method.

3. Describe the process by which the method was developed. Include a description of the theoretical basis, rationale for selection of content and procedures, and derivation of scores.

4. Provide evidence that the assessment method yields results that satisfy its intended purpose(s).

5. Investigate the performance of students with special needs and students from different backgrounds. Report evidence of the consistency and validity of the results produced by the assessment method for these groups.

6. Provide potential users with representative samples or complete copies of questions or tasks, directions, answer sheets, score reports, guidelines for interpretation, and manuals.

Users should select assessment methods that have been developed to be as fair as possible for students who have different backgrounds or special needs. Users should select methods that are appropriate for the intended purposes and suitable for the students to be assessed.

Users should:

1. Determine the purpose(s) for assessment and the characteristics of the students to be assessed. Then select an assessment method suited to that purpose and type of student.

2. Avoid using assessment methods for purposes not specifically recommended by the developer unless evidence is obtained to support the intended use.

3. Review available assessment methods for relevance of content and appropriateness of scores with reference to the intended purpose(s) and characteristics of the students to be assessed.

4. Read independent evaluations of the methods being considered. Look for evidence supporting the claims of developers with reference to the intended application of each method.

5. Ascertain whether the content of the assessment method and the norm group(s) or comparison group(s) are appropriate for the students to be assessed. For assessment methods developed in other regions or countries, look for evidence that the characteristics of the norm group(s) or comparison group(s) are comparable to the characteristics of the students to be assessed.

6. Examine specimen sets, samples or complete copies of assessment instruments, directions, answer sheets, score reports, guidelines for interpretation, and manuals and judge their appropriateness for the intended application.

7. Review printed assessment methods and related materials for content or language generally perceived to be sensitive, offensive, or misleading.

8. Describe the specialized skills and training needed to administer an assessment method correctly, and the specialized knowledge to make valid interpretations of scores.

9. Limit sales of restricted assessment materials to persons who possess the necessary qualifications.

10. Provide for periodic review and revision of content and norms, and, if applicable, passing or cut-off scores, and inform users.

11. Provide evidence of the comparability of different forms of an instrument where the forms are intended to be interchangeable, such as parallel forms or the adaptation of an instrument for computer administration.

12. Provide evidence that an assessment method translated into a second language is valid for use with the second language. This information should be provided in the second language.

13. Advertise an assessment method in a way that states it can be used only for the purposes for which it was intended.

7. Review printed assessment methods and related materials for content or language that would offend or mislead the students to be assessed.

8. Ensure that all individuals who administer the assessment method, score the responses, and interpret the results have the necessary knowledge and skills to perform these tasks (e.g., learning assistance teachers, speech and language pathologists, counsellors, school psychologists, psychologists).

9. Ensure access to restricted assessment materials is limited to persons with the necessary qualifications.

10. Obtain information about the appropriateness of content, the recency of norms, and, if applicable, the appropriateness of the cut-off scores for use with the students to be assessed.

11. Obtain information about the comparability of interchangeable forms, including computer adaptations.

12. Obtain evidence about the validity of the use of an assessment method translated into a second language.

13. Verify advertising claims made for an assessment method.

II. *Collecting and Interpreting Assessment Information*

Developers should provide information to help users administer an assessment method correctly and interpret assessment results accurately.

Users should follow directions for proper administration of an assessment method and interpretation of assessment results.

Developers should:

1. Provide clear instructions for administering the assessment method and identify the qualifications that should be held by the people who should administer the method.

2. When feasible, make available appropriately modified forms of assessment methods for students with special needs or whose proficiency in the original language of administration is inadequate to respond in the anticipated manner.

3. Provide answer keys and describe procedures for scoring when scoring is to be done by the user.

4. Provide score reports or procedures for generating score reports that describe assessment results clearly and accurately. Identify and explain possible misinterpretations of the scores yielded by the scoring system (grade equivalents, percentile ranks, standard scores) used.

5. Provide evidence of the effects on assessment results of such factors as speed, test-taking strategies, and attempts by students to present themselves favourably in their responses.

Users should:

1. Ensure that the assessment method is administered by qualified personnel or under the supervision of qualified personnel.

2. When necessary and feasible, use appropriately modified forms of assessment methods with students who have special needs or whose proficiency in the original language of administration is inadequate to respond in the anticipated manner. Ensure that instruments translated from one language to another are administered by persons who are proficient in the translated language.

3. Follow procedures for scoring as set out for the assessment method.

4. Interpret scores taking into account the limitations of the scoring system used. Avoid misinterpreting scores on the basis of unjustified assumptions about the scoring system (grade equivalents, percentile ranks, standard scores) used.

5. Interpret scores taking into account the effects of such factors as speed, test-taking strategies, and attempts by students to present themselves favourably in their responses.

6. Warn against using published norms with students who are not part of the population from which the norm or comparison sample was selected or when the prescribed assessment method has been modified in any way.

6. Interpret scores taking account of major differences between the norm group(s) or comparison group(s) and the students being assessed. Also take account of discrepancies between recommended and actual procedures and differences in familiarity with the assessment method between the norm group(s) and the students being assessed.

   Examine the need for local norms, and, if called for, develop these norms.

7. Describe how passing and cut-off scores, where used, were set and provide evidence regarding rates of misclassification.

7. Explain how passing or cut-off scores were set and discuss the appropriateness of these scores in terms of rates of misclassification.

   Examine the need for local passing or cut-off scores and, if called for, reset these scores.

8. Provide evidence to support the use of any computer scoring or computer generated interpretations. The documentation should include the rationale for such scoring and interpretations and their comparability with the results of scoring and interpretations made by qualified judges.

8. Ensure that any computer administration and computer interpretations of assessment results are accurate and appropriate for the intended use. If necessary, ensure that relevant information not included in computer reports is also considered.

9. Observe jurisdictional policies regarding storage of and subsequent access to the results. Ensure that computer files are not accessible to unauthorized users.

10. Ensure that all copyright and user agreements are observed.

III. *Informing Students Being Assessed*

Direct communication with those being assessed may come from either the developer or the user of the assessment method. In either case, the students being assessed and, where applicable, their parents/guardians should be provided with complete information presented in an understandable way.

Developers or Users should:

1. Develop materials and procedures for informing the students being assessed about the content of the assessment, types of question formats used, and appropriate strategies, if any, for responding.

2. Obtain informed consent from students or, where applicable, their parents/guardians in the case of individual assessments to be used for identification or placement purposes.

3. Provide students or, where applicable, their parents/guardians with information to help them decide whether to participate in the assessment when participation is optional.

4. Provide information to students or, where applicable, their parents/guardians of alternate assessment methods where available and applicable.

Control of results may rest with either the developer or user of the assessment method. In either case, the following steps should be followed.

Developers or Users should:

1. Provide students or, where applicable, their parents/guardians with information as to their rights to copies of instruments and completed answer forms, to reassessment, to rescoring, or to cancellation of scores and other records.

2. Inform students or, where applicable, their parents/guardians of the length of time assessment results will be kept on file and of the circumstances under which the assessment results will be released and to whom.

3. Describe the procedures that students or, where applicable, their parents/guardians may follow to register concerns about the assessment and endeavour to have problems resolved.

IV. *Implementing Mandated Assessment Programs*[3]

Under some circumstances, the administration of an assessment method is required by law. In such cases, the following guidelines should be added to the applicable guidelines outlined in Sections I, II, and III of Part B.

Developers and Users should:

1. Inform all persons with a stake in the assessment (administrators, teachers, students, parents/guardians) of the purpose(s) of the assessment, the uses to be made of the results, and who has access to the results.

2. Design and describe procedures for developing or choosing the methods of assessment, selecting students where sampling is used, administering the assessment materials, and scoring and summarizing student responses.

3. Interpret results in light of factors that might influence them. Important factors to consider include characteristics of the students, opportunity to learn,

and comprehensiveness and representativeness of the assessment method in terms of the learning outcomes to be reported on.

4. Specify procedures for reporting, storing, controlling access to, and destroying results.

5. Ensure reports and explanations of results are consistent with the purpose(s) of the assessment, the intended uses of the results, and the planned access to the results.

6. Provide reports and explanations of results that can be readily understood by the intended audience(s). If necessary, employ multiple reports designed for different audiences.

References

Code of Fair Testing Practices for Education. (1988). Washington, D.C.: Joint Committee on Testing Practices.

Guidelines for Educational and Psychological Testing. (1986). Ottawa, Ont.: Canadian Psychological Association.

Standards for Teacher Competence in Educational Assessment of Students. (1990). Washington: D.C.: American Federation of Teachers, National Council on Measurement in Education, and National Educational Association.

The membership of the Working Group (WG) that developed the *Principles for Fair Student Assessment Practices for Education in Canada* and of the Joint Advisory Committee that oversaw the development was as follows:

Marvin Betts	Michael Jackson	Jean Pettifor
Gary Broker	Michel Laurier (WG)	Sharon Robertson
Clement Dassa (WG)	Tom Maguire (WG)	Don Saklofske
Dick Dodds	Romulo Magsino	Marvin Simner
Tom Dunn (WG)	Linda McAlpine	Marielle Simon (WG)
Bob Gilchrist	Allan McDonald	Ross Traub (WG)
Nicholas Head	Stirling McDowell	Sue Wagner
Douglas Hodgkinson	Craig Melvin	Kim Wolff
Barbara Holmes (WG)	Kathy Oberle (WG)	Todd Rogers (Chair,
	Frank Oliva	Working Group and Joint
		Advisory Committee)

Notes

[1] The *Principles for Fair Student Assessment Practices for Education in Canada* was developed by a Working Group guided by a Joint Advisory Committee. The Joint Advisory Committee included two representatives appointed by each of the following professional organizations: Canadian Education Association, Canadian School Boards Association, Canadian Association for School Administrators, Canadian Teachers' Federation, Canadian Guidance and Counselling Association, Canadian Association of School Psychologists, Canadian Council for Exceptional Children, Canadian Psychological Association, and Canadian Society for the Study of Education. In addition, the Joint Advisory Committee included a representative of the Provincial and Territorial Ministries and Departments of Education.

Financial support for the development and dissemination of the *Principles* was provided principally by the Walter and Duncan Gordon Charitable Foundation, with additional support provided by various Faculties, Institutes, and Colleges of Education and Provincial and Territorial Ministries and Departments of Education in Canada. This support is gratefully acknowledged.

The Joint Advisory Committee invites users to share their experiences in working with the *Principles* and to submit any suggestions that could be used to revise and improve the *Principles*. Comments and suggestions should be sent to the Joint Advisory Committee at the address shown below.

The *Principles for Fair Student Assessment Practices for Education in Canada* is not copyrighted. Reproduction and dissemination are encouraged. Please cite the *Principles* as follows: ***Principles for Fair Student Assessment Practices for Education in Canada.* (1993). Edmonton, Alberta: Joint Advisory Committee. (Mailing Address: Joint Advisory Committee, Centre for Research in Applied Measurement and Evaluation, 3-104 Education Building North, University of Alberta, Edmonton, Alberta, T6G 2G5).**

[2] Boards, boroughs, counties, and school districts.

[3] The Joint Advisory Committee wishes to point out it has not taken a position on the value of mandated assessment and testing programs. Rather, given the presence of these programs, the intent of the guidelines presented in Section IV, when combined with applicable guidelines in the first three sections of Part B, is to help ensure fairness and equity for the students being assessed.

Glossary

This glossary of assessment terms focuses primarily on the terms used in this book.

Achievement Assessment A procedure that is used to determine the degree to which individuals have achieved the intended learning outcomes of instruction. It includes both paper and pencil tests and performance assessments, plus judgments concerning learning progress.

Achievement Test An instrument that typically uses sets of items designed to measure a domain of learning tasks and is administered under specified conditions (e.g., time limits, open or closed book).

Alternate Forms Two or more forms of a test or assessment that are designed to measure the same abilities (also called *equivalent* or *parallel forms*).

Alternative Assessment An assessment procedure that provides an alternative to paper and pencil testing.

Analytic Scoring The assignment of scores to individual components of a performance or product (e.g., evaluate a writing sample by using separate scores for organization, style, mechanics, etc.).

Anecdotal Record A brief description of some significant student behaviour, the setting in which it occurred, and an interpretation of its meaning.

Authentic Assessment An assessment procedure that emphasizes the use of tasks and contextual settings like those in the real world.

Checklist A list of dimensions of a performance or product that is simply checked present or absent.

Content Standard A broad educational goal that indicates what a student should know and be able to do in a subject area.

Correlation Coefficient A statistic indicating the degree of relationship between two sets of test scores or other measures.

Criteria A set of qualities used in judging a performance, a product, or an assessment instrument.

Criterion-Referenced Interpretation A description of an individual's performance in terms of the tasks he or she can and cannot perform.

Derived Score A score that results from converting a raw score to a different score scale (e.g., percentile rank, standard score).

Difficulty Index Percentage of individuals who obtain the correct answer on a test item or task.

Discrimination Index The degree to which a test item or task discriminates between high and low scorers on the total test.

Expectancy Table A twofold chart that shows the relationship between two sets of scores. It can be used to predict the chances of success on one measure (the criterion) for any given score on the other measure (the predictor), and it can be used for obtaining criterion-related evidence of validity.

Generalizability The extent to which an assessment procedure provides comparable results over different samples of similar tasks, different settings, and different administrations.

Grade Equivalent Score A derived score that indicates the grade level at which an individual's score matches the average score (e.g., a grade equivalent score of 4.5 indicates the raw score matches the average score of students in the middle of the fourth grade).

Holistic Scoring The assignment of a score based on an overall impression of a performance or product rather than a consideration of individual elements. The overall judgment is typically guided by descriptions of the various levels of performance or scoring rubrics.

Item Analysis Traditionally, a method for determining the difficulty and discriminating power of test items. It can also be used to determine the responsiveness of test items to instructional effects.

Kuder–Richardson Formula 20 (KR-20) A method for estimating reliability based on the internal consistency of a test (i.e., on the extent to which the test items correlate with each other).

Mastery Testing An assessment method used to determine whether an individual has met some predetermined level of performance.

Norm-Referenced Interpretation A description of an individual's performance in terms of how it compares to the performance of others (typically those in a norm group).

Normal Curve A symmetrical bell-shaped curve based on a precise mathematical equation. It is widely used in interpreting standardized test scores because of its fixed mathematical properties (e.g., when standard deviations are plotted along the baseline of the curve, each portion of the curve contains a fixed percentage of scores).

Norms Data that describe the performance of individuals in some reference group (e.g., national norms, local norms). Norms represent average or typical performance and are not to be interpreted as standards.

Objective Test A test that can be consistently scored by equally competent scorers (i.e., they obtain the same scores). This contrasts with subjective tests where the scores are influenced by scorer judgment (e.g., essay tests).

Parallel Forms (*See Alternate Forms*)

Percentage Correct Score The percentage of items that an individual answers correctly on a test, or the percentage of tasks an individual performs correctly on a performance assessment.

Percentile Rank The percentage of individuals in a group scoring at or below a given score. Not to be confused with the percentage correct score.

Performance Assessment A procedure that requires individuals to perform tasks while the process of the performance is judged using prespecified criteria.

Portfolio Assessment A preplanned collection of samples of student work, assessment results, and other data that represent the student's accomplishments. It is viewed by some as a basic type of performance assessment and by others as merely a convenient method for accumulating evidence of student performance.

Product Assessment Assessing student achievement through a product, using prespecified criteria.

Range The difference between the highest score and the lowest score in a distribution of scores.

Rating Scale A systematic procedure for guiding and recording judgments concerning the degree to which the characteristics of a performance or behaviour are present.

Raw Score The score that is obtained when first scoring a test or performance task (also called an obtained score). The raw score is frequently con-verted to some type of derived score for interpretation (e.g., percentile rank or standard score).

Reliability The degree to which assessment results are consistent from one measurement (or assessment) to another. Reliability estimates typically indicate the consistency of scores or judgments over different forms, different time periods, different parts of the instrument, or different raters. High reliability indicates greater freedom from error.

Reliability Coefficient The correlation between two sets of measurements taken from the same procedure.

Sampling Selecting a small number of tasks for the student to carry out, representing all similar tasks.

Scoring Key A set of criteria for a product or performance, with the weight for each criterion.

Scoring Rubric A set of scoring guidelines that describe the characteristics of the different levels of performance used in scoring or judging a performance.

Standard A prespecified level of performance that is considered satisfactory for the use to be made of the assessment results (e.g., minimum standards, mastery standards).

Standard Error of Measurement A method of expressing reliability that estimates the amount of error in test scores. It is the standard deviation of the errors of measurement and is used to compute the error bands (e.g., percentile bands) used in interpreting test scores.

Standardized Achievement Test A test constructed to fit detailed specifications, administered under prescribed conditions to selected groups, and scored using definite rules of scoring. Published standardized tests typically include a test manual that contains rules for administration and scoring, norms for interpretation, and validity and reliability data.

Stanine A standard score that ranges from 1 to 9 with a mean of 5. Each stanine is one-half of a standard deviation wide, except 1 and 9 at the ends of the distribution.

Table of Specifications A two-way chart that specifies the number or proportion of test items (or assessment tasks) to be designed for each area of content and each type of intended learning outcome when planning a test (or other assessment procedure).

Task An assessment exercise that requires students to demonstrate a knowledge, skill, or combination of attributes, by means of a performance or product (see *performance assessment*).

Test Battery Two or more tests standardized on the same sample of students, so that performance on the different tests can be compared using a common norm group.

Validity The extent to which inferences made from assessment results are appropriate, meaningful, and useful in terms of the purpose for the assessment. Validity is a unitary concept that depends on a variety of types of evidence, is expressed by degree (high, low), and refers to the inferences drawn (not the instrument itself).

Validity Coefficient The degree of relationship between a set of test scores and some criterion measure.

Weight The numerical value assigned to a criterion in a scoring key. The total value of the weights is the total possible mark.

Index

Accountability, 5–6
Achievement assessment
    characteristics of, 22–23
    definition of, 11
    feedback of, 22–29
    guidelines for, 25–29
    methods of, 22, 60–61
    planning for, 28, 55, 136–137
    relation to instruction, 12–18, 25
Achievement test, *see* Paper and pencil test
Action verbs, 67, 137
Administering the test, 80
Alternative assessment, 3, 10
    See also Authentic assessment
Analytic scoring, 144–145
Anecdotal records, 159
Answer sheet, 80
Application items, 89, 90
Assembling the test, 77–79
Assessment, *See* Achievement assessment,
    Performance assessment
Authentic assessment, 3, 10, 23, 137, 153–156
Checklist, 159
Checklist for
    assembled test, 79
    test plan, 76
Cognitive domain of the *Taxonomy*, 58
Cognitive skill, 140
Comprehension items, 87–89
Computation of
    composite scores, 183–186
    guessing formula, 78–79
    item difficulty, 80–82
    item discriminating power, 80–82
    mastery formula, 48–50
    percentile rank, 33
    rater agreement, 50
    Spearman-Brown formula, 47
    standard error, 48
Confidence band, 48
Content standards, 55
Correction for guessing, 79

Correlation coefficients, 40, 45
Criteria for assessment, 24, 27, 139, 144
Criterion-referenced assessments
    in test planning, 31
    interpretation of, 31
    reliability of, 48–50
    validity of, 38–39
    versus norm-referenced, 31–32
Criterion-referenced interpretation, 31–32
Diagnostic assessment, 12–13
Difficulty of items, 80–82
Directions, preparation of, 78
Discriminating power of items, 80–82
Distracters, 85, 99
Equivalent-forms method, 46
Error, 45
Error band, 48
Essay questions
    construction of, 125–128
    extended response, 124–125
    limitations of, 125
    nature of, 124–125
    restricted response, 124
    scoring of, 128–129
    strengths of, 125
    versus selection items, 123
Evaluating the test, 79
Expectancy table, 41
Fairness, 26, 74, 186–187
Feedback of results, 12, 17, 27–28
Formative assessment, 14–15
Functioning content, 74
Grade equivalent scores, 33
Grading
    absolute, 181
    and assessment, 28–29
    basis for, 179–182
    combining data, 183–186
    guidelines for, 186–187
    relative, 180–181
    weighting scores, 185
Guessing, correction for, 79

Holistic scoring, 129, 139, 144, 146, 161
Index of Difficulty, 80–82
Index of Discriminating Power, 80–82
Instructional Objectives, *See* Learning out-
      comes, Objectives
Instructional process and assessment, 12–16,
      25
Internal-consistency, 45, 47–48
Interpretative exercise, 112–116
Interpreting test results, 33
      See also Test scores
Item analysis
      difficulty, 80–82
      discriminating power, 80–82
      effectiveness of alternatives, 81
      interpretation of, 82
Item arrangement, 78–79
Item writing
      considerations, 70–71
      essay, 125–128
      guidelines for, 75–77
      interpretive exercise, 115–116
      matching, 111–112
      multiple-choice, 85–103
      performance tests, 148–158
      short-answer, 121–122
      true-false, 105–111
Item difficulty, 80–82
Item discriminating power, 80–82
Key-type item, 113
Knowledge items, 87
Learning and assessment, 16–18, 25
Learning outcomes, 25, 56, 65, 70, 73–74, 87,
      123–125, 126, 128
Mastery testing, 31, 48–50
Matching items, 111–112
Motivation, 17
Multiple-choice items
      assessment role, 85
      evaluation of, 103
      reasons for responses, 82
      rules for writing, 91–102
      strengths and limitations of, 91
      uses of, 87–90
      See also Application items,
            Comprehension items, Knowledge
            items
Norm-referenced assessment
      in test planning, 31
      interpretation of, 31

item analysis of, 80–82
      versus criterion-referenced, 31
Norm-referenced interpretation, 27, 31
Normal curve, 32
Objective items, *See* Selection items
Objective test, 21
Objectives
      defining, 57
      examples of, 57, 137, 138
      locating, 58–59
      stating, 56–58, 137–138
      taxonomy of, 58
Paper and pencil test, 29, 64–65, 67
Percentage correct score, 33
Percentile Rank, 33
Performance assessment
      characteristics of, 4–5, 22–24
      definition of, 11
      evaluating, 144–146, 161
      expanded, 137–144
      focus of, 137, 148
      identification, 155–156
      improving, 162
      objectives for, 151–152
      observation forms for, 136, 138, 144,
            158–161
      procedure, 151–156
      realism of, 153–154
      reliability of, 50–51
      scoring, 158–161
      simulated, 158
      standards for, 157, 159
      steps for, 136
      strengths and limitations, 22–24, 150
      structured, 156
      student projects, 138–143
      tasks for, 155–156
      types of, 22–24, 155–156
      verbs for, 151
      work sample, 158
Performance standards, 157, 159
Performance tasks, 148–150, 151
Performance tests, 156
Placement assessment, 12–13
Portfolio
      advantages of, 167–168
      definition of, 166–167
      entries, 170
      evaluating, 170–171
      maintaining, 171–172

planning for, 168–169
purpose of, 169
use in reporting, 188
Product assessment, 136–149, 137–149
Product scale, 146
Rating scale, 142, 159–161, 174, 188
Realism of tasks, 23, 153–154
Reliability
    and assessment planning, 29–30
    coefficient, 45
    of criterion-referenced tests, 48–50
    equivalent-forms method, 46–47
    factors that lower, 50, 52
    importance of, 30, 38
    internal-consistency method, 47–48
    Kuder-Richardson, 47
    meaning of, 30, 44–51
    methods of determining, 44–51
    of performance assessments, 50–51
    Spearman-Brown Formula, 47
    standard error, 48
    test-retest method, 45, 46
    ways to "build in" reliability, 30
Reporting, 187–188
Research study, 142
Reviewing items, 79
Score Band, 48
Score interpretation, *See* Test interpretation,
    Test scores
Scoring, 24, 80, 144–146
Scoring keys and rubrics, 24, 146, 174–175
Selection items
    characteristics of, 71–74
    interpretive exercise, 112–116
    matching, 111–112
    multiple-choice, 85–103
    true-false, 105–111
    types, 71, 119
Self-assessment, 17, 27–28, 173
Short-answer items, 120–122
Spearman-Brown formula, 47
Specifications for tests, 68–70
Split-half method, 47
Standard error of measurement, 48
Standardized achievement tests
    characteristics of, 32
    history, 2–3, 4
    interpreting results to others, 33
    norm-referenced interpretation, 33
Standards, 32, 139, 157, 179

Student projects, 142
Stanines, 34
Summative assessment, 15–16
Supply items
    characteristics of, 71–74, 119–120
    essay, 123–130
    short-answer, 120–122
    types, 71, 119
Table of specifications, 68–70
Taxonomy of Educational Objectives, 58
Teachers' standards, 18
Test administration, 80
Test directions, 78
Test format, 77–78
Test interpretation
    criterion-referenced, 31
    norm-referenced, 31
Test items
    analysis of, 80–82
    arrangement of, 77–78
    characteristics of, 72
    difficulty of, 31, 80–82
    evaluation of, 79
    improving, 74
    relating to outcomes, 73–74
    selection of, 71–72
    types of, 71
    See also Item writing, Selection items,
        Supply items
Test length, 75
Test planning
    defining learning outcomes, 66–68
    evaluating the test, 79
    evaluating the test plan, 76
    identifying learning outcomes, 59
    outlining subject matter, 68–69
    relating items to outcomes, 69–70
    specifications for a test, 68–70
    steps in planning, 65, 68
    table of specifications, 68–70
Test preparation
    arranging the items, 77–78
    evaluating the test, 79
    preparing directions, 78
    steps in preparing, 65
    See also Item writing, Test planning
Test-retest method, 45–46
Test scores
    grade-equivalent scores, 33, 34
    percentile ranks, 33

Test specifications, 68–70
Transfer of learning, 17
True-false items, 105–111
Verbs, for defining objectives, 67, 151
Validity
    and assessment planning, 29
    characteristics of, 38
    coefficient, 40
    concurrent study, 40
    consequences, 38, 43–44

    construct-related evidence, 42–43
    content-related evidence 38–39
    criterion-related evidence, 40–42
    expectancy table, 41
    factors that lower, 39
    meaning of, 29, 38–43
    predictive study, 40
    types of evidence, 38–40
    ways to "build in" validity, 30
Weighting scores, 184–185